Drupal 6 JavaScript and jQuery

Putting jQuery, AJAX, and JavaScript effects into your Drupal 6 modules and themes

Matt Butcher

PUBLISHING

BIRMINGHAM - MUMBAI

Drupal 6 JavaScript and jQuery

First published: February 2009

Production Reference: 2260209

Published by Packt Publishing Ltd.
32 Lincoln Road
Olton
Birmingham, B27 6PA, UK.

ISBN 978-1-847196-16-3

www.packtpub.com

Cover Image by Damian Carvill (damianc@packtpub.com)

Credits

Author

Matt Butcher

Reviewers

Dave Myburgh

Paul Lovvik

Senior Acquisition Editor

Douglas Paterson

Development Editor

Swapna V. Verlekar

Technical Editor

Amey Kanse

Copy Editor

Sneha Kulkarni

Indexer

Hemangini Bari

Production Editorial Manager

Abhijeet Deobhakta

Editorial Team Leader

Akshara Aware

Project Team Leader

Lata Basantani

Project Coordinator

Leena Purkait

Proofreader

Joel T. Johnson

Production Coordinator

Rajni R. Thorat

Cover Work

Rajni R. Thorat

About the author

Matt Butcher is a Drupal programmer for `Palantir.net`. He is a member of the Emerging Technologies Lab at Loyola University Chicago, where he is currently finishing a Ph.D. in philosophy. He has written five books for Packt Publishing, including *Learning Drupal 6 Module Development*, *Mastering OpenLDAP*, *Managing and Customizing OpenCms 6*, and *Developing Websites with OpenCms*. He has also contributed articles to various web sites and scholarly journals. He is an active contributor in several Open Source projects.

Thanks to Gábor Hojtsy and Ariel Hitron for helping with the sections on the JavaScript translation system. Greg Knaddison and a few others organized DrupalCamp Colorado, which was the test bed for many of the ideas and examples in the book. Douglas Paterson and Leena Purkait not only managed the process of putting this book together, but also worked with me to make this book the pilot for the RAW program. Thanks also to the DrupalCamp Chicago crowd, who provided feedback on the later chapters. John Forsythe was instrumental in getting the early chapters prepared for the RAW release. Dave Myburgh and Paul Lovvik provided copious comments on the book. Larry Garfield, Nate Striedinger, Ken Rickard, Greg Dunlap, John Wilkins, Sam Boyer, and the rest of the Palantir team, have (wittingly or unwittingly) been great sources of information and inspiration. Thanks also to Scott Dexter and Samir Chopra, whose work has continued to fortify my belief in FOSS ethics. Katherine, Anna, Claire, and Angie had to give up the occasional Sunday afternoon activities so that I could write this book. To them, I indubitably owe the greatest debt of gratitude.

About the reviewers

Dave Myburgh has been involved with computers even before the Web existed. He studied to be a molecular biologist, but discovered that he liked working with computers more than bacteria. He had his own computer business in South Africa (where he grew up), which involved technical support and sales. He even created a few static web sites for clients during that time.

He went back to science for a few years when he first came to Canada, and then got sucked into the world of Drupal when a friend wanted a site for a local historical society. Since then, he has once again started his own company that now builds web sites exclusively in Drupal (he doesn't "do static" anymore). There is no lack of work in the Drupal world, and he now balances his time between work and family. He has also reviewed several Drupal books, including Drupal 5 Themes and Drupal 6 Themes.

> I would like to thank my family for being so supportive of me and what I do. Working from home can be a mixed blessing sometimes, but having the opportunity to watch my son grow up makes it all worthwhile.

Paul Lovvik is a Principal Engineer at Acquia and a contributor of Drupal. He received his B.S. in Computer Science from California State University. He has spent the last 15 years developing software at various technology companies, including Parallax Graphics, Sun Microsystems, and Openwave Systems. He has experience with developing in C, C++, Java, JavaScript, and PHP.

Table of Contents

Preface

JavaScript: It's not just for calculators and image rollovers.

Drupal 6 is loaded with new features, not all of which are necessarily implemented in PHP. This unique book, for web designers and developers, will guide you through what can be done with JavaScript (and especially with jQuery) in Drupal 6.

With the combination of the powerhouse jQuery library, with its own robust set of JavaScript tools, Drupal 6 comes with a pre-packaged killer JavaScript environment. Cross-platform by nature, it provides all of the tools necessary to create powerful AJAX-enabled scripts, gorgeous visual effects, and view-enhancing behaviors. In addition, Drupal developers have ported some of its most powerful PHP tools (like a theming engine and support for localization and language translation) to JavaScript, making it possible to write simple scripts, where once only complex PHP code could be used.

This book gives you the keys to the toolbox, showing you how to use Drupal's JavaScript libraries to make your modules and themes more dynamic, interactive, and responsive, and add effects to make your Drupal site explode into life!

If you've dipped your toe in the water of theme or module development with Drupal 6, this is the book that will make the look and behavior of your work something special. With it's project-based approach, this book is carefully constructed to guide you from how JavaScript fits into the overall Drupal architecture, to making you a master of the jQuery library in the world of Drupal themes and modules.

What this book covers

Chapter 1 focuses on various languages and technologies used in Drupal. We will have a high-level overview of the Drupal architecture followed by an examination of some key Drupal concepts such as users, blocks, and nodes. From there, we will move on to developers tools and learn about a few utilities that can expedite Drupal JavaScript development.

Chapter 2 covers the basics on how JavaScript can be used within Drupal 6. We will begin by exploring how JavaScript is included in Drupal pages, and then create our first script for Drupal.

Chapter 3 focuses on jQuery. Initially, we will look at jQuery independently of Drupal, and then we will take a closer look at how jQuery is integrated with Drupal.

Chapter 4 focuses on Drupal Behaviors and the major utility functions provided by drupal.js, which provides functions for behaviors, translation, theming, as well as other utility functions.

Chapter 5 focuses on the translation system in Drupal, and the JavaScript tools that are used in conjunction with that system. We will look at installing and configuring multiple languages using JavaScript functions, and then extracting and translating strings.

Chapter 6 focuses on the JavaScript theming system. We will look at the JavaScript theming module, and examine some of the themes and user interface tools that it provides. We will implement our own template system based on HTML, CSS, and JavaScript.

Chapter 7 focuses on the AJAX family of tools. We will learn to use jQuery's built-in AJAX support to get content from Drupal, and also use JSON (JavaScript Object Notation) as a JavaScript-friendly way of sending data from Drupal.

Chapter 8 focuses on module development. We will discuss how modules work, and will learn how to create modules and use them for adding JavaScript features. We will also learn to make our JavaScript available to other modules.

Chapter 9 focuses on advanced topics. We will look at integrating existing Drupal JavaScript tools with our own site design, and then we will see how to extend the JavaScript libraries with the jQuery UI library. We will also extend jQuery's library with our own functions, building a jQuery plug-in in the process.

Who this book is for

This book is for web designers and developers who want to add JavaScript elements to Drupal themes or modules to create more flexible and responsive user interfaces.

You are expected to know about the basic operation of Drupal, and be familiar with the concept of theming and modules in Drupal. No experience with creating themes or modules is required.

You will also need to know the basics of client-side web development. This includes HTML, CSS, but you should also have a rudimentary grasp of JavaScript syntax. Familiarity with PHP programming will be an advantage, since we will be writing PHPTemplate files and (at the end) creating Drupal modules. However, PHP is covered thoroughly enough that even the PHP neophyte will not find the text too demanding. The book also covers the jQuery JavaScript library and its use in Drupal, but no knowledge of jQuery is expected. You will learn everything you need in this book.

Conventions

In this book, you will find a number of styles of text that distinguish between different kinds of information. Here are some examples of these styles, and an explanation of their meaning.

Code words in text are shown as follows, "We can include other contexts through the use of the `include` directive."

A block of code will be set as follows:

```
Drupal.behaviors.countParagraphs = function (context) {
  if ($('#lots', context).size() > 0) {
    return;
  }
  else if ($('p', context).size() > 5) {
    $('body').append('<p id="lots">Lots of Text!</p>');
  }
};
```

When we wish to draw your attention to a particular part of a code block, the relevant lines or items will be made bold:

```
if(sel.id == txtareaID && sel.start != sel.end) {
  txtareaEle.value = SimpleEditor.insertTag(
    sel.start,
    sel.end,
    $(this).hasClass('bold') ? 'strong' : 'em',
    txtareaEle.value
  );
  sel.start = sel.end = -1;
}
```

New terms and **important words** are introduced in a bold-type font. Words that you see on the screen, in menus or dialog boxes for example, appear in our text like this: "clicking the **Next** button moves you to the next screen".

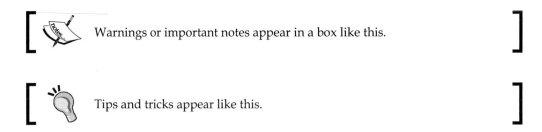

Warnings or important notes appear in a box like this.

Tips and tricks appear like this.

Reader feedback

Feedback from our readers is always welcome. Let us know what you think about this book, what you liked or may have disliked. Reader feedback is important for us to develop titles that you really get the most out of.

To send us general feedback, simply drop an email to feedback@packtpub.com, making sure to mention the book title in the subject of your message.

If there is a book that you need and would like to see us publish, please send us a note in the **SUGGEST A TITLE** form on www.packtpub.com or email suggest@packtpub.com.

If there is a topic that you have expertise in and you are interested in either writing or contributing to a book, see our author guide on www.packtpub.com/authors.

Customer support

Now that you are the proud owner of a Packt book, we have a number of things to help you to get the most from your purchase.

Downloading the example code for the book

Visit http://www.packtpub.com/files/code/6163_Code.zip to directly download the example code.

The downloadable files contain instructions on how to use them.

Errata

Although we have taken every care to ensure the accuracy of our contents, mistakes do happen. If you find a mistake in one of our books—maybe a mistake in text or code—we would be grateful if you would report this to us. By doing this you can save other readers from frustration, and help to improve subsequent versions of this book. If you find any errata, report them by visiting http://www.packtpub.com/support, selecting your book, clicking on the **let us know** link, and entering the details of your errata. Once your errata are verified, your submission will be accepted and the errata are added to the list of existing errata. The existing errata can be viewed by selecting your title from http://www.packtpub.com/support.

Piracy

Piracy of copyright material on the Internet is an ongoing problem across all media. At Packt, we take the protection of our copyright and licenses very seriously. If you come across any illegal copies of our works in any form on the Internet, please provide the location address or website name immediately so we can pursue a remedy.

Please contact us at copyright@packtpub.com with a link to the suspected pirated material.

We appreciate your help in protecting our authors, and our ability to bring you valuable content.

Questions

You can contact us at questions@packtpub.com if you are having a problem with some aspect of the book, and we will do our best to address it.

1
Drupal and JavaScript

If you're anything like me, you're reading this first paragraph with two questions in mind: Is this book going to cover the topics I need? And, is this book any good? (Again, if you're anything like me you're groaning already that the author has lapsed into indulgent first-person navel-gazing.)

Regarding the second question, I'm obviously not the person whose opinion you'll want. But here's the answer to the first question: The aim of this book is to provide a practical, hands-on approach to using the JavaScript scripting language to extend and customize the Drupal 6 Content Management System (CMS).

Drupal 6 offers JavaScript tools designed to enable developers to turn Drupal sites into Web 2.0 platforms. That's why this book exists. We're going to see how to use Drupal's JavaScript support to assemble the building blocks needed to enhance the client-side experience. Tools such as jQuery, language translation, and AJAX support—all included in Drupal's core—provide powerful features that we will explore. While we won't be developing word processors or webmail applications, we will be developing widgets and tools that can be assembled in many different ways to enrich the user's experience. Most importantly, we'll be doing this in a practical and hands-on way.

What do I mean by 'practical and hands-on'? I mean that every chapter after this one will be organized around one or more projects. While preparing my previous book, *"Learning Drupal 6 Module Development", Packt Publishing, 978-1847194442*, I came to appreciate the power of Drupal's well-integrated JavaScript libraries. In this book, we will use those libraries in conjunction with other Drupal technologies to create functional pieces of code that you can use. Or even better yet, use them as a starting point to create something even more well-suited to meet your own needs. We won't be agonizing over the details of every function, nor will we spend a lot of time looking at the theory. Instead, the pace will be crisp as we work on code, learn how it works, and how it can be used.

Let's start things off with a quick, high-level overview of Drupal. We will meet all of these components again, so a good grounding in them will be helpful. In this first chapter, we will cover the following:

- The core technologies and languages upon which Drupal is built
- The major components in Drupal and how they work together
- The tools that you, as a JavaScript developer, can use to make Drupal development easier

Once we've hurtled our way through this motley list of items, we'll embark in Chapter 2 on our first project.

 Unlike many technical books, we are not going to start off with a chapter on installing Drupal. There are many resources on this already, including the well-written Drupal installation notes that are included with Drupal. If you need to install Drupal, go to `http://drupal.org` and download the latest 6.x series Drupal package. The archive you download will contain a file named `INSTALL.txt` that contains detailed installation instructions.

Let's begin by looking at the languages in which Drupal is written.

Do you speak...?

Most of the time, people (including myself) talk about Drupal as a PHP-based CMS. **PHP** (a recursive acronym for **PHP: Hypertext Preprocessor**) is a web-centered programming language. Talking about Drupal as a PHP application makes sense as most of the server-side programming logic is indeed written in PHP.

But PHP is not the only language used by Drupal. Surprisingly, there are at least six different languages used in Drupal: PHP, **SQL (Structured Query Language)**, **HTML (HyperText Markup Language)**, **CSS (Cascading Style Sheets)**, **XML (eXtensible Markup Language)**, and—you guessed it—**JavaScript**.

 You might be asking, "At least six? Can there be more?" Yes, there can be more. Drupal can be extended to support innumerable languages. This can be done through its module system.

The focus of this book will be on JavaScript. We will make use of a lot of HTML, CSS, and also a subset of PHP. But Drupal's use of these technologies is fairly standard, and we won't be doing anything really startling with HTML or CSS. In Drupal, XML is used primarily to provide support for **RSS (Really Simple Syndication)** feeds and **AJAX (Asynchronous JavaScript And XML)**. In fact, we will be using Drupal's XML support for these things. We will make use of some light PHP programming—mainly for writing templates—but it won't play a major role in this book. We won't be using SQL at all.

While we encounter many Drupal technologies, we will stay on target. JavaScript will be our focus.

Okay, so Drupal makes use of several languages. Impressive, sure...but why? And how? Let's take a two-minute tour of each of these languages to learn about the roles they play.

PHP

PHP (`http://php.net`) is a procedural, object-oriented scripting language. Originally, it was designed to perform server-side HTML processing like the antiquated SSI (Service Side Includes) technology introduced in the mid-1990s. But while SSI grew stale and died off, PHP developers kept growing their language. With each release of the PHP engine, it grew in power and flexibility. As a result, it achieved superstar status among web developers. These days, you're likely to find PHP on Windows, Mac, Linux, and UNIX boxes across the Web. Since PHP can now be used to write shell scripts and even windowed applications, you might find it doing more than just driving a web site.

Drupal's server-side logic is written primarily in PHP. How so? When the web server hands Drupal a connection from a client, it is the PHP code that gets executed to handle the client's request. Other than the queries passed to the database, all of the processing that the server does is handled by PHP.

While this is a book on JavaScript, we will be writing some PHP code. Not a PHP developer? Don't worry. For the most part, we will be using a very small subset of PHP. We will be calling basic functions to handle formatting and layout from Drupal's template engine called **PHPTemplate**. The purpose of PHPTemplate is simple: Provide an easy method for inserting dynamic values into HTML. You only need know a handful of PHP functions to be able to use PHPTemplate. This book will cover those functions without assuming you're already a PHP ninja.

Here's a quick example of what PHPTemplate programming looks like:

```
<strong><?php print t("Good Day");?></strong>
```

The `<strong>` and `</strong>` tags are just you're regular old HTML tags. The `<?php ... ?>` part indicates that the enclosed information is PHP code that the server should execute. Inside that is the line `print t("Good Day")`, which simply uses the `t()` function to translate `Good Day` into whatever the user's language is. Then using the print directive, prints the results to the HTML. Assuming my preferred language is German, the previous code would generate something like this:

```
<strong>Guten Tag</strong>
```

That's the sort of PHP we'll be writing in this book.

 Drupal's translation features, which are available in JavaScript, will be covered in Chapter 4.

Towards the very end of the book, we will use a little more PHP to build a Drupal module. This might be a little more demanding, but those are the chapters you can skim if you don't want to learn PHP. If you're interested in learning more about PHP development, there are several other great books available, including (shameless plug) my book *Learning Drupal 6 Module Development Packt Publishing, 978-1847194442*.

SQL

SQL is an acronym for Structured Query Language. What do you query with SQL? A database! SQL is the industry standard for writing queries that relational database systems can then parse and execute. But while the language is standardized, there are multiple flavors of SQL. Each database program seems to use a slightly different version of SQL—supporting some subset of the standardized language while also adding on additional database-specific features.

Historically, Drupal development has targeted the open source MySQL database (`http://mysql.com`) as the "official" database. Another popular open source database, PostgreSQL (`http://postgresql.org`), is also supported by recent Drupal releases (though not all add-on modules currently support it).

While you will need to run a database in order to use Drupal, we won't be making much use of the SQL language in this book. Drupal provides built-in tools that we can use to get the content we need out of the database without having to write our own queries.

HTML

HTML is the primary format for web-based content. As you undoubtedly know, the purpose of HTML is to "mark up" a text using **tags**, sometimes with **attributes** to provide instructions on how the document is structured and how it should look when displayed in a browser.

Tags and elements

An HTML tag looks like this: `<p>`. Most tags in HTML are paired, with a start and end tag. A tag may also have attributes, such as `type="text/javascript"`, and may also surround some content. When we talk about the tag, plus the attributes and its content, we use the term **element**.

For example, to indicate that a piece of text is particularly important, we would put it inside of the `<strong></strong>` tags:

```
The <strong>important</strong> thing.
```

By default, most visual browsers render the content of the `<strong>` element as bold text as seen here:

The **important** thing.

HTML's evolution has been a rough one. Initially, it was designed just to provide structural information about the contents. But somewhere along the line, it also became a tool for encoding layout and styling information. Combining the two seemingly similar ideas of structure and style seemed like a good idea. But in practice, it made for some very messy code.

The family of HTML specifications can be found online at `http://www.w3.org/html/`.

On another front, XML (which we will look at in a moment) evolved separately. Then, at some point, reconciliation between the HTML standards and the XML standards was attempted. The outcome of this endeavor was XHTML (HTML in XML). XHTML is now considered to be *the right way* to write HTML. In this book, we will strive to use well-formed XHTML. You may notice this in the following ways:

- All tags and attribute names will be in lowercase.
- All tags will be closed. That means a tag will either appear in the opening and closing pairs (`<strong></strong>`), or as a single self-closing tag (`<br/>`—note the forward slash (/) before the closing angle bracket (>)).
- All documents will start with an XML declaration (`<?xml ... ?>`) and a document type declaration (`<!DOCTYPE html ...>`).

One of the primary roles of JavaScript (as we shall see many times) is to interact with the document represented in HTML. Consequently, we will be using HTML frequently in this book.

CSS

Another design principle driving XHTML is that the layout and styling information embedded directly in the HTML should be limited to what is absolutely necessary. Styling and layout should primarily fall in the purview of a style-specific language.

What language might that be? Cascading Style Sheets (CSS) is the *de facto* styling language in today's browsers.

 The CSS family of standards is found here: `http://www.w3.org/Style/CSS/`.

CSS is a declarative language whose central task is to map styles to patterns of markup in an XML or HTML document. Or, plainly speaking, CSS identifies certain pieces of HTML and tells the browser how those pieces should look.

Earlier we looked at this piece of HTML:

```
The <strong>important</strong> thing.
```

I noted that by default, a browser would display this as highlighted text. But with CSS, we can tell the browser to display it differently:

```
strong {
  font-weight: normal;
  font-size: 14pt;
  color: green;
  text-decoration: underline;
}
```

This little snippet of CSS tells the browser that the text inside of `<strong>`... `</strong>` should look like this:

- The weight of the font (how bold it is) should be normal, not bold.
- The font size should be 14 points high. Assuming that the surrounding text is 12 points, this will appear larger than surrounding text.
- The text color should be green.
- The text should be underlined.

Thus, when rendered through the browser, the text would look more like this:

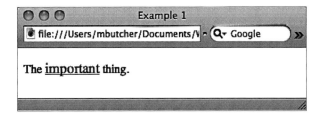

Another important use of JavaScript is to interact with the styles in a document. Thus, we will be using CSS throughout this book.

XML

HTML tags are strictly defined. But what if you want to use a tag-based structure, yet define your own tags? That's where XML comes in. Using XML, you can keep the markup syntax while defining your own tags and attributes.

For example, if we want to develop an XML-based document type that describes a pen, the markup might look something like this:

```
<?xml version="1.0"?>
<pen type="ballpoint">
  <ink>
    <color>black</color>
    <permanent>true<permanent>
  </ink>
  <shaft>
    <color>clear</color>
    <material>plastic</material>
  </shaft>
</pen>
```

Basically, it looks like an HTML document, but the tag names and attributes have been developed specifically for the purpose of describing a pen.

Creating special-purpose markup languages is certainly the most common use of XML. But there are many technologies that complement, co-operate with, and extend XML to provide advanced capabilities. You can peruse `http://w3.org` to get an idea of these technologies.

Here, we won't be using anything sophisticated. Our interest will be limited to plain old XML and a few standard XML-based formats (such as the RSS).

JavaScript

The star of the show has been saved for the last. JavaScript is an object-oriented scripting language designed to run within a web browser. Let's unpack this statement:

- **Object-oriented**: Like other object-oriented programming languages, JavaScript uses objects as a way of organizing code. (We will come back to objects later.) But JavaScript doesn't provide all of the usual object-oriented constructs you may have seen elsewhere. There are no classes in JavaScript, nor are there private and protected object methods. But, the bottom line is simply this: JavaScript employs the methodologies and principles espoused in other modern object-oriented languages. We will use this to our advantage.

> The use of the term "object-oriented" to describe JavaScript is contested. Sometimes, JavaScript is called **Object-Related** because it does not have all of the constructs that object-oriented languages typically contain. Currently, calling JavaScript object-oriented seems to be in favor, since JavaScript can be made to emulate any features that it does not have built-in. JavaScript 2.0 will be a fully object-oriented language.

- **Scripting language**: Many languages—such as Java, C++, and C#—are written in plain text, and then compiled into a format that is not readable by humans. The compiled code is then executed by the computer when the program is run. Scripting languages differ from these. They are not pre-compiled. Instead, they are delivered for execution as plain text files. Then an interpreter takes the responsibility for executing the script. JavaScript-enabled web browsers have JavaScript interpreters embedded inside.

- **Web browser-centered**: JavaScript was initially developed as a special-purpose language designed to provide interactivity to the otherwise static HTML pages. While talented software developers have found other uses for the JavaScript language, it is still the scripting language of choice for cross-browser web scripting. Our use of it will be limited to web programming with Drupal.

So why does Drupal use both PHP and JavaScript? Why not use just one? The reason has to do with where the code is executed.

In a web application, PHP is always executed *only on* the server. The server runs the PHP code and then sends the resulting information to the client. The information that is sent is usually in the form of HTML, CSS, or JavaScript.

The web browser will never see a line of PHP code. It will all be taken care of by the server.

So the PHP runs on the server and then sends the results to the client. The browser takes that information—HTML, CSS, and JavaScript—and uses it to display the page. As we saw earlier, HTML and CSS are used to describe and format the content.

The JavaScript serves a different purpose.

When the browser encounters a JavaScript file, it fires up the JavaScript interpreter and passes the script to the interpreter. Remember that this activity is happening on the client machine, not the server.

The script can then interact with the other content that the server has sent to the browser. The script can add or remove CSS styles. It can add or remove elements from the HTML. It can rearrange a web page. It can (using AJAX) request additional content from the server and then insert that content into the document. It can make the user interface more attractive and easier to use. In a nutshell, it can take a static page and add some interactivity.

Does this description make JavaScript sound like a toy language? A gimmicky way of adding glitz, but nothing more? That might have been the case in the beginning, but it's come a long way. Web-based applications driven by advanced JavaScript (Web 2.0) are today's Internet darlings.

That's where we are headed. In the coming chapters, we are going to use JavaScript to add client-side functionality to our Drupal site.

We've taken a high-level overview of the different languages that Drupal employs. Now we're going to take a different perspective. We're going to look at the many parts that make up Drupal and see how they all connect.

Drupal's architecture

As mentioned in the previous section, almost all of the server-side Drupal code is written in PHP. Just like a complex physical structure—a building or an airplane—this code is organized into units, each of which does a particular job.

Let's take a look at what might be called a blueprint of Drupal:

```
┌─────────────────────────────────────────────┐
│         ┌───────────────────────────┐         │
│         │          Browser          │         │
│         └───────────────────────────┘         │
│                                               │
│         ┌────┐ ┌────┐ ┌────┐ ┌──────┐         │
│         │HTML│ │CSS │ │ JS │ │Other │         │
│         └────┘ └────┘ └────┘ └──────┘         │
│                                               │
│    ┌──────────────────────────────────┐      │
│    │ Server                           │      │
│    │   ┌────────────────────────────┐ │      │
│    │   │ Theme Engine (PHPTemplate) │ │      │
│    │   └────────────────────────────┘ │      │
│    │   ┌──────────────────┐ ┌───────┐ │      │
│    │   │ Drupal Core (PHP)│ │Database│ │      │
│    │   ┌──┐┌──┐┌──┐┌──┐┌──┐          │      │
│    │   └──┘└──┘└──┘└──┘└──┘          │      │
│    │        Additional Modules        │      │
│    └──────────────────────────────────┘      │
└─────────────────────────────────────────────┘
```

Let's look at the pieces in the diagram.

This diagram is divided into two major components: the browser and the server. The majority of Drupal's processing is done on the server.

The PAC design pattern

On the server side, Drupal follows the **PAC (Presentation-Abstraction -Control)** design pattern. The Drupal Core provides the controller. It responds to user requests and routes them to the appropriate handlers. The theme system provides the presentation layer. The modules (including the built-in modules like Node) access and manipulate the data which is the job of the abstraction layer.

The Drupal Core

At the center of Drupal is the **Drupal Core**. This core consists of important libraries that Drupal must have in order to run. When a browser makes a request to Drupal, the Drupal Core is what oversees how Drupal responds to the request. The Drupal Core gathers data from various sources (including from the **database** where information is stored long-term), and then hands that data off to the Theme Engine.

The Drupal Core also includes some important modules. These are usually called **Core modules**. All of them provide features that are often used in CMS systems. But within the list of Core modules, there are a handful of modules that are absolutely essential for the proper functioning of a Drupal system. Though these are not as intimately connected with controlling the application, they provide services that Drupal needs. You might notice these modules when you look at the Modules page (in the Drupal administration interface: **Administer | Site Building | Modules**):

<table>
<tr><td colspan="4">▽   Core - required</td></tr>
<tr><th>Enabled</th><th>Name</th><th>Version</th><th>Description</th></tr>
<tr><td>☑</td><td>**Block**</td><td>6.0</td><td>Controls the boxes that are displayed around the main content.</td></tr>
<tr><td>☑</td><td>**Filter**</td><td>6.0</td><td>Handles the filtering of content in preparation for display.</td></tr>
<tr><td>☑</td><td>**Node**</td><td>6.0</td><td>Allows content to be submitted to the site and displayed on pages.</td></tr>
<tr><td>☑</td><td>**System**</td><td>6.0</td><td>Handles general site configuration for administrators.</td></tr>
<tr><td>☑</td><td>**User**</td><td>6.0</td><td>Manages the user registration and login system.</td></tr>
</table>

The screenshot shows the five absolutely necessary modules: **Block**, **Filter**, **Node**, **System**, and **User**.

While these modules are displayed with all of the other modules installed on the system, modules marked **Core – required** cannot be disabled.

Later in this chapter we will discuss the data types that three of these modules provide: nodes, blocks, and users.

The major JavaScript libraries, including `drupal.js` and `jquery.js`, are also managed as a part of the Drupal Core. These libraries are not encapsulated in modules, nor are they stored with the PHP libraries. They are maintained as part of the Core, and are included with Drupal.

Much of our attention in this book will be devoted to these core libraries. The enormously powerful jQuery library is introduced in Chapter 3, and will be used throughout the book. The `drupal.js` library is the subject of Chapter 4, 5 and 6, and is also used elsewhere in this book.

The Theme Engine

The job of the **Theme Engine** is to take the data given to it and format that data for display. It might, for example, use templates to build HTML or CSS. In some cases, it might be used to generate XML, or even email messages to be sent from the local mail server.

Once data has been formatted by the Theme Engine, it is sent back to the browser, typically in the form of HTML, CSS, or images.

JavaScript is a slightly more complex form. It is not usually passed through the Theme Engine. Instead, it is passed to the browser unmodified. Where does JavaScript come from? Sometimes it comes from libraries written by developers (the core Drupal library and jQuery are both examples of this). Sometimes it comes from a theme. At other times, the JavaScript comes from a module.

The Theme Engine is part of the theme system. The theme system provides an API for styling and laying out data. It loads the Theme Engine and hands that engine data for formatting. Why the distinction? Here is the reason. While the theme system API remains the same, you can actually substitute different Theme Engines for the default PHPTemplate engine (We will only use PHPTemplate, though). You can see a list of Theme Engines at the Drupal web site: `http://drupal.org/project/Theme+engines`.

Modules

Modules are the last part of server-side processing that we will look at. Drupal itself does not try to provide every possible feature that a web site might need. Instead, it provides common and important features and then provides a mechanism for plugging in additional functionality.

This mechanism is called the **module system**. Modules can provide additional functionality to the Drupal Core, the Theme Engine, or even JavaScript. But it is the Drupal Core that oversees how modules get loaded and executed, and what happens to the data they return.

There is a lot more that could be said of this system, but we have the main concepts covered. In this book, we'll be working primarily with themes, though we will make use of some modules as well. As we take a closer look at these technologies, we'll build on the overview given earlier.

For our current purposes, though, it's time to move on. We need to cover a few more high-level Drupal concepts.

Where does our JavaScript go?

As we will see in the next chapter, JavaScript can be used in both themes and modules. For the sake of simplicity, we will make more use of theme-based JavaScript than module-based JavaScript. By attaching JavaScript to themes (instead of modules), we will avoid having to write much PHP code. In the last two chapters of the book, though, we will create a few modules.

Users, nodes, and blocks

There are three terms that are crucial to understand when doing any kind of Drupal development: users, nodes, and blocks.

Since the user concept is the easiest to grasp, we'll start with that.

Users

One of the required core modules that Drupal provides is the **User module**. This module defines Drupal's concept of a user. As expected, a Drupal user is identified by a username and password (or in some cases by an OpenID URL). A bundle of information, including things such as name, email address, and preferences, is also associated with a user.

Users can be assigned roles. **Roles** determine what permissions a user has. By default, there are two roles: **anonymous user** and **authenticated user**. An anonymous user is one who has not signed in (and thus has no known username). An authenticated user is one who is a member of the site (and has already signed in).

Using the **Administer | User management | Permissions** tool, you can assign privileges to roles. For example, with this tool we could allow authenticated users to post comments, but not allow that privilege to anonymous users.

Along with being able to define custom permissions, you can also define custom roles. On sites that I administer, I often create an Administrator role. Users in that role are typically granted broad access to the administration features of Drupal.

A special user

The first user created on a Drupal site is treated as a special administrative user. This user is created during installation and will be allowed full administrative access to the server regardless of role.

As we work through this book, the users, roles, and permissions will play a part in our coding. We will be developing code intended to be not only functional and feature-rich, but also secure. Understanding how the user system works is a step in the direction of securing our code.

Blocks

The next important concept that we will look at is the block system. The core block features are provided by the **Block module**.

What is a block? In a nutshell, a block is a unit of organization that provides a way for small pieces of content to be displayed in designated areas on a Drupal page. Not terribly clear? Let's look at a screenshot:

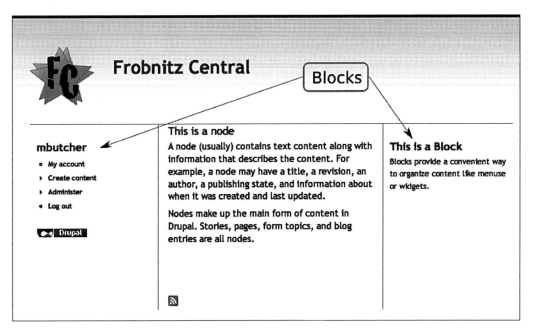

In this screenshot, there are two arrows pointing to a couple of blocks displayed on the page. On the left, there is a block showing the username and menu. This is the **Navigation** block. Its purpose is to provide context-sensitive navigation for the user. The Drupal logo shown beneath it is also a block, called **Powered by Drupal**.

On the right side is a block displayed from a custom module (the demoblock module that is included in the source code for this book). This block simply displays some text.

You can choose which blocks show up and where they will be displayed. This is done using the **Administer | Site building | Blocks** tool. For example, using that tool we can reorganize the screen shown earlier like this:

Frobnitz Central

This is a Block

Blocks provide a convenient way to organize content like menuse or widgets.

Drupal

This is a node

A node (usually) contains text content along with information that describes the content. For example, a node may have a title, a revision, an author, a publishing state, and information about when it was created and last updated.

Nodes make up the main form of content in Drupal. Stories, pages, form topics, and blog entries are all nodes.

mbutcher

- My account
- Create content
- Administer
- Log out

Notice that in the screenshot, the **This is a Block** and Navigation blocks have been swapped. This illustrates one of the main features of blocks: They can be repositioned.

So what is happening behind the scenes to generate blocks? Essentially this: Drupal modules have the ability to define blocks. When you configure a block to show up in some region of the page, Drupal tells that module to go through the process of creating the block.

When the module delivers its block content to Drupal, Drupal passes that information on to the theme system. This system styles the block itself, and then inserts that styled block into the main page template.

In the next chapter, we will be taking a closer look at the templates that come into play when theming. Later in the book we will use JavaScript to make a block more than just a static part of the page.

At this point, you should feel a little more comfortable with what a block is used for. Blocks define pieces of information—lists of links, short forms, images, text, or any other standard web content—that can be selectively displayed and positioned by an administrator. But blocks are rarely used to provide the main content of a page.

Let's turn our attention from blocks to nodes.

Nodes

Visually speaking, blocks typically show up as small bits of content. Nodes, in contrast, can be thought of as the big pieces of content. Stories and pages—the two types of content enabled by default in Drupal—are both types of nodes. Their role is to hold and display large pieces of textual content.

In fact, that is the general purpose of a node: It encapsulates a piece of content (usually a piece of text) and also provides additional information about that content.

Nodes typically have a body and a title. A node also tracks information about the version of the node, the owner, creation date, and publishing state of a node. In short, any information about that content is attached (in one way or another) to a node.

Most of the node information is stored in built-in Drupal tables in the database. But custom node types can be defined either programmatically (in code) or using modules such as the **CCK** (**Content Construction Kit**). In such cases, information is indeed attached to a node, but the underlying data storage mechanism is usually not limited to the built-in Drupal node table. Data may be spread out in the database.

Let's take another look at the screenshot we saw earlier:

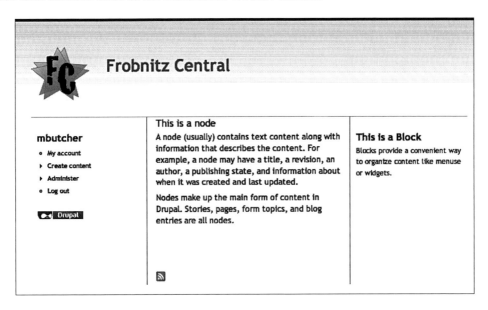

Right in the center of the page is the node object. In this case, it is a **Page** node created by clicking on the **Create content** link visible in the Navigation block on the left side, followed by clicking on the **Page** link.

On this page, we can see the node's title (**This is a node**) and a pair of paragraphs that make up its content.

There is more that can be done with a node than simply viewing it. We can get lists of nodes (imagine a table of contents or a list of recent stories). We can display just a selection from a node, as is often done on a Drupal front page. Also, with additional modules, we can get even more sophisticated. For example, the **ImageNode** module turns nodes into containers to which images may be attached. The **Services** module makes it possible to serve node content as XML or other formats.

But for the sake of brevity, the most useful way to think of a node is simply as a *piece of content* inside of the Drupal CMS.

How does Drupal go through the process of displaying a node? The process is similar to the block display process. When a node is requested, the Node module (and any necessary auxiliary modules) retrieves the node from the database. Then, the theme system formats the node's content for display, and then inserts that content into the main template. Once the node, blocks, and any additional content is placed in the template, the resulting HTML document is returned to the browser for display.

The behind-the-scenes logic for nodes is implemented in complex PHP code. But we won't be interacting with nodes at that level.

For us, we are more interested in the node content as it is styled by the Theme Engine and returned to the browser. JavaScript operates only on the already-rendered node content, so there is no need to delve into node internals.

We've now, taken a look at three major concepts that will be used throughout this book: users, blocks, and nodes. Next, we can turn our attention to the tools used to develop JavaScript.

Drupal JavaScript development tools

One of the nice things about JavaScript development is that you don't really need any other tools besides a text editor and a web browser. If you want to do your JavaScript development that way, you can.

While you don't *need* any other tools, you can become a more proficient developer by using some additional tools. In this section, I will introduce a few tools that make Drupal JavaScript development faster and easier.

A good editor

Any plain text editor can be used to write JavaScript. But there are many editors that provide features specific to JavaScript development. Features such as syntax highlighting (automatically color-coding code to make it easier to read), automatic code completion, and a debugger can help you write code more efficiently.

That said, there are hundreds of code editors—perhaps even thousands—that provide some degree of JavaScript support. So which editor or editors should *you* use? That will depend on your own preferences. In the open source world, editors like **jEdit** (cross-platform) and **Notepad++** (Windows) provide basic support without lots of frills. If you are also a PHP developer (or you write code in other languages), IDEs such as **Eclipse**, **Aptana**, and **NetBeans** provide good integration. Even **Vim** (Vi Improved) and **Emacs** provide JavaScript support. Also, there are many commercial packages, such as **TextMate** for the Mac, that provide environments for coding in JavaScript.

If you don't have an editor that you already feel comfortable with, I suggest trying a couple of different ones. Start with an easy-to-use editor like jEdit (http://jedit.org) or Notepad++ (http://notepad-plus.sourceforge.net/).

Firebug

Unlike editors, when it comes to debugging JavaScript, there is a clear candidate. The Firefox extension Firebug tool (https://addons.mozilla.org/en-US/firefox/addon/1843) is not only a good way of debugging your JavaScript code, but also a tool for analyzing HTML, the DOM, CSS, and network performance. With the built-in JavaScript command line, you can interactively execute JavaScript from within your browser.

For example, here's a screenshot of Firebug inspecting the HTML contents of the page we've been looking at:

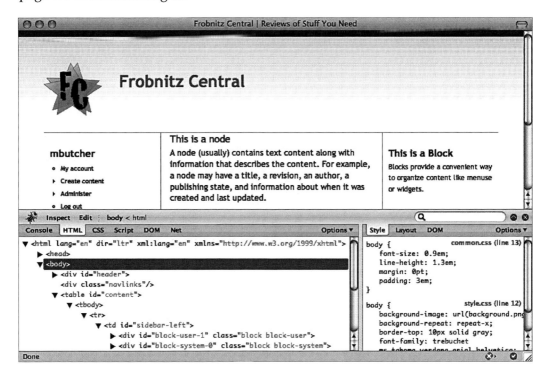

Firebug is running inside of Firefox (though I have hidden the Firefox toolbars to squeeze more into the screenshot). In the lower-left pane, Firebug is displaying an HTML representation of the current state of the document.

To the right of the HTML browser is the CSS browser, which is currently displaying the styles attached to the highlighted HTML element. Since the <body> tag is highlighted in the HTML, the CSS viewer is showing all styles related to the <body> element.

Using Firebug will help you find bugs, understand what is happening in the browser, and test out ideas right there. We will be using it in Chapter 3 to learn the basics of jQuery.

The Drupal Devel package

Seasoned Drupal developers have created special Drupal modules designed to make developing for Drupal easier. The Devel package contains some of the most useful developer modules.

Devel provides a suite of utilities to help developers work on Drupal. The Devel package can be downloaded from the Drupal website: `http://drupal.org/project/devel`. This package provides five modules:

1. **Devel**: The main developer module.
2. **Devel generate**: A tool to randomly generate users, nodes, and other data for developing and debugging.
3. **Devel node access**: Tools for learning about what nodes are currently being accessed.
4. **Macro**: A tool to help you automate form submission for development and debugging purposes.
5. **Performance logging**: A tool to help you identify bottlenecks and memory usage.
6. **Theme developer**: A tool to help theme developers determine what code is generating what part of the HTML output.

The Devel and Theme developer modules are particularly helpful for JavaScript development. Devel gives us a handful of tools to do things such as clear server-side caches, find out about the PHP engine, examine the server's session record, and even re-install modules. It also provides some information about how the current theme is structured. All of this can be useful while developing JavaScript and debugging client-server exchanges.

Devel must first be installed using **Administer | Site building | Modules**, and then the **Development** block must be added to one of the block regions using **Administer | Site building | Modules**.

 While developing themes and modules, it is often necessary to clear server-side caches. This module is worth installing just for the convenience of the cache-clearing feature.

The **Theme developer** module (also called **Themer**) provides an interface for finding out what template or Theme Engine call generates a particular piece of HTML. As with **Devel**, the **Theme developer** module must be installed in **Administer | Site building | Modules**. Once that is done, the **Theme developer** tool will show up in the lower left corner of all of your Drupal pages.

The tool looks like this:

If you check the box, then the main **Theme developer** tool will open. With this tool, you can click on any part of the page and the tool will display information about the Theme Engine's rendering of that piece of HTML as seen here:

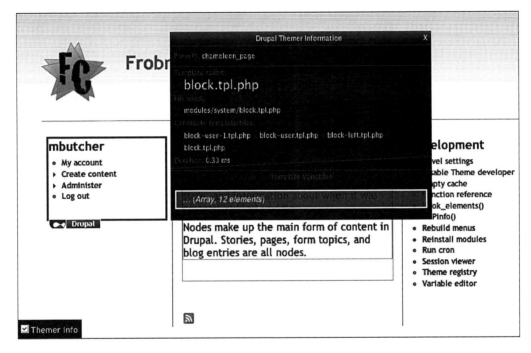

There are a few things to notice in the screenshot. First, around the Navigation block in the left-hand column, there is a gray box. The box appeared when I clicked on that block. It indicates that the HTML fragment is the one currently being examined.

Second, there is a gray semi-opaque pop-up window in the center of the image. That is the Themer tool. It displays information about the currently selected HTML fragment. In this case, it tells us what template file was used to generate the block and what theme that template came from. By clicking on the lighter gray box at the bottom of the Themer tool, we could also examine all of the variables passed to that theme.

Finally, if you examine the screenshot you might notice that there are also bordered boxes around the main node. Whenever the mouse hovers over a themeable element, a red box is drawn around that element.

In the screenshot, you might also notice the new block in the righthand navigation. This is the Developer block we discussed. To add this block to your own site, go to **Administer | Site building | Blocks** and add the Development module to the right sidebar..

Understanding the details of how this works is not important at present. Later, when we look at themes in more detail, you may want to use this tool to help locate which templates are responsible for generating various parts of the page. These are the main tools that you will be using when developing JavaScript for Drupal.

Summary

At this point we finished with our introduction to Drupal. We looked at various languages and technologies used in Drupal. We then had a high-level overview of the Drupal architecture followed by an examination of some key Drupal concepts, such as users, blocks, and nodes. From there we moved on to developers tools, learning about a few utilities that can expedite Drupal JavaScript development.

This chapter has been introductory in nature, and has been light on code. In the next chapter we'll make a practical turn, focusing on writing Drupal-centric JavaScript code. There, we will build our first JavaScript project.

2
Working with JavaScript in Drupal

The first chapter in this book introduced Drupal and JavaScript. It also explained the role that JavaScript plays in the Drupal 6 environment. We will now move beyond mere explanation and take a look at the practical details and examples.

In this chapter, we will be working with JavaScript inside of a Drupal environment. We will begin by exploring how JavaScript is included in Drupal pages, and then create our first script for Drupal. While we're not going to cover the basics of the JavaScript language (there are already lots of available resources on the topic), the code we create here will be simple and straightforward.

The purpose of this chapter is to cover the basics on how JavaScript can be used within Drupal 6. In that regard, this chapter will serve as a foundation for our future JavaScript development. Here are the topics that we're going to cover:

- Serving JavaScript from Drupal
- Creating a first script
- Creating a simple theme
- Adding JavaScript to a theme

Without further ado, let's get going.

How Drupal handles JavaScript

How is JavaScript typically used? Mostly, it is used to provide additional functionality to a web page, which is usually delivered to a web browser as an HTML document. The browser receives the HTML from the server and then begins the process of displaying the page. During this parsing and rendering process, the browser may request additional resources from the server such as images, CSS, or Flash. It then incorporates these elements into the document displayed to the user.

In this process, there are two ways that JavaScript code can be sent from the server to the browser. First, the code can be placed directly inside the HTML. This is done by inserting code inside the `<script>` and `</script>` tags:

```
<script type="text/javascript">
 alert('hello world');
</script>
```

This is called including the script **inline**.

Second, the code can be loaded separately from the rest of the HTML. Again, this is usually done using the `<script>` and `</script>` tags. However, instead of putting the code between the tags, we use the `src` attribute to instruct the browser to retrieve an additional document from the server.

```
<script type="text/javascript" src="some/script.js"></script>
```

In this example, `src="some/script.js"` points the browser to an additional script file stored on the same server as the HTML document in which this script tag is embedded. So, if the HTML is located at `http://example.com/index.html`, the browser will request the script file using the URL `http://example.com/some/script.js`.

The </script> tag is required

When XML was first standardized, it introduced a shorthand notation for writing tags that have no content. Instead of writing `<p></p>`, one could simply write `<p/>`. While this notation is supported by all modern mainstream browsers, it cannot be used for `<script></script>` tags. Some browsers do not recognize `<script/>` and expect that any `<script>` tag will be accompanied by a closing `</script>` tag even if there is no content between the tags.

If we were developing static HTML files, we would simply write HTML pages that include `<script></script>` tags anytime we needed to add some JavaScript to the page. But we're using Drupal, not static HTML, and the process for adding JavaScript in this environment is done differently.

Where Drupal JavaScript comes from?

As with most web content management systems, Drupal generates HTML dynamically. In the previous chapter, we talked about how this is done through interactions between the Drupal core, modules, and the theme system. A single request might involve several different modules. Each module is responsible for providing information for a specific portion of the resulting page. The theme system is used to transform that information from PHP data structures into HTML fragments, and then compose a full HTML document.

But this raises some interesting questions: What part of Drupal should be responsible for deciding what JavaScript is needed for a page? And where will this JavaScript come from?

In some cases, it makes sense for the Drupal core to handle JavaScript. It could automatically include JavaScript in cases where scripts are clearly needed.

JavaScript can also be used to modify the look and feel of a site. In that case, the script is really functioning as a component of a theme. It would be best to include the script as a part of a theme.

JavaScript can also provide functional improvements, especially when used with AJAX and related technologies. These features can be used to make more powerful modules. In that case, it makes sense to include the script as a part of a module.

So which one is the best: modules, themes, or core? Rather than deciding on your behalf, Drupal developers have made it possible to incorporate JavaScript into all three:

- The Drupal core handles including the core JavaScript support as needed. The Drupal and jQuery libraries are included automatically when necessary.
- When theme developers needs to add some JavaScript, they can do so within the theme. There is no need to tamper with the core, or to accompany a theme with a module.
- Finally, module developers can add JavaScript directly to a module. In this way, modules can provide advanced JavaScript functionality without requiring modification of the theme.

In this book we will add scripts to themes and modules. As we get started with this chapter, we will begin with a theme.

Module or theme?

How do you decide whether your script ought to go in a theme or in a module? Here's a basic guideline. If the script provides functionality specific to the layout details of a theme, it should be included in a theme. If the script provides general behavior that should work regardless of the theme, then it should be included in a module.

Sometimes it is hard to determine when a script belongs to a theme and when it should to be placed in a module. In fact, the script we create here will be one such a case. We are going to create a script that provides a printer-friendly version of a page's main content. Once we have the script, we will attach it to a theme. Of course, if we want to provide this functionality across themes, we might instead create a module to house the script.

Since modules require some additional PHP development, we will delay examining them until Chapter 8. We will start out simply with a JavaScript-enabled theme.

Project overview: printer-friendly page content

As we continue through this book, each chapter will have at least one project. In this chapter, we are going to write one piece of JavaScript and then create a theme to utilize the JavaScript.

The JavaScript that we will write creates a pop-up printer-friendly window, and automatically launches the **print** dialog. This is usually launched from **File | Print** in your browser's menu.

Once we write the script, we will incorporate it into a theme, and add a special printing feature to the page(s) displayed with that theme. As we walk through this process, we will also create our first theme. (Technically, it will be a subtheme derived from the Bluemarine theme.)

By the end of this project, you should know how to create Drupal-friendly JavaScript files. You will also know how to create themes and add scripts to them. These are foundational tasks upon which we will build in subsequent chapters.

The first step in the process is to write the JavaScript.

The printer script

Our script will fetch the main content of a page and then open a new window, populating that window's document with the main content of the page. From there, it will open the browser's print dialog, prompting the user to print the document.

Since this is our first script, we will keep it simple. The code will be very basic, employing the sort of classical procedural JavaScript that web developers have been using since the mid-1990's. But don't expect this to be the norm. In the next chapter we will dive into what John Resig, creator of jQuery, calls the "New Wave JavaScript."

To minimize clutter and maximize the reusability of our code, we will store this new script in its own script file. The file will be named `printer_tool.js`:

```javascript
// $Id$
/**
 * Add printer-friendly tool to page.
 */

var PrinterTool = {};

PrinterTool.windowSettings = 'toolbar=no,location=no,' +
  'status=no,menu=no,scrollbars=yes,width=650,height=400';

/**
 * Open a printer-friendly page and prompt for printing.
 * @param tagID
 *    The ID of the tag that contains the material that should
 *    be printed.
 */
PrinterTool.print = function (tagID) {
  var target = document.getElementById(tagID);
  var title = document.title;

  if(!target || target.childNodes.length === 0) {
    alert("Nothing to Print");
    return;
  }

  var content = target.innerHTML;

  var text = '<html><head><title>' +
    title +
    '</title><body>' +
    content +
```

```
     '</body></html>';
  printerWindow = window.open('', '', PrinterTool.windowSettings);
  printerWindow.document.open();
  printerWindow.document.write(text);
  printerWindow.document.close();
  printerWindow.print();
};
```

Since this is our first piece of Drupal code, we are going to dwell on the details a little more than we will in future sections.

First, let's talk about some of the structural aspects of the code.

Drupal coding standards

In general, well-formatted code is considered a mark of professionalism. In an open source project such as Drupal, where many people are likely to view and contribute to the code, enforced coding standards can make reading and understanding what the code does easier.

When contributing code to the Drupal project, developers adhere to a Drupal coding standard (`http://drupal.org/coding-standards`). Add-on modules and themes are expected to abide by these rules.

It is advised that you follow the Drupal standards even in code that you do no anticipate submitting to the Drupal project. Along with keeping your code stylistically similar to Drupal's, it will also help you develop good coding habits for those occasions when you do contribute something to the community.

For the most part, the official Drupal coding standards are focused on the PHP code. But many of these rules are readily applicable to JavaScript as well. Here are a few important standards:

* Every file should have a comment near the top that has the contents `$Id$`. This is a placeholder for the version control system to insert version information.

Drupal uses **CVS (Concurrent Versioning System)** for source code versioning. Each time a file is checked into CVS, it will replace `$Id$` with information about the current version of the software. To learn more about CVS, visit `http://www.nongnu.org/cvs/`.

- Indenting should be done with two spaces (and no tabs). This keeps the code compact, but still clear.
- Comments should be used wherever necessary.
  - Doxygen-style documentation blocks (`/** ... */`) should be used to comment files and functions.
  - Any complex or potentially confusing code should be commented with `//` or `/* ... */`.
  - Comments should be written in sentences with punctuation.
- Control structure keywords (`if`, `else`, `for`, `switch`, and so on) should appear at the beginning of a line, and be followed by a single space (`if ()`, not `if()`). Here's an example:

```
if (a) {
  // Put code here.
}
else if (b) {
  // Put code here.
}
else {
  // Put code here.
}
```

- Operators (`+`, `=`, `*`, `&&`, `||`, and so on) should have a single space on each side, for example: `1 + 2`. The exception to this rule is the member operator (`.`), which is used to access a property of an object. There should be no spaces surrounding these. Example: `window.document` (never `window . document`).

Stylistic differences between PHP and JavaScript

Not all PHP coding standards apply to JavaScript. PHP variables and function names are declared in all lower case with underscores (_) to separate words. JavaScript typically follows different conventions.

JavaScript variables and functions are named using **camel case** (sometimes called **StudlyCaps**). For a variable or function, the first word is all lower case. Any subsequent words in the variable or function name are capitalized. Underscores are not used to separate words. Here are some examples:

```
var myNewVariable = "Hello World";
function helloWorld() {
  alert(myNewVariable);
}
```

While this convention is employed throughout the Drupal JavaScript code, there is currently no hard-and-fast set of JavaScript-specific coding conventions. The working draft, which covers most of the important recommendations, can be found at `http://drupal.org/node/260140`.

Here is a summary of the more important (and widely followed) conventions:

- Variables should always be declared with the `var` keyword. This can go a long way towards making the scope of variables explicit. As we will see later in the book, JavaScript has a particularly broad notion of scope. Functions inherit the scope of their parent context, which means a parent's variables are available to the children. Using `var` makes it easier to visually identify the scoping of a variable. It also helps to avoid ambiguous cases which may lead to hard-to-diagnose bugs or issues.
- Statements should always end with a semicolon (`;`). This includes statements that assign functions, for example, `myFunction = function() {};`. Our `print` function, defined earlier, exhibits this behavior.

Why do we require trailing semicolons?

In JavaScript, placing semicolons at the end of statements is considered optional. Without semicolons, the script interpreter is responsible for determining where the statement ends. It usually uses line endings to help determine this. However, explicitly using semicolons can be helpful. For example, JavaScript can be compressed by removing whitespace and line endings. For this to work, every line must end with a semicolon.

- When an anonymous function is declared, there should be a space between the function and the parentheses, for example, `function () {}`, not `function() {}`. This preserves the whitespace that would be there in a non-anonymous function declaration (`function myFunction() {}`).

There are other conventions, many of which you will see in this book. But the ones mentioned here cover the most frequently needed.

With coding standards behind us, let's take a look at the beginning of the `printer_tool.js` file.

The first lines

Let's take another look at the first ten lines of our new JavaScript:

```
// $Id$
/**
 * Add printer-friendly tool to page.
 */
```

```
var PrinterTool = {};

PrinterTool.windowSettings = 'toolbar=no,location=no,' +
  'status=no,menu=no,scrollbars=yes,width=650,height=400';
```

The first line is a comment with the `$Id$` tag required by the coding standards. If this file were checked into CVS, the line would be replaced with something like this:

```
// $Id: print_tools.js,v 1.0 2008/07/11 08:39 mbutcher Exp $
```

As you can see, CVS will add some information about the version of the file. This information includes the name of the file, its version number, when it was checked in, and who checked it in.

Directly beneath the ID comment is the file-wide documentation block.

Documentation blocks use a special comment style beginning with a slash and two asterisks: `/**`. Automated documentation tools can later scan the file and pick out the documentation blocks, automatically generating API documentation for your script.

The role of the file-wide documentation block is to explain what the code in the file does. The first line should be a single-sentence description of the file. Additional paragraphs may be added.

In the following line, we define our `PrinterTool` object:

```
var PrinterTool = {};
```

This code is declaring the PrinterTool variable and assigning it an empty object literal (`{}`). This line plays an interesting role in the structure of our application, and we will see constructs like this both within Drupal and in the later chapters of this book.

> An object literal is a notation for defining an object by using its symbolic delimiters, rather than by using a new constructor. That is, instead of calling the `new Object()` constructor, we use the symbolic representation of an empty object, `{ }`, to declare an empty un-prototyped object. We will use this method frequently in this book.

The role of the `PrinterTool` object is to serve as a **namespace** for our application. A namespace is an organizational tool that allows the software developer to collect various resources together . This is done without having to worry that these resources will be in conflict with those created by other developers.

> Objects that function as namespaces should always begin with an initial capital letter, such as `Drupal` or `PrinterTools`.

Let's consider an example. The main function in our `printer_tool.js` file is named `print()`. But `print` is a very common name, and the built-in JavaScript `window` object already has a function named `print()`. So how do we distinguish our `print()` from `window`'s `print()`?

One popular method of solving this problem is to assign objects to namespaces. Then the developer can explicitly specify which `print()` ought to be used.

Let's look at the next line of the script for an example:

```
PrinterTool.windowSettings = 'toolbar=no,location=no,' +
    'status=no,menu=no,scrollbars=yes,width=650,height=400';
```

Here we create the `windowSettings` string object, assigning it a long value that will later be used when calling JavaScript's built-in `window.open()` function.

But `windowSettings` is defined as a member of the `PrinterTool` namespace.

If we were to insert the following code directly beneath the previous line, what would happen?

```
alert(windowSettings);
```

We would get an error since there is no object in the current context named `windowSettings`. To retrieve the value of the `windowSettings` object, we would need to write this instead:

```
alert(PrinterTool.windowSettings);
```

Now the alert dialog would be created and populated with the string `'toolbar=no, location=no,status=no...'`.

That is how namespaces function. If we were to call `print()`, it would use the `window.print()` function. Remember, `window` is the default scope for browser-based JavaScript. To call the `print()` function, which this script defines, we would have to provide the full namespace `PrinterTool.print()`.

Since we are talking about it already, let's take a closer look at the `PrinterTool.print()` function.

The print() function

The `PrinterTool.print()` function looks like this:

```
/**
 * Open a printer-friendly page and prompt for printing.
 * @param tagID
```

```
 *    The ID of the tag that contains the material that should
 *    be printed.
 */
PrinterTool.print = function (tagID) {
  var target = document.getElementById(tagID);
  var title = document.title;

  if (!target || target.childNodes.length === 0) {
    alert("Nothing to Print");
    return;
  }

  var content = target.innerHTML;

  var text = '<html><head><title>' +
    title +
    '</title><body>' +
    content +
    '</body></html>';

  printerWindow = window.open('','',PrinterTool.windowSettings);
  printerWindow.document.open();
  printerWindow.document.write(text);
  printerWindow.document.close();
  printerWindow.print();
};
```

The function starts with a documentation block. As with a page-level documentation block, this begins with a single sentence describing the function. If more information is needed, we could include additional sentences after this first line.

In this documentation block, we also have a special keyword `@param`. This indicates to the documentation processor that we are about to describe one of the parameters for this function. The `@param` keyword should be followed by the names of the arguments it describes. In our case, there is only one param, `tagID`. These are the only two things that should be on this line.

The next line should be indented two more spaces, and should describe the parameter.

Order Matters

`@param` tags should always describe arguments in order. If we have a function with the signature `myFunction(paramA, paramB)`, then the documentation block should have the `@param paramA` section before the `@param paramB` section.

Our function here does not have a return value. If a return value were to exist, that too would need to be documented. Consider this example function:

```
function sum(a, b) {
    return a + b;
}
```

The documentation block for such a function might look like this:

```
/**
 * Add two numbers.
 *
 * This function adds two numbers together and returns
 * the sum.
 *
 * @param a
 *    The first number.
 * @param b
 *    The second number.
 * @return
 *    The sum of a and b.
 */
```

An automated documentation tool, such as Doxygen, can use such a well-formatted comment to create a helpful API reference.

Let's continue and look at the next part of the code.

First, we assign a function to `PrinterTool.print`:

```
PrinterTool.print = function (tagID) {
```

Essentially, what we have done is created a method named `print()` attached to the `PrinterTool` object. The function takes one argument: `tagID`. This will be the ID of an element in the HTML document.

 A function defined with the form `name = function () {}` is called a **function expression**. For all intents and purposes, it works the same as a typical **function declaration** of the form `function name() {}`. The subtle differences are explained in the official Mozilla JavaScript documentation: `http://developer.mozilla.org/En/Core_JavaScript_1.5_Reference:Functions`.

Inside the function, we begin by getting information from the document that the browser is currently displaying:

```
PrinterTool.print = function (tagID) {
    var target = document.getElementById(tagID);
```

```
var title = document.title;
if (!target || target.childNodes.length === 0) {
  alert("Nothing to Print");
  return;
}
var content = target.innerHTML;
```

There are two major pieces we want to retrieve from the document. These pieces are the title of the document and the contents of some specified element. We start by finding that element.

To find the element, we search the document for an element with an ID passed in as `tagID`. The **DOM (Document Object Model) API**, which defines standard objects that describe HTML and XML documents, provides a method called `getElementById()`. It searches the DOM for an element with the given ID, and returns the element if it is found.

> The DOM API is standardized by the World Wide Web Consortium (`http://w3.org`), and is implemented by all major web browsers. With the DOM, we can manipulate HTML and XML documents from JavaScript.

We store the desired element in the `target` variable. We then get the `title` of the current document.

Next, we check to make sure that target is set and that it has content. This is done using the conditional `if (!target || target.childNodes.length === 0)`. If `target` is `null` or undefined, `!target` will return `true`. If the `target` element has no children, then the `childNodes.length` will be 0. In either of these circumstances, the function will alert the user of the problem and return without opening a printer-friendly page.

> **Strong Equality and Type Coercion**
>
> When comparing two objects for equality in JavaScript, we usually do something like this: `if (a == b) { /* do something */ }`. In this case, the JavaScript interpreter will try to convert both a and b to the same type before comparing them. So the string "0" is equal to the integer 0. Often times this is good. However, sometimes coercion can cause problems, as it might give the faulty impression that two values are equal when they are not. To avoid this problem, use the **strong equality operator** (===). As a programmer, you should keep this difference in when as you write your code.

Once the script has made it beyond this test, we know there is content inside of the `target` element. We want the content of `target` to be a string (rather than as mere DOM objects), so we access that information using target's `innerHTML` property.

At this point, we have the two major pieces of information we need: the `title` of the page and the `content` that we want to print.

Next, we want to put this information into a new window and prompt the user to print the contents of that window:

```
PrinterTool.print = function (tagID) {
  var target = document.getElementById(tagID);
  var title = document.title;

  if(!target || target.childNodes.length == 0) {
    alert("Nothing to Print");
    return;
  }

  var content = target.innerHTML;

  var text = '<html><head><title>' +
    title +
    '</title><body>' +
    content +
    '</body></html>';

  printerWindow = window.open('', '', PrinterTool.windowSettings);
  printerWindow.document.open();
  printerWindow.document.write(text);
  printerWindow.document.close();
  printerWindow.print();
}
```

The portion we are concerned with is highlighted in the function.

First, we create the `text` variable, which holds the HTML for our new printer-friendly version. This document is sparse. All it has is a `title`, the `content` that we want to print, and the required HTML tags.

Next, we open a new window with `window.open()`. This is where we use the `PrinterTool.windowSettings` property that we defined earlier. The new window will have a default blank document. We open that document for writing (`printerWindow.document.open()`), write `text` to it, and then close it for writing.

Now we have a new window with the content that we want to print. The last highlighted line, `printerWindow.print()`, opens the printer dialog.

Our first JavaScript tool is now written. Next, we will create a new theme and incorporate this tool into the theme.

Creating a theme

As we saw in Chapter 1, Drupal separates layout and styling information from processing code. HTML is usually stored in templates or theme functions. The CSS along with other styling information (including some images) are also stored separately from the functional code.

A **theme** is a collection of resources, (usually template files, CSS, JavaScript, and images) that can be plugged into Drupal to provide layout and styling to a site.

If we want to change the look and feel of a site, the best place to start is with a theme.

W've already created a JavaScript file that provides additional printing functionality. In this section, we are going to create a new theme, and then incorporate our new script.

Typically, a theme must provide the following things:

- HTML markup for common Drupal structures such as pages, blocks, comments, and nodes. This will include navigational elements.
- Any styles needed. This is typically done in the CSS files.
- Any necessary images or media elements that will play a substantial role in layout.
- Information about the theme, including a screenshot.

In addition to these, many themes will also provide:

- JavaScript files that may be necessary for added functionality.
- Other sorts of media, such as Flash animations, may occasionally be needed.
- PHP code that performs complex layout tasks may sometimes be used.

A theme must have at least one pre-defined file (the theme's `.info` file). Commonly though, full themes have eight or more files.

Full themes and subthemes

The first step in creating our theme is deciding whether we want to start from scratch or begin with an existing theme. If we were to start from scratch, we would create a **full theme**. But if we wanted to build on another theme, we could create another kind of theme called a **subtheme**.

To create a full theme, we would need to implement all of the required features of a theme, and perhaps add on some other features as well. Typically, this would involve creating all of the necessary templates, a couple of CSS files, and a couple of helper files.

Sometimes, it is more expedient to begin with an existing theme and just override the things we want to change. This is the capability that subthemes, a new addition in Drupal 6, provide.

From a technical perspective, creating a full theme is not difficult, but it is time-consuming. In contrast, a subtheme can be created quickly. Since our focus is on JavaScript, and not theming, we will be creating a subtheme. That way, we can make the most of an existing project and keep our work to a minimum.

As the name implies, a subtheme is derived from another theme. Therefore, we will need to pick a theme to start with. Drupal comes with six themes pre-installed, and these vary in method and complexity. For example, **Garland** is a complex theme with templates, JavaScript, CSS, and lots of special PHP. In contrast, **Chameleon** generates simpler HTML, but does all of this in pure PHP code, without reliance on template files.

Since we want to focus our attention on JavaScript, it would be best to start with a simple theme. From there, we will selectively override only what we need.

Our theme of choice will be the **Bluemarine** theme, which has a very basic PHPTemplate-based structure that is easy to customize.

 Looking for a good base theme to start with? Check out the **Zen** theme in the contributed themes at `http://drupal.org/project/zen`. It's built to enable subtheming. You will need to create some CSS content, but the HTML structure is all in place.

We will with Bluemarine and create a new subtheme, borrowing as much as possible from the base theme.

Creating a theme: first steps

To create a theme, we will do the following:

1. Create a directory for the theme.

2. Create the theme's `.info` (dot-info) file.

3. Add our first files.

After we've finished these three short steps, we will add our JavaScript to the theme.

A precaution for theme developers

To get build our theme correctly, we will need to be able to view it. But to view it, we will need to have it enabled. What if we make a mistake that prevents Drupal from rendering correctly? We could lock ourselves out of the administration page. To prevent this from happening, it is wise to set the administration theme to one of the default themes. This is done in **Administer | Site configuration | Administration theme**.

Creating a theme directory

Every theme should have its own directory.

When you install Drupal, one of the directories created is called `themes/`. If you take a look inside that directory, you will see all of the top-level (non-subtheme) themes that Drupal provides. Do not put your themes in there. This directory is only for themes that come with Drupal's core.

Themes, like modules, go inside the `sites/` subtree. The `sites/` area also appears inside the Drupal directory and is created when you install Drupal. Inside the `sites/` directory, two folders are created by default: `sites/all/` and `sites/default/`.

To better understand these two directories, keep in mind that one installation of Drupal can serve multiple sites. For example, if I have a site called `example.com` and a site called `anotherexample.com`, I can use one installation of Drupal to serve both.

The first site I install will be installed in `sites/default/`. The next site I install will need to go in its own folder (for example, `sites/anotherexample.com/`). Content that only belongs to a single site should go in that site's directory.

For example, if I want to install a special theme for `anotherexample.com`, I should put the theme in `sites/anotherexample.com/themes/`.

In other cases, I may want to share a theme or module across all sites. In these cases, files would go in `sites/all/`. In this book, we will be putting all of our themes and modules in `sites/all/themes/` and `sites/all/modules/`.

If in doubt, put files in `sites/all/`. This makes it easier to share your work between sites.

With that background material behind us, let's create our theme directory. The name we give to this directory will be the name of our theme.

Theme and module names should always be in a lower case, and may be composed only of letters, numbers, and underscores. In the `.info` file, we will be able to attach a human-readable name to the theme. That may use spaces, capital letters, and other special characters.

Our first theme will be in `sites/all/themes/frobnitz/` as seen in the following screeshot:.

If this is the first theme you create, you may also need to create the `sites/all/themes/` directory.

Once the directory is created, we need to add a special file to tell Drupal about the theme.

Creating the .info file

Inside `sites/all/themes/frobnitz/`, we need to create a file to provide important information about our theme. The file will always be named after the theme, and end with the extension `.info`. Because of the extension, it is usually called the theme's **dot-info file**.

We will create `frobnitz.info`, and add the following contents to the file:

```
; $Id$
name = Frobnitz
description = Table-based multi-column theme with JavaScript
enhancements.
version = 1.0
core = 6.x
base theme = bluemarine
```

The `.info` file contains a handful of lines with the form `name = value`. These entries provide basic information about the theme.

Some of this information is displayed to the user (for example, `name` and `description`). Some information is used by Drupal to make sure that this theme will work with the installed version of Drupal. The `core` parameter is used for that.

Later in this chapter, we will see some other entries that contain information directly related to the display of the theme. With those parameters, we can change the way the theme looks and behaves just by altering the values.

The `name`, `description`, `version`, and `core` fields are required for all themes.

- The `name` field is used to give our theme a human-friendly name. You can use capital letters and spaces in this field.
- The `description` parameter is used to provide a one-sentence explanation of what the theme does.
- The `version` field should indicate which version number of this theme is. As with most software, you typically start with `1.0`.
- Finally, the `core` field should indicate what version of Drupal this theme works with. For us, it will always be `6.x`.

There's one additional parameter in our file:

```
base theme = bluemarine
```

The `base theme` parameter is what we use to inform Drupal that our theme is a subtheme, derived from `bluemarine`. If we were creating a theme from scratch, we would not include this line.

For the time being, this is all we need in our theme file. Later, we will add more.

Modifying .info files and clearing the cache

To improve performance, Drupal caches theme information, particularly the theme's `.info` file. When you change the contents of that file (for example, when you add a new script or stylesheet), you will need to clear the theme information cache to force Drupal to re-read the `.info` file. The most reliable way to do this is through **Administer | Site configuration | Performance**. At the bottom of that page is a button labeled **Clear cached data**. Press that button to clear the cache.

Adding files to the theme

At this point, we've actually created a working theme. Only the theme's directory and `.info` file are required. With just those two elements, we can now go to **Administer | Site building | Themes** and select our **Frobnitz** theme.

Of course, all Frobnitz will be at this point is an exact duplicate of Bluemarine The following screenshot shows a sample of the Frobnitz theme:

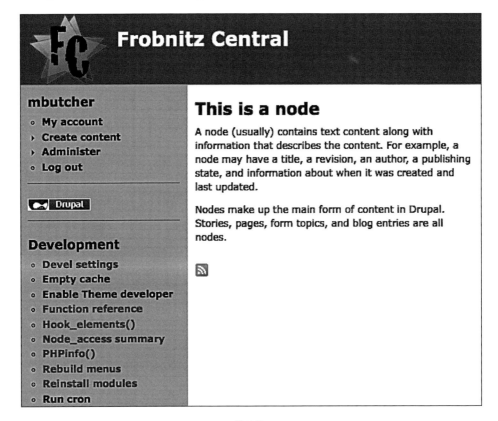

The logo image, titles, and all other information in the screenshot is showing through the regular site configuration. The look and feel should be identical whether we choose Bluemarine or our new Frobnitz style.

What we want to do now is add something new to our theme, and what better place to start than with a stylesheet.

Our theme will import all of the stylesheets of its parent. So in our theme, we inherit `style.css` from Bluemarine. Looking at the HTML source for a page rendered with Frobnitz, we would see a line like this:

```
<link type="text/css" rel="stylesheet" media="all"
      href="/drupal/themes/bluemarine/style.css" />
```

If we didn't want that style to be loaded from Bluemarine, we could simply create another file named `style.css` in our own theme's directory. This new file would override Bluemarine's.

But we don't want to start over and rebuild the stylesheet. We just want to add a few extra styles. To do this, we will create a new stylesheet called `frobnitz.css`. This CSS file will also go inside our `sites/all/themes/frobnitz/` folder.

 Like PHP and JavaScript, the Drupal project defines coding standards for CSS. You can learn more about these here: `http://drupal.org/node/302199`.

To begin, all we will do is add a black, one-pixel border on the right side of the lefthand column. The stylesheet looks like this:

```
#sidebar-left {
    border-right: 1px solid black;
}
```

 Cascade: the 'C' in 'CSS'.

Drupal will add styles in a specific order, with theme styles added last. Because of this, you can predictably make use of the CSS cascading behavior. The previous declaration will be added to the declaration made in Bluemarine's `style.css` file. That means we will get the combination of styles in `style.css` and `frobnitz.css`, with `frobnitz.css`'s declarations taking precedence.

But before our new stylesheet will have any effect, we need to tell Drupal to include it as part of the theme. This is done with a simple addition to the `frobnitz.info` file:

```
; $Id$
name = Frobnitz
```

```
description = Table-based multi-column theme with JavaScript
enhancements.
version = 1.0
core = 6.x
base theme = bluemarine
stylesheets[all][] = frobnitz.css
```

Only that last line, which is highlighted, is different. This informs Drupal that there is a stylesheet that should be used on all format types for this page, and is named `frobnitz.css`.

The `all` keyword indicates that this stylesheet applies to all media format types. CSS format types include `print` (for printed media), `screen` (for screen displays), and other types.

While this directive uses an array-like syntax, it does not function like an array. You cannot, for example, refer to `stylesheets[all][1]`.

The empty square brackets on the end emulate the PHP array assignment operation. This stylesheet is added to a list of stylesheets. This array-like syntax, which we will see again in the next section, indicates that an attribute can be used multiple times. For example, we could add another stylesheet using `stylesheets[all][]` = `anotherstyle.css`.

The base path for a stylesheet included using `stylesheets[][]` is always the path of the theme. In other words, `stylesheets[all][]` = `frobnitz.css` will point to `sites/all/themes/frobnitz/frobnitz.css`.

Remember to clear the theme cache to see the updates after changing this file (see the information box a few pages back).

Now, after clearing the cache, we can see the results of our labor:

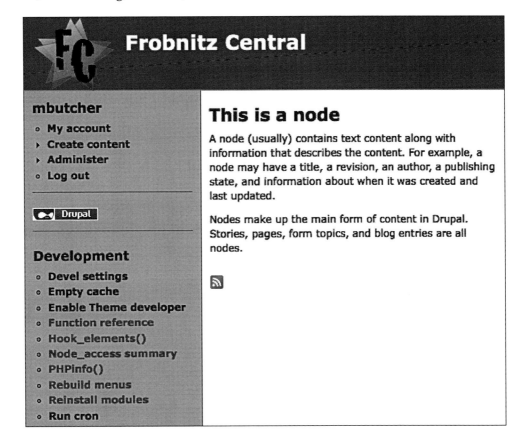

Notice the black line between the lefthand menu and the main page contents. That's what we added with our new stylesheet.

These last three segments were a rushed tour through the process of creating a new theme. We will continue to build on our theme throughout this book. In the next section, we will work with theme templates and theme JavaScript. However, this is not a comprehensive introduction to themes.

If you are interested in learning more about theming in Drupal 6, the best place to start is with the official theming handbook: `http://drupal.org/theme-guide`.

The CSS file

Next, we need to make a quick addition to the CSS file—the `frobnitz.css` file mentioned in the last section. This will provide a very simple style for the tool we are going to add. Here is what it looks like:

```
#printer-button {
  float: right;
  font-weight: bold;
  padding-right: 20px;
}
```

This CSS simply adds a definition for some element with the ID of printer-button. We will see that element a little later in this chapter. The styles here will float that element to the right side of the screen, add a little padding, and make the font bold.

Adding JavaScript to a theme

We now have a shiny new theme to work with. Let's turn our attention to incorporating our JavaScript print tool into that theme.

This will require three short steps:

1. Add a template that will display a **Print** link.
2. Make a minor adjustment to the stylesheet to make this link stand out.
3. Add the JavaScript to our page.

Let's start with the template.

Overriding a template

Bluemarine already has all of the templates required for displaying Drupal. However, we want to add a link on the righthand side of the main content display that will show a **Print** link. When clicked, this link will run our JavaScript.

To do this, we want to **override** Bluemarine's `page.tpl.php` file. In other words, we want to provide a Frobnitz template that will be used instead of Bluemarine's. Since we want it to primarily look the same, we will start by copying `themes/bluemarine/page.tpl.php` into `sites/all/themes/frobnitz/`.

 The **page template** (`page.tpl.php`) is responsible for rendering the main structure of a Drupal page, including the main body of the HTML.

Let's take a quick look at the page template just to see howit's structured. Don't worry about the details. Most of it is just boilerplate HTML:

```php
<?php
// $Id: page.tpl.php,v 1.28 2008/01/24 09:42:52 goba Exp $
?>
<!DOCTYPE html PUBLIC "-//W3C//DTD XHTML 1.0 Strict//EN"
  "http://www.w3.org/TR/xhtml1/DTD/xhtml1-strict.dtd">
<html xmlns="http://www.w3.org/1999/xhtml"
      lang="<?php print $language->language ?>"
      xml:lang="<?php print $language->language ?>"
      dir="<?php print $language->dir ?>">

<head>
  <title><?php print $head_title ?></title>
  <?php print $head ?>
  <?php print $styles ?>
  <?php print $scripts ?>
  <script type="text/javascript"><?php /* Needed to avoid Flash of
Unstyle Content in IE */ ?> </script>
</head>
5<body>
<table border="0" cellpadding="0" cellspacing="0" id="header">
  <tr>
    <td id="logo">
      <?php if ($logo) {
        ?><a href="<?php print $front_page ?>"
          title="<?php print t('Home') ?>"><img
          src="<?php print $logo ?>"
          alt="<?php print t('Home') ?>" /></a><?php } ?>
      <?php if ($site_name) { ?><h1 class='site-name'><a
        href="<?php print $front_page ?>"
        title="<?php print t('Home') ?>"><?php
        print $site_name ?></a></h1><?php } ?>
      <?php if ($site_slogan) { ?><div class='site-slogan'>
<?php print $site_slogan ?></div><?php } ?>
    </td>
    <td id="menu">
      <?php if (isset($secondary_links)) { ?><?php print
      theme('links', $secondary_links,
        array('class' => 'links', 'id' => 'subnavlist'))
      ?><?php } ?>
      <?php if (isset($primary_links)) { ?><?php
        print theme('links', $primary_links,
          array('class' => 'links', 'id' => 'navlist'))
```

```
        ?><?php } ?>
        <?php print $search_box ?>
      </td>
    </tr>
    <tr>
      <td colspan="2"><div><?php print $header ?></div></td>
    </tr>
  </table>
  <table border="0" cellpadding="0" cellspacing="0" id="content">
    <tr>
      <?php if ($left) { ?><td id="sidebar-left">
        <?php print $left ?>
      </td><?php } ?>
      <td valign="top">
        <?php if ($mission) { ?><div id="mission"><?php
          print $mission ?></div><?php } ?>
        <div id="main">
          <?php print $breadcrumb ?>
          <h1 class="title"><?php print $title ?></h1>
          <div class="tabs"><?php print $tabs ?></div>
          <?php if ($show_messages) { print $messages; } ?>
          <?php print $help ?>
          <?php print $content; ?>
          <?php print $feed_icons; ?>
        </div>
      </td>
      <?php if ($right) { ?><td id="sidebar-right">
        <?php print $right ?>
      </td><?php } ?>
    </tr>
  </table>

  <div id="footer">
    <?php print $footer_message ?>
    <?php print $footer ?>
  </div>
  <?php print $closure ?>
  </body>
  </html>
```

There are a few important things to note about the template.

First, templates are the only place in Drupal where you will see this mix of PHP code and HTML. By design, Drupal keeps programming logic separate from layout. Themes are the only area where these two converge.

PHP logic will always be enclosed inside the **PHP processor instruction** tag: `<?php ... ?>`

Second, the PHP code in templates is generally restricted to the following:

- Simple print statements (`print $variable_name`)
- A handful of function calls, usually to either the theming subsystem (`theme()`) or to the translatation subsystem (`t()`)
- Control structures, like `if/else` and `foreach`, to determine what needs to be displayed

If you are not a PHP expert, you can learn these techniques just by reading the themes.

Finally, the page template creates the basic framework for the page. Smaller sections are created by other templates, and provided to this template late in the rendering process.

For example, in Bluemarine, blocks are themed with `block.tpl.php`. Then the themed blocks are put in their designated regions. In this example, all of the blocks that are displayed in the lefthand column will be formatted and placed in the siderbar-left region, which is designated in the `page.tpl.php` file by the `$left` variable. Then the `page.tpl.php` file simply prints `$left`:

```
<table border="0" cellpadding="0" cellspacing="0" id="content">
  <tr>
    <?php if ($left) { ?><td id="sidebar-left">
      <?php print $left ?>
    </td><?php } ?>
    <td valign="top">
      <?php if ($mission) { ?><div id="mission"><?php
        print $mission ?></div><?php } ?>
      <div id="main">
```

There are many variables to keep track of in the `page.tpl.php` template (`block.tpl.php` is much simpler). Fortunately for us, we won't be dealing with all of the variables directly. We're more interested in the HTML and JavaScript.

The Garland theme (`themes/garland/`) is very well-documented. You can get an idea of what each variable stands for by reading the comments at the top of Garland's templates.

What we now want to do is add a snippet of HTML to this theme that will add our new link. Here is our addition:

```
<table border="0" cellpadding="0" cellspacing="0" id="content">
  <tr>
    <?php if ($left) { ?><td id="sidebar-left">
      <?php print $left ?>
    </td><?php } ?>
    <td valign="top">
      <?php if ($mission) { ?><div id="mission"><?php print $mission
                                       ?></div><?php } ?>
      <!-- New Content -->
      <div id="printer-button"><a
        href="javascript:PrinterTool.print('main')" >
        Print</a></div>
      <!-- End new content -->
      <div id="main">
        <?php print $breadcrumb ?>
        <h1 class="title"><?php print $title ?></h1>
        <div class="tabs"><?php print $tabs ?></div>
        <?php if ($show_messages) { print $messages; } ?>
        <?php print $help ?>
        <?php print $content; ?>
        <?php print $feed_icons; ?>
      </div>
    </td>
    <?php if ($right) { ?><td id="sidebar-right">
      <?php print $right ?>
    </td><?php } ?>
  </tr>
</table>
```

This section of code occurs about thirty five lines into `page.tpl.php`. The highlighted lines are highlighted are the only ones we've added. In these lines we create a new `<div></div>` tag, and then put a `Print` link inside. When clicked, this link executes the JavaScript function `PrinterTool.print('main')`.

Recall that `PrinterTool.print()` takes as an argument the HTML ID (the value of `id=""` in an HTML tag). Taking a glance at `page.tpl.php`, we can quickly see what element this ID belongs to. In fact, it's directly below the link we just added:

```
<div id="main">
  <?php print $breadcrumb ?>
  <h1 class="title"><?php print $title ?></h1>
```

```
    <div class="tabs"><?php print $tabs ?></div>
    <?php if ($show_messages) { print $messages; } ?>
    <?php print $help ?>
    <?php print $content; ?>
    <?php print $feed_icons; ?>
</div>
```

This is the section of the template the print function will load into a new window for printing. Of course, all of the PHP calls will be replaced with HTML content.

We have one short step left before we can test out our new JavaScript-enabled theme.

Adding the script file

When we add a new CSS file, we need to inform Drupal about this by adding an entry to the .info file. Adding a JavaScript file is done in the same way.

The first step in adding our JavaScript file will require copying the script into the sites/all/themes/frobnitz/ directory, and then editing the frobnitz.info file.

```
; $Id$
name = Frobnitz
description = Table-based multi-column theme with JavaScript
enhancements.
version = 1.0
core = 6.x
base theme = bluemarine
stylesheets[all][] = frobnitz.css
scripts[] = printer_tool.js
```

Again, we're making only a one-line change. We're adding printer_tool.js to the list of scripts automatically included by this theme.

Before viewing, don't forget to refresh the theme cache by either clearing it or visiting the **Administer | Site building | Themes** page.

Now when we visit a page on our site, it should have the **Print** link as seen here:

Clicking on this new link should execute the JavaScript and launch our new script, which will load a printer-friendly page into its own window. It will then launch the browser's print dialog:

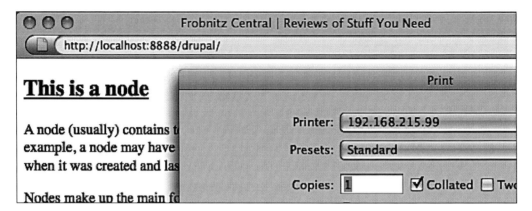

We've just completed our first project. We have added JavaScript to a theme.

Summary

In this chapter we have undertaken our first project. We have created a new JavaScript library and a new theme. We also added some JavaScript functionality to the new theme.

Our task here has been fine for the purpose of illustration. But, as we shall see in the coming chapters, we can accomplish much more (often with much less code) using the JavaScript libraries included with Drupal.

In the next chapter, we will look at one library (newly added in Drupal 6) that is generating a lot of excitement both in and outside of the Drupal community—jQuery, which will be our focus in Chapter 3.

3
jQuery: Do More with Drupal

In the last chapter, we built our first Drupal JavaScript. There, we used only standard JavaScript functions and tools to build our printing library. One of the benefits of working with Drupal is having access to libraries bundled with the core Drupal platform.

In this chapter, we will look at one such library: jQuery. Specifically, we will look at the following:

- An overview of the jQuery library
- The basics of using jQuery
- Using jQuery within Drupal
- Building a sticky node rotation tool with jQuery
- jQuery effects, DOM manipulation, and events

As of Drupal 6, jQuery plays a major role in Drupal-centered JavaScript. For this reason, we will make a heavy use of jQuery in the remainder of this book. By the end of this chapter, you will be able to understand jQuery code. This will be a tremendous help not only in the rest of this book, but in your future Drupal JavaScript development.

jQuery: the write less, do more library

I wrote my first JavaScript code in the year 1995. It ran in Netscape 2.0, and looked something like this:

```
alert("Welcome to our site!");
```

In the next few years, I wrote lots of calculators, image rollovers, and scrolling status bar messages. My overall impression of JavaScript, which I suspect was the attitude shared by most web developers at the time, was that JavaScript was a low-powered tool for adding cutesy effects to web pages.

I've never been happier to eat my words.

With the birth of dynamically refreshing page renderers and the **XMLHttpRequest (XHR)** object (or control), JavaScript suddenly became a much more powerful tool for manipulating the contents of a page without requiring a full round trip to a remote web server.

 XMLHttpRequest and AJAX (Asynchronous JavaScript And XML) will be the subject of Chapter 5.

But with all of this new power came a fair amount of complexity. The core JavaScript libraries—the tools bundled in the major browsers—have remained relatively small. And, as newer versions of browser have been released, writing working code often requires an awful lot of boilerplate "cross-browser compatibility" code.

Where changes have been made, they are often complex. The event model in Microsoft's IE and the one in Mozilla-based browsers diverged quite a while ago. The DOM API, implemented on all major browsers, is anything but simple. Anyone who has written an AJAX library from scratch will be quick to voice an opinion on the trials and tribulations of getting that library to work on all major browsers. Even manipulating a stylesheet from JavaScript has come with its share of subtle implementation differences.

In short, even while the capabilities of JavaScript had reached new heights, the JavaScript developer was often forced to use complex APIs and work around lots of compatibility issues while building a program.

As JavaScript's capabilities and usefulness grew, another change was occurring. This was a culture change among the JavaScript developers.

For a long time, the online JavaScript developers released useful snippets of code. These were not libraries in the proper sense of the word, but short snippets of code that could be copied and pasted into a project, tweaked, and then reused.

As JavaScript matured, so did the community around it. The focus shifted (to some degree at least) from producing "useful doodads" to creating polished libraries designed for reuse in a wide variety of settings.

Today's popular libraries, such as Prototype, YUI, Dojo, and the like, have all been built for general use.

One of these libraries, jQuery, has enjoyed a meteoric rise to fame, and deservedly so. Why has it been so successful? It's because the focus of the library has been on taking the really difficult (but important) JavaScript tools and making them easy to use. Thus, in the words of its creators, jQuery is the "Write Less, Do More JavaScript Library."

The jQuery site is a great source for API documentation, tutorials, plug-ins, and additional tools: `http://jquery.com`.

With a library like this, less time must be spent on writing boilerplate code or trying to address cross-browser compatibility issues. Instead, more time can be spent on creating a powerful and robust JavaScript code.

 jQuery is an open source software, dual-licensed under either the GPL (the GNU General Public License) or the MIT license. Just as the Drupal developers included jQuery in Drupal 6, so can you use jQuery on your own sites and web applications.

jQuery provides a single, compact library focused on simplifying the following tasks:

- Finding things in a document
- Manipulating a document through the DOM
- Interacting with a document's CSS
- Working with events
- Providing flexible AJAX tools

Moreover, the library works on all major browsers—Internet Explorer, Firefox, Opera, and Safari.

As if this weren't enough, there's one more feature of jQuery that makes it a compelling tool for developers: It uses a tremendously compact syntax that makes it easy to accomplish surprisingly complex tasks in just a line or two of code. With a simple plug-in architecture (with hundreds of plug-ins already available), it can be extended to provide additional functionality.

 One popular addition to jQuery is **jQuery UI**. This library provides complex widgets such as calendars, accordions, and tabs. It also provides support for drag-and-drop, sorting, and other similar tasks. You can learn more about it at `http://ui.jquery.com`.

Okay, so what's the catch?

There is one aspect of jQuery that gets criticized on occasion. jQuery code looks different from other JavaScript, and this can make that initial jump into jQuery seem daunting. But once you've made that leap, it will change the way you write JavaScript.

Hopefully, this chapter will help make that first step an easy one. Let's take that first step now.

A first jQuery script

When you read the first few pages of this chapter, you must have noticed that very little was said about Drupal. jQuery is a standalone library with no dependency on Drupal, which means it can be used on its own.

In fact, that's the way we are going to dip our toes into the topic. Don't worry though. We will be coming back to Drupal just a little later in the chapter.

We are going to start out with a static HTML document and take a look jQuery in this simplified context. In the next section, we will apply this knowledge in the Drupal environment.

Getting jQuery

For our examples here, you will need the jQuery library. At this point, you have two options. You can either download a copy from `http://jQuery.com` or you can make a copy of the jQuery library that comes with Drupal. It's located in `misc/jquery.js`.

The copy that comes with Drupal is packed. Extraneous whitespace (such as newlines) has been removed, and long variable names have been replaced with short computer-generated names. That makes it difficult to read the jQuery library code, should you so desire.

For that reason, I suggest going to jQuery.com and downloading the **Uncompressed** version (it's right there on the front page).

 For more about packing code with **Packer**, see `http://dean.edwards.name/packer/`

Once you have the `jquery.js` file (or `jquery.1.2.X.js`), just make sure it is in the same directory as the HTML we will create in the next part.

Again, since Drupal already includes jQuery, there is no need to worry about putting this file where Drupal can see it. In fact, you should not put this in a Drupal directory.

Now, let's work up some simple HTML for a few examples.

Starting with a basic HTML document

Here is a very basic HTML document that will serve as a starting point. Notice that we are including the jQuery library in the `<script></script>` tag in the document's head.

```
<!DOCTYPE html PUBLIC "-//W3C//DTD XHTML 1.0 Transitional//EN"
    "http://www.w3.org/TR/xhtml1/DTD/xhtml1-transitional.dtd">
<html xmlns="http://www.w3.org/1999/xhtml"
    xml:lang="en" lang="en">
<head>
    <meta http-equiv=»Content-Type»
        content=»text/html; charset=utf-8»/>
    <title>sample</title>
    <script src="jquery.js" type="text/javascript"></script>
</head>
<body>
    <h1 id="title">Title</h1>

    <p class="odd">Paragraph 1</p>
    <p class="even">Paragraph 2</p>
    <p class="odd">Paragraph 3</p>
    <p class="even">Paragraph 4</p>
</body>
</html>
```

This document is just a standard XHTML document. We are concerned mainly with the highlighted sections. The first highlighted section loads jQuery with the file `jquery.js`. If you grab a copy from `jQuery.com`, it may have a name such as `jquery.1.2.X.js`. You can either rename that or change the `src` attribute to point to your version.

The second highlighted section exhibits the elements that we will be using in this section. Nothing should look unfamiliar here. It's just a header and four paragraphs.

Notice that the `<h1></h1>` has an id, `id='title'`. Also, the paragraph elements have `class` attributes. The even paragraphs have the `even` class, and the odd paragraphs have the `odd` class.

We are going to make use of these `id` and `class` attributes.

Now we're ready for some jQuery.

Querying with jQuery (and the Firebug console)

We could demonstrate jQuery by adding a script to the previous HTML code. But that would require us to write a complete script first. For a gentler method of introducing jQuery, we will start out with the Firebug console introduced in Chapter 1, instead.

Firebug is a Firefox add-on that provides a debugging and inspection environment for web development—particularly for HTML, CSS, and JavaScript. One of the tools it provides is a **JavaScript console**, which can be used to interactively run JavaScript. That's exactly what we are going to do.

While we will use Firebug here, the Safari browser also includes similar developer tools that can be enabled by opening Safari's preferences window and then checking the **Show Develop menu in menu bar** check box. The examples that follow can also be duplicated on Safari's **Web Inspector** console.

To start off, let's use jQuery to find the `<h1></h1>` element in our document. Locating parts of an HTML document was, after all, the original purpose of using jQuery.

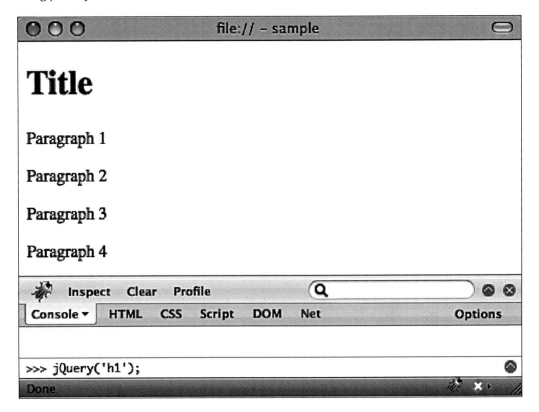

In the previous screenshot, we are entering the command `jQuery('h1')`. When we run this command, it should search the document and return a jQuery object that wraps a list of all `<h1></h1>` elements found in the document.

So if we hit *ENTER* to run the command, we will get something that looks like this:

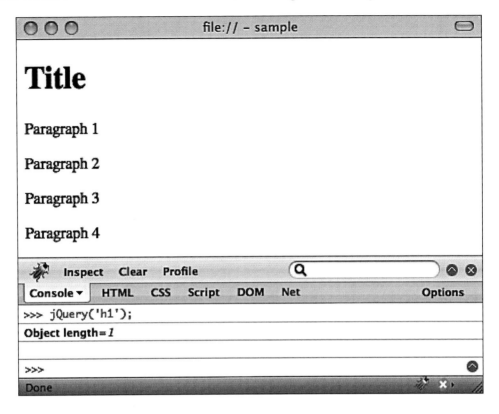

In this case, when we executed `jQuery('h1')`, it returned an object with a `length` property set to 1. We know that there is only one `<h1></h1>` element in our document, so this length is what we would expect. In fact, if we re-ran the command as `jQuery('p')`, we would get the output: **Object length=4**. The length is four because there are four `<p></p>` tags in our document.

What is the output on the console?

When you run a command on the console, Firebug always prints a representation of the returned value to the screen. In this way, you can get an idea of what is coming back from any executed function. If you come from a Ruby or Python background, this behavior is similar to the interactive shells of these languages.

But what is the object? It's a jQuery object. To show this, we could enter the following command into the console:

```
jQuery('h1') instanceof jQuery
```

The `instanceof` operator will compare the object type on the left hand with the type on the right hand. It will return **true** if both objects are of the same type. More specifically, if the object on the left side has the type of the object on the right side, the result will be true. Since prototypes are chainable, they may not have exactly all the same prototypes).

It should come as no surprise that the returned value is **true**. In fact, even if we were to search for an element that does not exist in our document, `jQuery()` will still return a `jQuery` object (though the `length` of this object will be `0`).

How do you run a function called `jQuery()` without the `new` keyword, and get a `jQuery` object? The short answer is that `jQuery()` acts like a **factory method**. This function simply creates a new `jQuery` object and then returns that object. For this reason, there is no need to use `new jQuery()`. Instead, just `jQuery()` will suffice.

 This method of creating a new `jQuery` object resembles the Factory pattern. The **Factory** is a common design pattern in object-oriented programming, where one object (the factory) takes responsibility for creating new instances of another object. Of course in jQuery's case, the `jQuery` object is responsible for creating new `jQuery` objects. The flexibility of JavaScript's prototyping system allows this sort of thing to be done.

What else can we query with jQuery?

We can get elements by their `id` attribute:

```
jQuery('#title');
```

To find an element by ID, we prefix the ID with a "#" (pound sign).

We can also get elements by class:

```
jQuery('.even');
```

Just as an ID is prefixed with #, a class is prefixed with a "." (dot).

Now we've seen four jQuery query strings: `h1`, `p`, `#title`, and `.even`. Do these look familiar? If you have worked with CSS stylesheets before, they should. jQuery's query language is none other than the CSS selector language.

To style all the even paragraphs in CSS, you might write a CSS statement like this:

```
p.even {
/* style info */
}
```

That same selector, `p.even`, can be used in jQuery to find all even paragraphs like this: `jQuery('p.even')`. Since jQuery supports all CSS selectors through CSS version 3, you can even build more complex queries. For example, we could grab only the first `even` paragraph with this:

```
jQuery('p.even:first');
```

This looks for all paragraphs with the `even` class, and then returns only the first of those. Incidentally, since CSS 3 defines a pseudo-class for selecting the even and odd children, we could drop the `odd` and `even` classes altogether and use queries such as `jQuery('p:nth-child(even):first')` or even `jQuery('p:even:first')` (We've just used the "`:`" (colon) symbol to indicate that we are using a built-in CSS pseudo-class instead of the even class we defined ourselves.)

Throughout this book we will be using these CSS selectors to create queries. But if you are eager to gain a detailed insight into selectors, you might want to take a look at the W3C's current CSS 3 draft standard at `http://www.w3.org/TR/css3-selectors/`.

Bye bye, jQuery(); hello $()

We've seen our last `jQuery()` function call.

From now on, we will be using an alias for that function. Instead of calling `jQuery('h1')`, we will be making calls such as `$('h1')`.

What is this "`$`" thing?

Surprising as it may seem, the `$` (dollar) sign is a legal character for function or variable names in JavaScript. That means `iNeed$`, `$tar`, and `my$amount` are all legal tokens in JavaScript. And as it turns out, so is `$`.

Making use of this, the jQuery developers aliased the `jQuery()` function to `$()`. That saves you five whole characters of typing. And it looks cool.

Generally speaking, you (as the software developer) can use either or both of these names to call jQuery. But the Drupal JavaScript convention suggests using the `$()` version. And so we shall.

Doing more with jQuery

We now have a glimpse of how we can find parts of a document with jQuery. But a querying engine alone doesn't get us too far. We need the ability to manipulate the information we've retrieved. Of course, jQuery provides such tools.

To start, let's get the text content of our `<h1></h1>` element. This is done with the `text()` function:

```
var title = $('h1');
title.text();
```

The first line retrieves a `jQuery` object containing our `<h1></h1>` element and stores this in the `title` variable. The second line calls the `jQuery` object's `text()` function. This will return all of the text inside of that element. Any HTML tags will be removed. (If you want the HTML content, use `html()` instead of `text()`.) Running this pair of statements would cause Firebug to output **"Title"** to the console.

Likewise, if we wanted to change the title of our document, we could call:

```
var title = $('h1');
title.text('New Title');
```

Immediately, the bolded text in the document would be changed as if we had written `<h1>New Title</h1>` instead of `<h1>Title</h1>`. What would Firebug output to the console when we set text? A string representing the `jQuery` object (for example **Object length=1**). This means that even a setter function returns an object. As we will see in a moment, this is an important aspect of the jQuery library.

Our two-line text-getting scriptlet is functional, but we can shorten it down to one line by making use of a convention called **function chaining** or **method chaining**. When we call a function that returns an object, we often store that object in a variable—as we did with the `title` variable. That way, we can use the object later by referring to `title`.

Sometimes we don't need to store the object, we just need to call one of its functions. Rather than storing the object in a variable, we can just use the dot operator (`.`) to chain the function to the function that returned the object.

Sounds confusing? An example will clear it up. We can rewrite our previous scriptlet like this:

```
$('h1').text('A New Title');
```

The `text()` function operates on whatever `jQuery` object the `$()` function returns.

> This is one of the important reasons why `$()` returns a `jQuery` object even if it doesn't find any matches to the query. Otherwise, scripts would be plagued with errors when a chain returned, say, a `null` instead of an object.

Just as with the earlier code, the previous line will find the `<h1></h1>` element and change its content.

jQuery makes greater use of the chaining concept by using a design pattern called the **Fluent Interface**. In a fluent interface, any member function that would normally return void (that is, nothing) returns its parent object instead.

> A **member function** is a function that belongs to an object. In most object-oriented languages, all functions are members of an object.

The jQuery object provides this type of fluent interface. So when we call `$('h1').text('A New Title')`, the title is changed; but we also get the `jQuery` object returned again.

How is this useful? Well, we can combine several tasks into the same line. Let's say we not only want to change the text of the title, but also want to underline the title. This additional step would involve changing the `<h1></h1>` element's CSS. We can chain another function to our code to accomplish this:

```
$('h1').text('New Title').css('text-decoration', 'underline');
```

The result should look something like this:

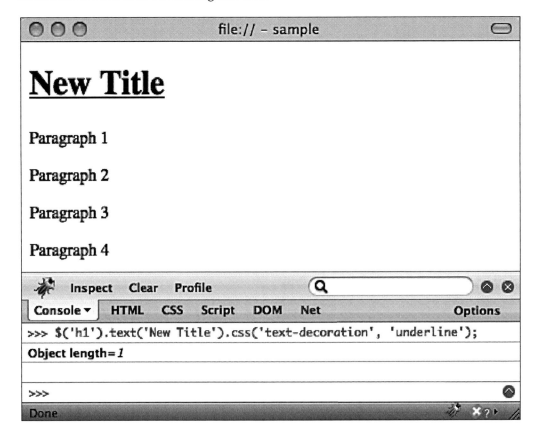

There are two things to notice here.

First, the title and text decoration have indeed changed.

Second, as you can see in the console output, the `css()` function still returned our `jQuery` object. That means we could continue our chain if we so desired.

Not every function returns a jQuery object

Before we get too addicted to the fluent interface, we should take another look at an earlier example as an illustration (or perhaps a reminder) that not all jQuery functions return `jQuery` objects.

In our first example of the `text()` function, we saw that running `$('h1').text()` returned the string `Title`.

In this case, we have a string object, not a jQuery object. Sure, we could continue chaining, but we could only call functions of the string object. For instance, the following would work just fine:

```
$('h1').text().substring(0,1);
```

The `text()` function returns a string, and `substring()` is a member function of a `string` object. However, we could not do this:

```
$('h1').text().css('color','red');
```

This would generate an error looking something like this: **TypeError: $("h1").text().css is not a function**. That happens because a `string` object does not have a `css()` function.

At this point, the important things to understand about jQuery are:

- How queries can be composed from CSS selectors
- How `$()` and `jQuery()` return `jQuery` objects (that often wrap lists of elements from the document)
- That jQuery function calls are often chained together to produce longer lines that do more

We will pick up more about jQuery as we proceed.

Feeling comfortable with the basic concepts of jQuery? Now it's time to get back to Drupal. We will be making use of jQuery to build Drupal-centric JavaScript.

Using jQuery in Drupal

So far, we have seen just a few lines of jQuery code. But, our examples have been independent of Drupal. How can we use jQuery inside of Drupal?

The answer is simple. If we write our JavaScript "the Drupal way", then Drupal will make it very easy to use jQuery. Here's what I mean.

How do we include JavaScript files in Drupal themes? By using the `scripts[]` directive in the theme's `.info` file. And if you're a PHP programmer, you can use the `drupal_add_js()` function in either a theme or a module.

If you use either of these means, then Drupal will automatically include the basic JavaScript libraries, including `drupal.js` and `jquery.js`. That's right. Drupal not only includes jQuery in its core distribution, but automatically includes it for you.

To see an example of this, we need not look further than the code we wrote in the previous chapter. Looking in the `<head></head>` section of the HTML for our theme, we can see the following `<script></script>` tags:

```
<script type="text/javascript"
        src="/drupal/misc/jquery.js"></script>
<script type="text/javascript"
        src="/drupal/misc/drupal.js"></script>
<script type="text/javascript"
        src="/drupal/sites/all/themes/frobnitz/printer_tool.js">
</script>
<script type="text/javascript">
        jQuery.extend(Drupal.settings, { "basePath": "/drupal/" });
</script>
```

All we added to our `.info` file was `scripts[] = printer_tool.js`. Drupal took care of adding the other two script files. But what is that last section? Well it is:

```
jQuery.extend(Drupal.settings, { "basePath": "/drupal/" });
```

This is another use of jQuery. It provides a few functions for extending an object, which assigns new attributes to an existing object on the fly.

In this case, the `extend()` function is taking the `Drupal.settings` object and adding a new property, `basePath`, with the value `/drupal/`. Here, `/drupal/` is the absolute web path to Drupal. That is, my Drupal installation resides at `http://localhost/drupal/`. The `basePath` property can then be used for constructing URLs.

Using the Firebug console, we can see the result of this extension. If we enter `Drupal.settings.basePath` on the console, Firebug will print **/drupal/**.

Using the jQuery object without constructing a new instance

In the Drupal-generated code that we just saw, you might notice that `jQuery` was referenced as an object, not as a function (note the missing parentheses after `jQuery`). Some jQuery functions do not need a list of elements or other contents before they can operate. Effectively, they can be used as static functions. The `extend()` function is such an example. In such cases, we don't need to build a new `jQuery` object. We can just use the main `jQuery` object.

The point to be made here is simply this: When we allow Drupal to manage our JavaScript, it handles the basic including necessary to make use of jQuery, and even initializes some things for us.

Of course, there's a converse side to this.

Don't do it yourself!

There may be a temptation to do things "the old fashioned way." One may be inclined to simply edit the `page.tpl.php` template and add `<script></script>` tags manually. After all, isn't this how we do things when we write HTML by hand?

Don't do it.

When you start adding scripts by hand, you are circumventing Drupal's JavaScript system. Drupal doesn't inspect the HTML to see what files are included in the template. So you may not get the default script files included automatically (unless some other part of the theme or some module triggers the automatic inclusion).

In addition to perhaps not getting the autoloading that we saw, adding scripts by hand can also lead to conflicts. For example, a library can get loaded manually, and then get loaded by a module. If the library versions are different (or if two libraries share functions with the same name), the results can be surprising.

There's one more thing in addition to these two: If you are planning on submitting your code as a theme or module, hardcoding scripts this way will no doubt prompt experienced Drupal developers to file bug reports against your code.

The moral of this story is simply to let Drupal handle the JavaScript library loading.

That's all there is to using jQuery within Drupal. We are now ready to move on to a project.

Project: rotating sticky node teasers

Now we're ready to start our first jQuery project. We're going to write some code that rotates sticky node teasers. With a description like that, it's got to be good!

Seriously, the phrase "rotating sticky node teasers" is pretty jargon-laden. Here's what I mean.

On various Drupal pages, the main content area of the page is composed of node teasers. The following front page is one such example:

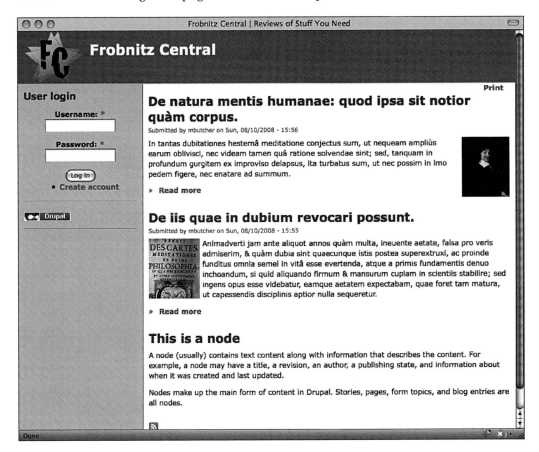

In the content shown in the screenshot, there are three different nodes displayed. But only the teaser version is shown. (One would have to click on **Read more** to see the full story.)

By default, items are arranged from the newest to the oldest. The newest node is listed first on the page.

But what if we wanted to have a node that was always displayed on the top?

This can be accomplished by marking a node as **sticky**. A sticky node floats to the top of the list of nodes on a page.

Nodes are marked as sticky using the content editor. Near the bottom of the editor page, there is a collapsed section called **Publishing options**. In that section, there are three checkboxes: **Published**, **Promoted to front page**, and **Sticky at top of lists**. This third box influences an item's stickiness. In the examples to follow, we will check all three to display sticky items on the front page. You can also mark a node as sticky by going to **Administer | Content management | Content**, checking the desired node, and selecting **Make sticky** from the drop-down list of **Update options**.

If we were to configure three items to be sticky at the top, the result would look something like this:

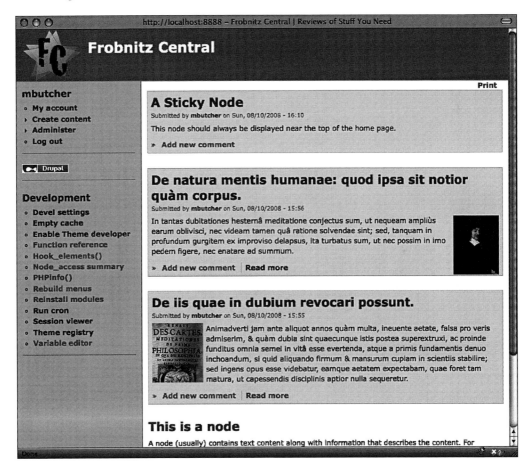

In the screenshot, the three nodes with light gray backgrounds are marked as sticky. Even when we add new nodes, these three will remain at the top of the page.

The screenshot also provides the basis for understanding the project we are about to do.

Having three sticky nodes at the top is in some ways counterproductive, for only one of those is really at the top. The others are de-emphasized in virtue of being displayed in a lower position on the page.

In addition, the regular content (like the important **This is a node** story we created in Chapter 2) is in danger of disappearing beneath the browser's fold. A viewer has to scroll down on the page to see what's new. This isn't an attractive feature.

So, we're going to change the display of sticky nodes. We're going to build a tool, enlisting the help of jQuery, which will rotate through the sticky nodes. It will display them one at a time, in sequence.

After the first node has been displayed for a period of time, it will "fade out" into the background, and then the second sticky node will "fade in". It, too, will be displayed before fading out again. This process will continue as long as the page is displayed. This is a process often referred to as **rotating** a list.

This is what the phrase "rotating sticky node teasers" means.

Using this technique, all of our sticky nodes will be displayed in the page's top slot. In addition, the standard content display will begin in the second spot (rather than the fourth spot in the case of our earlier screenshot). Since sticky items no longer take up a lot of space, we can make four, five, or even six nodes sticky without making the display cumbersome to the visitor.

And we hope this will be an attractive, eye-catching feature for our visitors as well.

That's our goal. Let's move on to the code.

The StickyRotate functions

We are going to continue building on the `frobnitz` theme we created in the previous chapter. To start off, we are going to create a new JavaScript file called `sticky_rotate.js`. As usual, this will go in the `sites/all/themes/frobnitz` directory. And once again we will have to edit the `frobnitz.info` file in that directory.

```
; $Id$
name = Frobnitz
description = Table-based multi-column theme with JavaScript
enhancements.
version = 1.0
core = 6.x
base theme = bluemarine
```

```
stylesheets[all][] = frobnitz.css
scripts[] = printer_tool.js
scripts[] = sticky_rotate.js
```

Only that last highlighted line is new. It adds the sticky_rotate.js script to the list of scripts automatically loaded by the theme. Remember that you may need to clear the theme cache before Drupal adds this new script to the rendered output.

From here, we will begin editing the sticky_rotate.js file. The code we create will come in at around sixty lines, some of which is just comments.

Again, let's take a quick glance at the lines at the top of the file:

```
// $Id$
/**
 * Rotate through all sticky nodes, using
 * jQuery effects to display them.
 */

// Our namespace:
var StickyRotate = StickyRotate || {};
```

We start the file with the Id keyword as explained in the last chapter. Again, this is used by the version control system. (CVS is the official version control system for Drupal.)

Next, we have a documentation block describing the contents of the file. This is standard practice in Drupal. It is not always treated as required for JavaScript (though it is required for PHP). However, it's a good idea to include it.

Finally, once again we create a new object that we will use as a namespace for our library. In this case, StickyRotate will be our namespace, and all of our functions and public variables will be attached to that namespace.

Using the "or" operator for default assignment

In the previous code, the StickyRotate function is assigned StickyRotate || {}. The "||" (or) operator works in the following manner: If the StickyRotate variable already exists, it will be assigned to the StickyRotate variable on the lefthand side, and the Boolean logical operator will short circuit. But if StickyRotate doesn't already exist, then the right half of the || will be evaluated, and StickyRotate will be assigned an empty object ({}). In short, this construct allows us to assign StickyRotate a default value, only if StickyRotate is not already defined. This idiom is used frequently in JavaScript, and you will notice it in many Drupal files.

First, we will start out by writing a function that will take care of initializing the process.

The init() function

To accomplish our node rotation effect, we will need to do some setup when the page first loads. Our first function will take care of initializing sticky rotation:

```
/**
 * Initialize the sticky rotation.
 */
StickyRotate.init = function() {
  var stickies = $(".sticky");

  // If we don't have enough, stop immediately.
  if (stickies.size() <= 1 || $('#node-form').size() > 0) {
    return;
  }

  var highest = 100;
  stickies.each(function () {
    var stickyHeight = $(this).height();
    if(stickyHeight > highest) {
      highest = stickyHeight;
    }
  });
  stickies.hide().css('height', highest + 'px');
  StickyRotate.counter = 0;
  StickyRotate.stickies = stickies;

  stickies.eq(0).fadeIn('slow');
  setInterval(StickyRotate.periodicRefresh, 7000);
};
```

Taking a quick glance over the function we just saw, we will notice more than a few invocations of jQuery's $() function. In fact, we will be using jQuery to provide DOM and CSS manipulation, and also to provide some nice visual effects.

Let's take a closer look at the first few lines of the function:

```
StickyRotate.init = function() {
  var stickies = $('.sticky');

  // If we don't have enough, stop immediately.
  if (stickies.size() <= 1 || $('#node-form').size() > 0) {
    return;
  }

  /* The rest of the code... */
};
```

The first line is our function assignment. Just as we did in the previous chapter, we make use of JavaScript's ability to assign anonymous function declarations to variables. So this function can be called as `StickyRotate.init()`.

On the first line of this function, we create a local variable: `stickies`. It is assigned a jQuery object containing the results of the `$('.sticky')` query. As we saw earlier in the chapter, when jQuery is given the query string `.sticky`, it will search the document for elements assigned the CSS class named `sticky`.

 Effectively, this is the same as saying that it will search for all elements with the attribute declaration `class="sticky"`. However, one should keep in mind that the class may be added by JavaScript. Thus, it may not be visible when viewing the raw HTML source.

So what is this `sticky` class and where does it come from? Drupal's theming system assigns the `sticky` class to all sticky nodes. To see this for yourself, view the `node.tpl.php` in Bluemarine or Garland. (The class can also be set in PHP code. In Chameleon, which is a PHP-driven theme, this happens in a theming function `chameleon_node()`.)

In other words, we can rely upon Drupal to flag those sticky nodes for us. Our jQuery needs only to look for the right class.

So `stickies` should contain a jQuery-wrapped list of all of the sticky nodes on the page.

We only want to apply our effect on pages where there is more than one sticky node preview. After all, it wouldn't be all that useful or attractive to rotate through a list of one.

To address this situation, we add the next conditional:

```
// If we don't have enough, stop immediately.
if (stickies.size() <= 1 || $('#node-form').size() > 0) {
    return;
}
```

jQuery's `size()` function retrieves the number of items that the jQuery object is currently wrapping. Since our `stickies` variable refers to a jQuery object, we can call the `size()` function to determine whether our list is long enough to warrant rotating through it.

A `jQuery` object also has a public attribute named `length`, which contains the same information. We saw this attribute in the output of the Firebug console earlier in the chapter. Determining which one to use is a matter of preference, as both provide identical information. Some might argue that `length` is faster, since it is a property. However, `size()` just returns that property, so there is no real performance impact.

But that's not all our conditional does. It also runs another query to make sure that the current document does not contain an element with the ID `node-form`.

Why? This takes care of one possible place where our JavaScript might cause confusion. When a user is previewing a node, the node may show up twice (as a preview of the teaser version and of the full version). In such cases, it might appear that there are two sticky nodes, when really it's just the same node displayed twice. For example, take a look at the following screenshot:

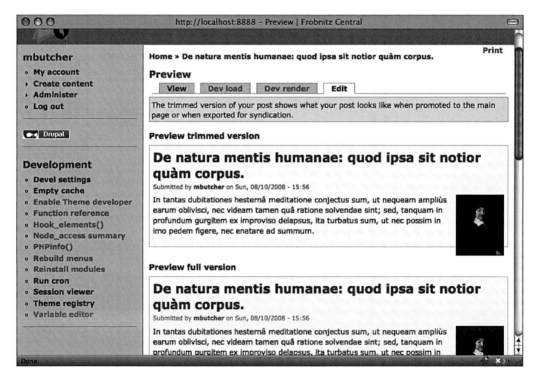

Unfortunately, there are no obvious cues in the node display that might make it easy for us to avoid the situation. But fortunately, preview screens also include the node-editing form. And the node-editing form always has the `node-form` ID.

So in that one corner case, we can avoid adding our effect when `$('#node-form').size()` is greater than `0`.

In the case where there is only one sticky node on a page, or when the sticky node is displayed as part of a content editing preview, the function simply returns without doing anything.

But if neither of those conditions is met, initialization continues. Let's take a look at what's next:

```
StickyRotate.init = function() {
  var stickies = $(".sticky");

  // If we don't have enough, stop immediately.
  if (stickies.size() <= 1 || $('#node-form').size() > 0) {
    return;
  }

  var highest = 100;
  stickies.each(function () {
    var stickyHeight = $(this).height();
    if(stickyHeight > highest) {
      highest = stickyHeight;
    }
  });
  /* The rest of the code... */
};
```

We are interested in the highlighted portion of the code. The focus of this snippet of code is the height of the area where our sticky nodes will be displayed.

Looking back at our three sticky nodes, we have two fairly large teasers (the two Latin Descartes' quotes), but we also have a very short one. The node entitled **A Sticky Node** has a one-line teaser: **This node should always be displayed near the top of the home page**.

What we don't want is for a short node like this to cause the page layout to shift significantly. We don't want the content to slide up for the short node, and then slide back down to make room for longer nodes.

What we do want then, is to control the height of the sticky nodes. We want them all to take up the same amount of screen space.

The code we just saw is designed to find the largest sticky node, get that node's height, and then use that as the height for all of the sticky nodes.

The `highest` variable will store the size of the highest node. By default, we set it to `100` pixels.

Next, we make use of another jQuery feature. Along with the rest of the jQuery goodies, there are a handful of basic list-traversing functions. One of these is the `each()` function, which iterates through each item in the list of nodes wrapped by a `jQuery` object. On each object, it executes the function passed into the `each()` function.

 There are actually two jQuery `each()` functions: One that iterates through the contents of a `jQuery` object, and one that iterates through any list-like object. The list-iterating version is called on the main jQuery object like this: `jQuery.each(myList, function () {})`.

So this version of `each()` takes one argument—a function object.

In our case, we are going to supply the `each()` function with an anonymous function that will do the height comparison:

```
stickies.each(function () {
  var stickyHeight = $(this).height();
  if(stickyHeight > highest) {
    highest = stickyHeight;
  }
});
```

When that anonymous function is executed, the `this` variable is set to the current list item. In our case, this will contain the current DOM element in the list of stickies.

 This method of formatting inline anonymous functions is conventional, and you will see the same formatting throughout jQuery and Drupal.

It is important to note that `this` is a DOM element object, not a `jQuery` object. We want to find the height of that object, but the easiest way to get the height of an element is to use the jQuery library. So in the second line, we pass `this` into `$()` to get a new `jQuery` object, Then we use jQuery's `height()` function to find out the element's height. This is all packed into the line that reads: `var stickyHeight = $(this).height()`.

While the first two lines of this code sample are complex, the next part is straightforward:

```
if(stickyHeight > highest) {
  highest = stickyHeight;
}
```

All we do here is check to see if the height of the current element is higher than the current highest (again, 100px by default). If it is higher, then the value of `stickyHeight` is assigned to `highest`. All we're doing, then, is finding the highest element and setting `highest` to that element's height.

There is one point of interest here. The `highest` variable is local to the `init()` function, and is declared outside of the anonymous function declaration. Doesn't it seem like this variable ought to be out of scope for the function inside our `each()` loop?

Yet, as the previous example shows, it is still accessible inside of the function's body.

This works because in JavaScript, functions inside other functions retain access to the variables of their parent functions. In other words, if function `a()` (the outer function) encloses the definition of function `b()` (the inner function), then function `b()` will have access to all of function `a()`'s local variables.

By the time the `each()` function returns, `highest` should be set to the pixel height of the highest sticky node that we will display.

We're ready to move onto the next part of the `init()` function:

```
StickyRotate.init = function() {
  var stickies = $(".sticky");

  // If we don't have enough, stop immediately.
  if (stickies.size() <= 1 || $('#node-form').size() > 0) {
    return;
  }

  var highest = 100;
  stickies.each(function () {
    var stickyHeight = $(this).height();
    if(stickyHeight > highest) {
      highest = stickyHeight;
    }
  });

  stickies.hide().css('height', highest + 'px');
  StickyRotate.counter = 0;
  StickyRotate.stickies = stickies;

  stickies.eq(0).fadeIn('slow');
  setInterval(StickyRotate.periodicRefresh, 7000);
};
```

These last several lines do all of the visible work.

To start off, we know that we currently have three sticky nodes. By default, they all will be displayed, each at its own height.

But we want them to be hidden initially, displaying them only one at a time. We also want to give them all the same height—the height of the tallest sticky node.

Making use of jQuery's chaining features, we can do this all in one line of code:

```
stickies.hide().css('height', highest + 'px');
```

What this will do is take all of the items wrapped in the `stickies` jQuery object and hide them (`hide()`), and then assign each the CSS property `height` set to the height of the highest element.

 PHP programmers should note that the "+" (plus) operator in JavaScript is used for string concatenation—a task done by the . (dot) operator in PHP.

Just as we saw earlier, in many cases, when a jQuery function is called on a `jQuery` object, every item that that `jQuery` object wraps is affected. Both the `hide()` and `css()` functions are examples of this.

Now that the list is hidden, we can get to work displaying the items one at a time.

First, we initialize a few public variables, `StickyRotate.counter` and `StickyRotate.stickies`. This first will help the later functions determine the index position of the currently displayed item. The second will provide our other functions with access to our jQuery `stickies` object.

 These variables are public because their scope is such that they can be accessed from anywhere in the script being currently executed.

Preparation is done. The next thing to do is display the first sticky node. And we want to do that with some panache. Specifically, we want to make it fade in.

```
stickies.eq(0).fadeIn('slow');
```

On this line, we take the stickies list and reduce it to just the first item. The `eq()` jQuery function is used to reduce a list to just one item, and take as a parameter the index of the item. We pass it `0` because we want the first item in the list.

Next, we use another jQuery function, `fadeIn()`, to provide us with an effect.

jQuery comes with several built-in effects, including `fadeIn()`, `fadeOut()`, `slideDown()`, and `slideUp()`. We use the `fadeIn()` effect here to gradually alter the opacity from transparent to completely opaque. For example, the following screenshot illustrates what a node item looks like when it's about a third of the way through the fading-in process:

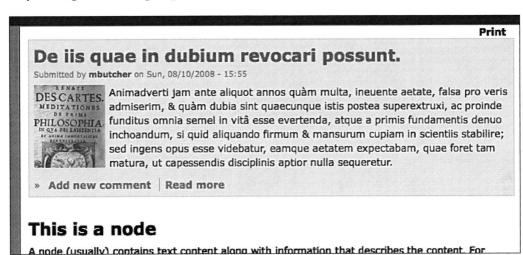

The `fadeIn()` function takes up to two parameters—the speed of the effect and a callback function. We will look at the callback later in this chapter. The first is the speed of the effect. It can be specified either as an integer representing the number of milliseconds that the effect should take, or one of three keywords: `slow`, `def` (or `normal`), and `fast`.

We used `slow` in our example.

The full effect of this, then, is to gradually fade-in only the first sticky node. The others remain hidden.

Finally, we are up to the last line in our `init()` function. This line sets up a time-delayed loop that will handle the fading-out and fading-in of the subsequent node displays.

```
setInterval(StickyRotate.periodicRefresh, 7000);
```

The `setInterval()` function is a built-in JavaScript function that takes as arguments a callback function and an interval in milliseconds. In this case, every `7000` milliseconds (seven seconds), the `StickyRotate.periodicRefresh()` function will be executed.

It is important to note that when we pass the function name to `setInterval()`, we do not add parentheses at the end of the function name. That would result in sending the results of that function to the `setInterval()` function.

Instead, we want to pass the function object so that `setInterval()` can call that function at the appropriate interval.

If we wanted to get really fancy, we could rewrite this function to pass a closure to the `setInterval()` function. In such a case, we wouldn't need to set any public variables. For the sake of simplicity (and performance), we will stick to our current implementation.

Of course, the `StickyRotate.periodicRefresh()` function has not been written yet. Let's turn to that now.

The periodicRefresh() function

This is the second (and the last non-anonymous) function in our project. As we saw earlier, it is called by the `setInterval()` function. In fact, barring some interruption, it will be called every seven seconds.

Fortunately, this new function makes use of the same tools just introduced, so our review of the function should go quickly.

```
/**
 * Callback function to change show a new sticky.
 */
StickyRotate.periodicRefresh = function () {
  var stickies = StickyRotate.stickies;
  var count   = StickyRotate.counter;
  var lastSticky = stickies.size() - 1;

  var newcount;
  if (count == lastSticky) {
      newcount = StickyRotate.counter = 0;
  }
  else {
      newcount = StickyRotate.counter = count + 1;
  }

  stickies.eq(count).fadeOut('slow', function () {
    stickies.eq(newcount).fadeIn('slow');
  });
};
```

Let's break this function into two chunks. Here is the first:

```
StickyRotate.periodicRefresh = function () {
  var stickies = StickyRotate.stickies;
  var count   = StickyRotate.counter;
  var lastSticky = stickies.size() - 1;

  var newcount;
  if (count == lastSticky) {
    newcount = StickyRotate.counter = 0;
  }
  else {
    newcount = StickyRotate.counter = count + 1;
  }

  /* More code... */
};
```

To make things easier on ourselves, we use `stickies` and `count` to store local copies of the `StickyRotate.stickies` and `StickyRotate.counter` variables. This makes for a cleaner code and reduces the chances for mistakes to be made when typing variable names.

The `lastSticky` stores the index number of the last sticky in the `stickies` list. (Actually, `stickies` is a jQuery object wrapping the list of stickies.)

At this point, we have the list of stickies, the index (`count`) of the current sticky, and the index (`lastSticky`) of the last sticky. Based on this, we can compute what item should be displayed next.

That is done with the simple conditional:

```
var newcount;
if (count == lastSticky) {
  newcount = StickyRotate.counter = 0;
}
else {
  newcount = StickyRotate.counter = count + 1;
}
```

 On a stylistic note, we could omit the curly braces for the `if` and `else` blocks. However, Drupal's coding standards strongly encourage developers to leave these braces in, for the sake of readability. For that same reason, it is also often suggested that the `if` or `else` statement be used rather than the ternary (? :) operator. However, in simple cases where the ternary is easier to read, it is acceptable.

Our conditional is basically checking to see if we have reached the last sticky node. If we have, then we want to start over again with the first node. Otherwise, we want to keep going through the list.

One interesting aspect of the previous code is that we want to set two variables at once. We want a local variable, `newcount`, pointing to the index of next sticky node. We also want to set the `StickyRotate.counter` variable to this new value so that future invocations of our `preiodicRefresh()` function will access the correct item in the list of sticky nodes.

To accomplish this, we use the double assignment:

```
newcount = StickyRotate.counter = 0;
```

Both variables will be assigned the value 0 if the current `count` is equal to `lastSticky`. Otherwise, `newcount` and `StickyRotate.counter` will be set to `count + 1`.

Now there are only a couple of additional lines to investigate:

```
StickyRotate.periodicRefresh = function () {
  var stickies = StickyRotate.stickies;
  var count   = StickyRotate.counter;
  var lastSticky = stickies.size() - 1;

  var newcount;
  if (count == lastSticky) {
    newcount = StickyRotate.counter = 0;
  }
  else {
    newcount = StickyRotate.counter = count + 1;
  }

  stickies.eq(count).fadeOut('slow', function () {
    stickies.eq(newcount).fadeIn('slow');
  });
};
```

The highlighted lines take care of fading-out the old sticky node, and fading-in the next sticky node in the list.

This is accomplished by (again) getting a single item from our list of stickies using the `eq()` function, and then calling the `fadeOut()` function.

This time, we call the `fadeOut()` function with both of its arguments. We set the speed to `slow`, and then give it an anonymous callback function.

The callback function uses the `newcount` variable to select the next item from the list of `stickies` and fades it in.

At first, a glance at these three lines of code might make it look unnecessarily complex. After all, can't we write something like the following instead?

```
stickies.eq(count).fadeOut('slow');
stickies.eq(newcount).fadeIn('slow');
```

This won't work as expected. Instead of getting a full fade-out followed by a fade-in, both will happen at the same time. In this case, two sticky node teasers will be displayed at the same time. This, in turn, means that the viewer will temporarily see two stacked sticky nodes. Then the top one will go away and the bottom one will slide up.

It's ugly.

The reason behind this is that the fading process takes time. For all practical purposes, though, fading is handled in a separate "thread". As soon as the fade is started, the script interpreter continues to execute the next line of the script. So the fading-in process will begin before the fading-out process has completed.

To work around this, we use the anonymous callback function that jQuery will fire when it has finished the fading-out. While this might seemingly lead to more complexity, it's only gained us a line of code. And as we will see in later chapters, being able to launch multiple effects at the same time can have its benefits.

Now we have two functions that, when used together, will provide our sticky node a rotation feature.

There's only one thing left to do. We need to make sure that our little `StickyRotate` tool gets started when a page loads.

Adding an event handler with jQuery

When a page loads, we want to start our `StickyRotate` tool. Practically speaking, we want to have the browser execute the `StickyRotate.init()` function when the page is done loading and is ready to add effects.

 We want it to be loaded because we want first, all of our sticky nodes to be loaded, and second, all of the CSS styles to be applied so that they don't override the styles we set dynamically. But we don't really want to wait for the images to load first.

Unfortunately, the two popular ways of accomplishing this have significant drawbacks.

The first method of calling the `init()` method is to embed a snippet of JavaScript somewhere in the page. For example, a section of code like this might be inserted somewhere in the document's body:

```
<script>
  StickyRotate.init()
</script>
```

What's wrong with this? For starters, it's messy. In order to make sure that it is executed correctly, we have to put the script somewhere in the HTML after the last sticky node. Otherwise, we run the risk of having the script execute before the HTML is completely loaded. This means that we have to hack the `page.tpl.php` file to insert the code in the appropriate place. This, in turn, can end up being a pain to maintain (and it is not very portable).

Instead, we might try to fire the event by adding `onload="StickyRotate.init()"` to the `<body></body>` element. This has two drawbacks. First, it means we have to hack `page.tpl.php`, which is undesirable. Second, `onload` is not implemented consistently across browsers, and it may take longer to fire than we would like (or it may fire before the document is really ready).

Fortunately for us, jQuery provides a third alternative. We can write a few lines of JavaScript that will attach an event handler to a special jQuery `ready` event. According to the jQuery documentation, the `ready` event is fired *the instant the DOM is ready to be read and manipulated*. (See `http://docs.jquery.com/Events/ready` for details.)

Here and throughout the book, we will use this method to execute code as soon as we can reliably do so.

Here's how we will do it for our present code:

```
$(document).ready(StickyRotate.init);
```

This code doesn't go in the HTML body, and does not need to be launched from `onload` or another HTML attribute. Instead, it is included in our `sticky_rotate.js` file.

Here's how this line works.

`$(document)` creates a `jQuery` object that wraps the `document` object. The `ready()` function assigns an event handler to the `ready` event of that object. This `ready` event is a special jQuery event that fires when the DOM is ready for manipulation. Roughly, though, it functions like the `(on)load` event, and should almost always be used instead of an `onload` handler.

The `ready()` function takes a function as a parameter. Often, developers will write an inline anonymous function to do the initialization. But we've already created an `init()` function that is suitable for our needs. So all we have to do is pass in that function object, and jQuery takes care of the rest.

But what if we have multiple scripts that need to do something when the document is ready? Do we need to write a master function to handle all of the initialization?

No we do not. One of the nice things about jQuery's event model design is that we can register multiple handlers for the `ready` event (or any other event)—and we can even do this in different script files. So, we can use `$(document).ready()` multiple times.

Now we have a tool that will rotate through sticky nodes, displaying them in order. Using the fade effect provided by jQuery, it will smoothly transition from one sticky node to the next. It will accomplish our goals of keeping the important information right at the top, while not occupying too much space (and subsequently pushing other information further down the page).

More importantly, we've gotten to see jQuery in action, providing querying tools, DOM manipulation features, effects, and event handlers. This will lay groundwork for later chapters.

A brief look backward

Now that we've seen the possibilities that come with jQuery, let's briefly reconsider how we built the printer tool in Chapter 2.

To build that tool, we had to make changes within the HTML of our theme, and we had to work with various DOM methods such as `getElementById()`.

With jQuery, we could have skipped the template part altogether, using the `ready()` function (and other jQuery event handlers) to create the printing link as the page was created. In fact, we will do something like this in the coming chapter.

Likewise, we could probably have trimmed down the size of our script by making use of jQuery's chaining feature.

But in the interest of moving forward, we will not spend time revising that code. Instead, the next chapter will cover some of the additional JavaScript functionality provided by Drupal.

Summary

This chapter has focused on jQuery. Initially, we looked independently at jQuery. We manipulated a static HTML document using jQuery. From there, we took a closer look at how jQuery is integrated with Drupal. Our main project in this chapter explored how jQuery can interact with HTML created by Drupal. We created a tool to take Drupal's default display of sticky nodes. We transform it into a rotating display, fading one item into view, and then fading it out again, only to fade-in the next item.

As we move on from here, we will explore more Drupal libraries. In the next chapter, we will look at Drupal behaviors—another powerful component in Drupal JavaScript development. But this isn't the last you will see of jQuery. On the contrary, it figures prominently in Drupal 6 JavaScript development.

4
Drupal Behaviors

In the previous chapter, we spent some time getting to know jQuery. We will now look at another library that comes bundled with Drupal. In fact, the library we will see here is Drupal-specific. The `drupal.js` library is composed of tools commonly used in Drupal-centred JavaScript.

There are four major sets of tools in `drupal.js`: translation functions, theming system, some utility functions, and the core code for Drupal Behaviors. In this chapter, we are going to focus on Drupal Behaviors and then examine some of the utility functions. Translation and theming will each get their own chapter.

In this chapter we will cover the following:

- The basics of the `drupal.js` library
- Understanding and using Drupal Behaviors
- Avoiding pitfalls in Drupal Behaviors
- Using utility functions

We will also do two projects in this chapter. The first project, a short one, will focus on behaviors. The second project will be grander in scope. We will combine our jQuery tools with the features we discover in `drupal.js` in order to create a simple text editor.

The drupal.js library

In the *Using jQuery in Drupal* section of the previous chapter, we saw how Drupal will automatically include the jQuery library when it detects that the page request uses JavaScript. When a theme or module, for example, includes a JavaScript file with a `scripts[]` entry in the `.info` file, Drupal will automatically include the standard JavaScript libraries.

Let's take another look at the scripts that get included:

```
<script type="text/javascript"
  src="/drupal/misc/jquery.js"></script>
<script type="text/javascript"
  src="/drupal/misc/drupal.js"></script>
<script type="text/javascript"
    src="/drupal/sites/all/themes/frobnitz/printer_tool.js">
</script>
<script type="text/javascript">
jQuery.extend(Drupal.settings, { "basePath": "/drupal/" });
</script>
```

Drupal generated this code from our printer tool script developed in Chapter 2. There are three JavaScript files included here. The first one is `jquery.js`, which was the focus of the previous chapter. The last one is `printer_tool.js`, the script we created in Chapter 2.

Sandwiched between them is `drupal.js`. Like `jquery.js`, `drupal.js` plays a prominent role in Drupal's client-side scripting efforts, which is included by default on any page that includes JavaScript.

But what exactly does it do?

Essentially, it is composed of four classes of tools:

1. Theming functions
2. Translation functions
3. Utility functions
4. Support for Drupal Behaviors

Theming functions provide a partial JavaScript implementation of the Drupal theming system. Using the theming system, we can theme JavaScript objects just like the PHP developers do on the server side.

Translation functions, which we will explore in the next chapter, provide language translation facilities to JavaScript. Just as is the case with the theming system, the translation system is designed to provide an API similar to the server-side PHP translation system.

Some of the tools provided by `drupal.js` cater to commonly needed services. I am referring to these as **Utility functions**.

Finally, Drupal offers a framework for adding scripted behaviors to a page. When the page is loaded, these behaviors are automatically "attached" to the page, and immediately take effect. This framework is called **Drupal Behaviors** (often shortened to just *behaviors*). If this all sounds unclear, don't worry. We will look at this topic in more detail later in this chapter.

Now we are ready to move on to a discussion of behaviors.

Drupal JavaScript behaviors

As I mentioned at the beginning of the chapter, the `drupal.js` library is Drupal-specific. The main advantage of using a tightly-coupled library is that the tools provided are aware of the Drupal structure and do things the Drupal way.

Behaviors are a good example.

The Drupal Behaviors feature provides a standard method for attaching some particular information (called a **behavior**) to zero or more elements on a page. To understand this admittedly vague description, let's start with an example and build a better explanation.

In the previous chapter we looked at registering a handler for the jQuery `ready` event—`jquery('document').ready()`. We can use that function to run some JavaScript as soon as the DOM is ready for manipulation.

For example, we might write a JavaScript snippet that dynamically adds a new `class` attribute to all paragraph tags:

```
$(document).ready(function () {
  $('p').addClass('fancy');
});
```

This script finds all paragraph elements and adds the `fancy` class. Since it is executed during the ready event, it will happen as soon as the DOM is ready for manipulation.

But what if we have a script that executes a little later and adds a new paragraph?

```
$('body').append('<p>Another paragraph</p>');
```

Now we have a paragraph that doesn't have the `fancy` class because it was added to the DOM after the ready event was handled.

Defining a behavior to handle repeatable events

The `ready` event that jQuery defines (and that we saw at the end of the previous chapter) is fired as soon as the DOM is ready for manipulation. But that's the only time it fires.

The DOM can undergo many changes between the time the page loads and when the user leaves the page. Some of those DOM changes may have an impact on how the other JavaScript works. In cases like this, we want to be able to re-run our query to add the `fancy` class whenever a new paragraph is inserted into the DOM.

This is the sort of case that Drupal Behaviors were designed to address. Instead of having our paragraph query run (once) when the `ready` event fires, we can define this as a behavior. In essence, we would be creating a behavior that says, "`<p></p>` elements should behave this way."

When we define a behavior, we describe what elements should be modified and how they should be modified. We then let Drupal take care of the attaching.

 I have heard some Drupal JavaScript developers state that behaviors are a replacement for `jQuery.ready()`. But this is not an accurate description. Behaviors should be used when you are attaching some behavior to elements in the DOM—and only when you want those behaviors to be attached to new (matching) content when it is inserted into the DOM. Treating behaviors as a better `ready event` can cause unexpected errors and less efficient code.

When you define a new behavior, Drupal takes over the management of that behavior. When a page is loaded, the behavior is executed. When other important DOM-altering events occur, Drupal re-runs the behaviors.

However, when writing JavaScript in Drupal, there are a couple of things you need to do to keep behaviors—both yours and others'—working correctly:

- When writing behaviors, to make sure you don't accidentally attach the same behavior to the same thing multiple times. We'll see how to do this later.
- When writing code that modifies the DOM, remember to notify the behaviors system that behaviors may need reattaching. This is done using the `Drupal.attachBehaviors()` function, and we will see examples of this later.

Let's take a look at an example that re-implements our early code—this time as a behavior:

```
Drupal.behaviors.addFancy = function (context) {
    $('p:not(.fancy)', context).addClass('fancy');
};
```

This three line behavior essentially does the same thing as our previous jQuery snippet, with only minor exceptions. Let's look at the differences.

First of all, a behavior is a function that is attached to the `Drupal.behaviors` object. In our case, the function will be named `Drupal.behaviors.addFancy()`.

When Drupal executes a behavior, it passes one parameter, `context`.

The `context` object contains information about the part of the document that is being evaluated. This should always be a *location within the DOM*. When behaviors are first attached (in a call to `$(document).ready()`), the `document` object is passed in as the context. In other cases, only a smaller subset of DOM may be passed in.

Generally, it is advised that a behavior restricts its changes to the `context` (though that is not always a good idea, and we will discuss the point later in the chapter). So we will add the `fancy` class only to elements in our given context:

```
$('p:not(.fancy)', context).addClass('fancy');
```

Notice that the second argument to `$()` is the `context` object. That optional argument provides the object that jQuery should query.

There's another item of note here: The query has been modified. Originally, we began with `$('p')`. Now we have `$('p:not(.fancy)', context)`. What is the `:not(.fancy)` part for? The `:not()` is a pseudo class in CSS. It tells jQuery to not match anything inside of that query. So `<p></p>` will match and therefore be included in the returned results, but `<p class='fancy'></p>` will not.

 The `:not()` functions with an implicit AND. Any matching query must match the initial query and not the query within `:not()`.

So the jQuery line, if translated into plain English, would read "Find all paragraphs that don't have the class `fancy` and give them that class."

Technically in this particular situation, it is not necessary to add the `:not(.fancy)` part. There's no way to add two of the same classes to an element, and jQuery will gracefully handle the situation. But this illustrates a point: in many cases, you want to ensure that your behavior does not do the same thing twice.

When we work on our project later in the chapter, we will see another way of using CSS classes to make sure that a behavior isn't attached twice when it should only be attached once.

Telling Drupal to attach behaviors

After modifying a portion of the document, it might be desirable to notify Drupal so that behaviors can be re-attached. This is done with yet another function from `drupal.js`: `Drupal.attachBehaviors()`.

When should attachBehaviors() be called?

There are some DOM modifications which probably don't warrant calling `Drupal.attachBehaviors()`. For example, just changing the text of a node (without altering any elements) can usually be done safely. Also, there are other elements, such as `<br/>`, that rarely have behaviors attached. In these cases, you should not run `Drupal.attachBehaviors()`. On the converse, any time you load HTML from an AJAX/AHAH call you should run `Drupal.attachBehaviors()`.

Let's look at an example of `Drupal.attachBehaviors()`. At the beginning of the part entitled *Drupal JavaScript behaviors*, we inserted a paragraph using jQuery. We did this with a quick jQuery one-liner:

```
$('body').append('<p>Another paragraph</p>');
```

We will now build on that example:

```
var context = $('<p>Another paragraph</p>')
   .appendTo('body').get(0);
   Drupal.attachBehaviors(context);
```

Whoa! This new snippet of code looks a lot different. But surprisingly, it functions similarly. Let's take a closer look at the jQuery call:

```
$('<p>Another paragraph</p>').appendTo('body').get(0);
```

Just as with our initial example, this jQuery chain adds a new paragraph to the end of the body element. However, it does so in reverse order. Instead of finding the body and adding an element, this code creates the new element and then appends it to the body.

Along with the other things the `$()` function can deal with, it can also recognize HTML embedded in strings. It converts this information to a DOM fragment. By default, this value is held in its own DOM. It is not immediately put into the document that is being displayed.

So in this example, the `$()` call returns a jQuery, wrapping a paragraph element that is currently not a part of the main document. The next thing to do is to append this element to the `document` object at the end of the body. That is done with the `appendTo()` method, which takes a jQuery query string (a CSS selector).

The call to `appendTo()` returns a jQuery object that is still wrapping the `<p></p>` element. But now, that element is part of the main document. The `appendTo()` call took care of that.

> **append() and appendTo(): don't overlook the differences!**
>
> An easily overlooked difference between `append()` and `appendTo()` is in the return value; both return `jQuery` objects. But where `append()` returns a `jQuery` object wrapping the thing(s) that have been appended to, the `appendTo()` call returns the elements that were appended.

The final function in that chain is `get()`. This too is a jQuery function. It extracts the object(s) wrapped by jQuery and return(s) those objects. It takes an optional index value. Since jQuery stores its elements in an indexed list, we can get the wrapped objects by position. In our case, we want the first paragraph (there should be only one), so we use `get(0)`.

The return value of `get(0)` is stored in the `context` variable. So context is now pointing to the `<p></p>` element that we just created.

The last line in our script looks like this:

```
Drupal.attachBehaviors(context);
```

This simply tells Drupal to try to attach behaviors.

If we had called `Drupal.attachBehaviors()` with no arguments, then a default context would have been built for us. That context would have been the `document` object. Since we know that our script only inserted this one paragraph tag, we can reasonably restrict the context to just new `<p></p>` elements.

In general, it's better to set the context appropriately. The more specific the context, the faster the code runs. So in our case, we have created a very limited context.

But beware! This might not always be the best choice, for the impact of inserting one element—even at the end of a document—might extend well beyond the intended target.

Context and behaviors: bug potential

In some cases, working with the context and behaviors can get tricky, leading to bugs that may be difficult to debug.

For example, let's look at another behavior that we assume would work with the one we just created:

```
Drupal.behaviors.countParagraphs = function (context) {
  if ($('#lots', context).size() > 0) {
    return;
  }
  else if ($('p', context).size() > 5) {
    $('body').append('<p id="lots">Lots of Text!</p>');
  }
};
```

The previous code snippet does the following:

- It checks to see if an element with the ID `lots` exists. If it does, that means this behavior has already been properly processed. So it returns early.
- If the `lots` ID does not exist, it checks to see if there are more than five paragraphs.
- If there are more than five paragraphs, a short piece of text `Lots of Text!` is appended to the end of the document. The ID of the paragraph that wraps this text is `lots`. So we know this has already been processed (and that there are more than five paragraphs) by the existence of the `lots` ID.

Another important thing to notice is that both queries (the checking queries) use the context. This is the recommended procedure, but it can have unanticipated results, as we shall see.

We have two behaviors, both making use of the context in the recommended way. In our code that attaches the new paragraph we call `attachBehaviors()`, passing it the most narrow context we can (the paragraph that was inserted).

So what happens when the number of paragraphs in the document exceeds five? Nothing.

Here's an example from Firebug's console:

```
>>> $('p').size();
5
>>> var cxt = $('<p>Sixth paragraph</p>')
    .appendTo('body').get(0);
>>> Drupal.attachBehaviors(cxt);
>>> $('p').size();
6
>>> $('#lots').size();
0
```

At the beginning of this script, our document had five paragraphs. On the next two lines, we added a sixth and re-attached behaviors.

But the `<p id="lots">Lots of Text!</p>` was not added to the document We can tell this in two ways—First, by the fact that it would have added a seventh paragraph. Second, `$('#lots').size()` would have returned 1. That means our `Drupal.behaviors.countParagraphs()` behavior did not run.

This happened because our behaviors are configured to use the context. Our `attachBehaviors()` call keeps the context limited to just the changed elements. This is correct, isn't it? But in this case, our zeal to optimize actually caused the failure.

Let's look at why it fails.

Here's how the context is set up:

```
var cxt = $('<p>Sixth paragraph</p>').appendTo('body').get(0);
Drupal.attachBehaviors(cxt);
```

The context object, `cxt`, points *only* to the new paragraph.

So `Drupal.attachBehaviors(cxt)` only passes that one paragraph to all of the registered behaviors.

Now, let's look at the behavior that counts paragraphs:

```
Drupal.behaviors.countParagraphs = function (context) {
  if ($('#lots', context).size() > 0) {
    return;
  }
  else if ($('p', context).size() > 5) {
    $('body').append('<p id="lots">Lots of Text!</p>');
  }
};
```

The highlighted line is the problematic one. Since the context is limited to just one paragraph, the jQuery chain `$('p', context).size()` will always return 1 when our `Drupal.attachBehavior(cxt)` function is executed. So regardless of how many paragraphs the actual document contains, the content's `else if` statement won't get executed.

This is a simple case, but we could imagine fairly elaborate ones that come from similar problems. In order to be sure that a call to `Drupal.attachBehaviors()` will not result in a bug like the one we just saw, you must be familiar with all of the behaviors that might run in your Drupal instance. (If you are creating portable code, you should have some way to ensure that no other code could possibly have problems like what was just described.)

What's the solution?

There are two possible solutions:

1. In your behaviors, ignore `context`.
2. When you call `Drupal.attachBehaviors()`, don't specify context.

The first solution has two problems. First, it goes against the design of behaviors. Second, it would require that all the developers implement it before we could be sure that it was working. Since behaviors are supposed to be context-aware, it would be hard to achieve this.

I'm inclined to suggest that the second solution is the best. The context should not be narrowed. That is, behaviors should use the `document` object as the context. In practice, what this means for you is that you should call `Drupal.attachBehaviors()` with no arguments. While it may result in a (small) performance hit, it will prevent bugs like the one seen previously.

Project: collapsing blocks

In this project, we will write a very simple behavior that will be attached to blocks on a page. We will make blocks collapsible. Clicking on a block's title will cause the body of the block to slide up or slide down.

Here are the contents of a file called `behaviors.js`, which is part of the Frobnitz theme, included in using a `scripts[]` directive in `frobnitz.info`:

```
// $Id$
/**
 * Defines behaviors for Frobnitz theme.
 * @file
 */

/**
 * Toggle visibility of blocks (with slide effect).
 */
Drupal.behaviors.slideBlocks = function (context) {
  $('.block:not(.slideBlocks-processed)', context)
    .addClass('slideBlocks-processed')
    .each(function () {
      $(this).children(".title").toggle(
        function () {
          $(this).siblings(".content").slideUp("slow");
        },
```

```
        function () {
          $(this).siblings(".content").slideDown("slow");
        });
      });
  };
```

In the code, we define one behavior named `Drupal.behaviors.slideBlocks()`. When attached, this behavior will add a toggle to *all blocks* on the page. When a block's title is clicked, the block will slide up and disappear. Here's a screenshot of the sliding in progress:

When the slide is complete, only the title — **mbutcher** — will be displayed.

When the title is clicked again, the contents will slide back down until they are fully visible.

Since our code is operating on blocks, it will be helpful to take a quick look at the HTML that Drupal generates for a block.

Here's the menu section as generated by the Frobnitz theme (which is inheriting this from the Bluemarine theme):

```
<div class="block block-user" id="block-user-1">
  <h2 class="title">mbutcher</h2>
  <div class="content">
    <ul class="menu">
      <li class="leaf first">
        <a href="/drupal/user/1">My account</a>
      </li>
      <li class="collapsed">
        <a href="/drupal/node/add">Create content</a>
      </li>
      <li class="collapsed">
        <a href="/drupal/admin">Administer</a>
      </li>
      <li class="leaf last">
        <a href="/drupal/logout">Log out</a>
```

```
        </li>
      </ul>
    </div>
  </div>
```

This shows the complete contents of one specific block. We are more interested in the generic structure that all blocks share. To see this, we can simplify the previous code to something like this:

```
<div class="block" id="some_id">
  <h2 class="title">Title</h2>
  <div class="content">Content</div>
</div>
```

That's about all there is to a generic block. Every block has three structural pieces, and these are identified by `class`. There's a `block` that contains a `title` and some `content`.

Returning to our code, let's look at the behavior function:

```
Drupal.behaviors.slideBlocks = function (context) {
  $('.block:not(.slideBlocks-processed)', context)
    .addClass('slideBlocks-processed')
    .each(function () {
      $(this).children(".title").toggle(
        function () {
          $(this).siblings(".content").slideUp("slow");
        },
        function () {
          $(this).siblings(".content").slideDown("slow");
        });
    });
};
```

Our behavior first tries to find all of the blocks that haven't already been processed by this behavior. The query to do this is: `.block:not(.slideBlocks-processed)`. As we saw in the previous HTML, the class `block` indicates that a piece of HTML is a block.

Again, we want to prevent our behavior from being run twice on the same element. To do this, we write the behavior in such a way that it attaches its own class to an element once the element has been processed. In this case, the class is `slideBlocks-processed`, following one of the conventions used when defining behaviors.

Any block that gets processed by our `slideBlocks` behavior will be assigned the `slideBlocks-processed` class. So when we do the initial query, we can avoid blocks that have already processed by using `.block:not(.slideBlocks-processed)`. The resulting jQuery object will only contain blocks that have not been processed.

The first thing we do with these matching blocks is append the `slideBlocks-processed` class to them. That way, later calls to `Drupal.attachBehaviors()` won't result in the behavior being attached again.

Let's continue in the jQuery chain:

```
$('.block:not(.slideBlocks-processed)', context)
  .addClass('slideBlocks-processed')
  .each(function () {
    $(this).children(".title").toggle(
      function () {
        $(this).siblings(".content").slideUp("slow");
      },
      function () {
        $(this).siblings(".content").slideDown("slow");
      });
  });
```

The `each()` function, which we saw in Chapter 3, will iterate through each item in the `jQuery` object and call the anonymous function on each item.

Inside this anonymous function, the `this` keyword will point to the current item in the list. So if there are four blocks on the page, the anonymous function will be called four times, with `this` being set first to the first item in the list, then to the second item in the list, and so on.

Since our query is returning elements that are blocks, iterations through `each()` will set `this` to point to a block element.

What we want to do is get the title of each block and add an event handler to it, so that each time the title is clicked, the content slides up or slides down. In the code just shown, here's how this is done:

```
$(this).children(".title").toggle(
  function () {
    $(this).siblings(".content").slideUp("slow");
  },
  function () {
    $(this).siblings(".content").slideDown("slow");
  });
```

Remember, `this` contains a block element (`<div class='block'>...</div>`). We wrap that in a jQuery object again, and then use the `children()` jQuery function to find all of the children of the current block that have the `title` class.

There will always be only one title per block.

To that title we want to attach an event handler that will fire when the title is clicked. But we want it to do one thing (slide up) the first time it is clicked, and another thing (slide down) the second time it is clicked.

The jQuery `toggle()` event handler is just what we need. It will fire the first function on odd clicks (1, 3, 5, and so on), and the second function on even clicks (2, 4, 6, and so on).

So on odd clicks it will execute this function:

```
function () {
  $(this).siblings(".content").slideUp("slow");
};
```

The `this` variable is set to the element that was clicked, which is the block's title. We want to add the slide up effect to the content. Recall that the general structure of a block looks like this:

```
<div class="block" id="some_id">
  <h2 class="title">Title</h2>
  <div class="content">Content</div>
</div>
```

The title and block sections of a node are next to each other at the same level in the DOM tree. In other words, they are **siblings**. To get from our current title to the content sibling, we wrap the title element in a jQuery object and then use the jQuery `siblings()` function, passing it a CSS selector that will match the element with the `content` class.

Why don't we look for div.content?

Why do we search for `.content` instead of the more specific `div.content`? This is done mainly for the sake of portability. Possibly, a themer will want to change the HTML structure, perhaps using a `<span>` tag or wrapping the content inside a table. We wouldn't want such changes to break our JavaScript. So we do our best to decouple the CSS selector from the HTML tags.

Once we've got the `content` sibling, we simply add the `slideUp()` effect, setting the speed parameter to `'slow'`.

The second toggle function performs an analogous task:

```
function () {
  $(this).siblings(".content").slideDown("slow");
};
```

Here, instead of sliding up, this function causes the content to slide down. Otherwise, the functions are identical.

That's all there is to our behavior. When the page is loaded (and the `ready` event fires), all of the registered behaviors, including this one, will be attached. So from the moment the user can first interact with the page, she or he will be able to click on block titles and cause block contents to slide up until they disappear, and then (with another click) slide back down.

In the coming chapters, we will make use of the `Drupal.attachBehaviors()` function to make sure that new blocks that are added dynamically from JavaScript will also be given this behavior.

Utilities

At the beginning of the chapter, I listed the four toolsets that can be found in `drupal.js`: behaviors, translations, theming, and utilities. We've already looked at behaviors. Translations and theming will the subjects of the next two chapters. But before we continue, let's look at some of the more important utilities.

All of the utilities covered in this section are part of the `drupal.js` library and will be available any time you include JavaScript files in your theme or module.

Checking capabilities with Drupal.jsEnabled

The first utility we will check out is not a function. It's a property of the `Drupal` object: `Drupal.jsEnabled`. This variable indicates whether or not the browser will support `drupal.js` and `jquery.js`.

The name of this property is slightly misleading. It doesn't actually indicate whether JavaScript is enabled. (That wouldn't be all that useful, would it? If JavaScript was truly disabled, a JavaScript variable would be worthless.)

Instead, this flag is set to `true` if the *requisite level* of JavaScript is supported. Some browser, such as antiquated desktop browsers and bare-bones embedded browsers, have a limited level of JavaScript support. But they don't provide a full implementation like what you would find in modern editions of IE, Firefox, Safari, or Opera.

When `drupal.js` loads, it will evaluate whether the JavaScript implementation supports DOM manipulation of the sort that jQuery and `drupal.js` rely upon. If the correct functions exist then this flag will be set to true. Otherwise, the flag will be set to false.

Internally, Drupal uses this flag to determine if behaviors are supported. If `Drupal.jsEnabled` is `false`, then `Drupal.attachBehaviors()` doesn't attempt to attach any behaviors. It just silently returns.

Also, Drupal uses this flag to set a cookie. If `Drupal.jsEnabled` is `true`, a cookie is set which indicates that JavaScript support is sufficient. This way, server-side code can send back appropriate responses based on a browser's JavaScript capabilities. (This cookie is named `has_js`, and is available in PHP using `$_COOKIE['has_js']`.)

Feel free to use `Drupal.jsEnabled` whenever you are concerned that a browser might not support the necessary JavaScript for DOM manipulations. But don't get overly concerned about checking with the use of this flag. Most jQuery functions will silently fail if JavaScript support isn't good enough, and the main Drupal features (like behaviors) will be skipped as well.

The Drupal.checkPlain() function (and the jQuery alternative)

The first function we will look at is the `Drupal.checkPlain()` function. If you have already written some Drupal PHP code, you will probably recognize the name.

The `Drupal.checkPlain()` function takes a string and prepares it for display, escaping symbols that have a special meaning in HTML. While the use of the term `check` implies that this will return a Boolean value (`true` if the text is plain, `false` if otherwise), it actually performs the escaping, and returns the escaped string.

So what does it escape? Let's look at an example. While viewing a node on our Drupal system, we can use the Firebug console to manipulate the document:

```
>>> myString = "A string with <em>HTML</em> embedded.";
"A string with <em>HTML</em> embedded."
>>> $('.node .content').html(myString);
Object length=1
```

The first line creates a new string named `myString`. Note that the contents of this string contain embedded HTML: **A string with HTML embedded**

In the second line we use jQuery to find the main content section for the node displayed on the current page, and replace the existing contents of that section with the value of `myString`. Since this involves a little bit of new jQuery, let's look at it closely.

The query we use here is `.node .content`. The most important character in this query is the space between `.node` and `.content`. It indicates a descendent relationship between `.node` and `.content`. We might rephrase this query as "find all elements with class `node`, and then find any elements that are descendants of this node and that have the class `content`."

Descendants and children

A descendant relationship is not limited to just children of the selected node. Child nodes are directly under the selected node. A descendant may be more than one level beneath a node. If you are interested in only children, you can use the > operator instead of the empty space: `$('.node > .content')`. Note that in this case the whitespace around the > is treated as insignificant.

So this query will select the main content for the main node or nodes displayed on the page. Why do we use this more complex form of the query? Why not just use `$('.content')`? That's because even blocks use the `.content` class, and we don't want to select the content of our blocks.

The second part of our jQuery chain is the `html()` method. This replaces the entire HTML under the current node with the string passed in. The string is interpreted and inserted into the DOM, so HTML tags in the string are actually recognized as HTML markup.

Let's look at the results of running this command to see how the string is interpreted:

Notice that `<em>HTML</em>` is displayed above as *HTML* (in italics).

What if we wanted to display the HTML tags and not have them interpreted? That's where the `Drupal.checkPlain()` function comes in. Let's take a look at a similar snippet of code:

```
>>> myString = "Add a line break using the <br/> tag.";
"Add a line break using the <br/> tag."
>>> escapedString = Drupal.checkPlain(myString);
"Add a line break using the &lt;br/&gt; tag."
>>> $('.node div.content').html(escapedString);
Object length=1
```

If we were to look at this in the browser, it would look something like this:

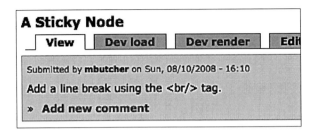

In the screenshot, the `<br/>` tag is displayed as is, and doesn't appear to be treated as HTML. What's going on behind the scenes?

Take a look at the second command entered on the console: `escapedString = Drupal.checkPlain(myString);`. Here, we use the `Drupal.checkPlain()` function to escape the contents of `myString`. The output displayed on the console shows what happens when we do so:

```
"Add a line break using the &lt;br/&gt; tag."
```

The tag `<br/>` that we originally entered in `myString` has now been converted to `&lt;br/&gt;`. The `<` and `>` characters were encoded into their HTML entity equivalents. The `Drupal.checkPlain()` function encodes four characters:

- `<` becomes `&lt;`.
- `>` becomes `&gt;`
- `"` (double quote) becomes `&quot;`
- `&` becomes `&amp;`

Why escape these four? They all represent HTML elements. By escaping them, we can ensure that we are not inserting HTML elements into the string. So there is no danger that the HTML is interpreted by the browser.

There is good reason for doing this. Not only does it allow us to display HTML tags, but it adds a layer of security when we are dealing with user-entered data. We wouldn't want the string `<script>doSomethingBad();</script>` to get rendered!

So when should you use `Drupal.checkPlain()` in your scripts? The usual answer is anytime you are displaying unknown or untrusted information. Actually, the situation is compounded by the fact that jQuery handles most cases where you'd use `Drupal.checkPlain()`, and it does so gracefully.

Earlier, when we inserted our new content, we did this:

```
>>> myString = "Add a line break using the <br/> tag.";
"Add a line break using the <br/> tag."
>>> escapedString = Drupal.checkPlain(myString);
"Add a line break using the &lt;br/&gt; tag."
>>> $('.node div.content').html(escapedString);
Object length=1
```

We could have done this with jQuery — and in a more succinct way:

```
>>> myString = "Add a line break using the <br/> tag.";
"Add a line break using the <br/> tag."
>>> $('.node div.content').text(myString);
Object length=1
```

In this case, instead of using the `Drupal.checkPlain()` function to do the encoding and then using the jQuery `html()` function to insert the content, we just use the jQuery `text()` function. It implicitly handles the encoding and the insertion.

The guideline for using the `text()` function is simple: Any time you are inserting text that should not contain HTML (including, for example, user-entered text), you should insert it with `text()` instead of `html()`.

So when should `Drupal.checkPlain()` be used? It should be used in cases where you need to encode a string, but not insert it into a document.

The Drupal.parseJson() function

Some of the functions in `drupal.js` were created before comparable functions existed in jQuery. One such function is `Drupal.parseJson()`.

This function was intended to be used for parsing AJAX data that was returned from the server in the JSON (JavaScript Object Notation) format. JSON data looks like JavaScript. Here's an example describing a person's name:

```
jsonString = "{'first': 'Matt', 'last': 'Butcher'}";
```

If we were to remove the double quotes, we would have a literal JavaScript object declaration. That's the idea behind JSON. As a part of an AJAX exchange, a server can send the client JSON data, which the client can then parse into JavaScript objects.

We will see JSON in action in Chapter 7. Until then, here's a short example of how the `Drupal.parseJson()` function works:

```
>>> jsonString = "{'first': 'Matt', 'last':'Butcher'}";
"{'first': 'Matt', 'last':'Butcher'}"
>>> name = Drupal.parseJson(jsonString);
```

```
Object first=Matt last=Butcher
>>> name.first
"Matt"
```

The line **Object first=Matt last=Butcher** in the code shows the main feature of `Drupal.parseJson()`. The string is parsed and converted to an object. We can then use that object directly in JavaScript.

This function may be of limited use as the version of jQuery that ships with Drupal 6 already contains functions for dealing with JSON content during AJAX calls. When we look at AJAX later in the book, we will see how jQuery functions can be used to handle JSON data.

The Drupal.encodeURIComponent() function

Earlier, we looked at encoding HTML with `Drupal.checkPlain()`. Here, we will look at another encoding function — one designed for encoding pieces of a URL or URI.

Drupal PHP programmers may also recognize this function. It essentially performs the same task as the `drupal_urlencode()` PHP function. Those familiar with JavaScript will recognize this as having the same name as a built-in JavaScript function.

The built-in JavaScript function, `encodeURIComponent()`, is used to encode values that will be used when constructing a query string or a URI. Certain values, such as a slash (/), have special meaning in URLs. A slash indicates a directory.

How do we write a request for a document on the server named `pros/cons.html`, where the slash is part of the file name and not an indicator that `pros/` is a directory? It should be escaped with "/" replaced by a hexadecimal representation of the character. We can see how this is done with the built-in browser function `encodeURIComponent()`:

```
>>> encodeURIComponent('pros/cons.html');
"pros%2Fcons.html"
```

Looking at the Firebug output, we can see that the slash was replaced by `%2F`, where `2F` is the ASCII hexadecimal representation of the / character.

But Drupal presents something of a special case. It uses paths as query parameters. So we would expect strings, such as `node/1/edit` with the slashes left as is. At the same time, we would want other special characters, such as `%`, to be escaped correctly.

That's where `Drupal.encodeURIComponent()` comes in. It correctly converts other characters while preserving the slashes. To see this in action, let's compare how the two different functions convert the fiction link `node/1/calc%`:

```
>>> myString = 'node/1/calc%';
"node/1/calc%"
>>> encodeURIComponent(myString);
"node%2F1%2Fcalc%25"
>>> Drupal.encodeURIComponent(myString);
"node/1/calc%25"
```

In this example we can see the difference: The `Drupal.encodeURIComponent()` call preserved the slashes in the path.

In general, `Drupal.encodeURIComponent()` should be used any time you are constructing links back to Drupal. However, when making calls to other non-Drupal services, you should continue to use the browser-defined `encodeURIComponent()` function.

The Drupal.getSelection() function

The last utility function that we will look at is the `Drupal.getSelection()` function. This tool is used to find out what portion of a text area (`<textarea></textarea>`) is selected.

For example, when you select a section of text with your mouse, this function can be used to find out the starting and ending locations of the selection.

The `Drupal.getSelection()` function returns an object with two attributes: `start` and `end`. These two properties are integers which represent the beginning and ending of the selection. In our next project, we will see this function in action.

There are a few other functions in the `drupal.js` file that may be used in rare circumstances, but the ones we have seen here are the ones you are most likely to use in your own scripts. In the last part of this chapter, we will do another project. We will create a simple editor with jQuery and some of the Drupal capabilities we have seen in this chapter.

Project: a simple text editor

In this project we are going to create a simple text editor. We are going to begin with text areas and add a couple of buttons that insert HTML tags for us. In doing this project, we will make use of the jQuery techniques we learned in the previous chapter, as well as behaviors and some of the utility functions we saw earlier in this chapter.

There are already several rich text editors available for Drupal, all of which are more advanced than the simple tool we will create here. The **WYSIWYG API** module is poised to become the *de facto* text editor going forward. It can be found at `http://drupal.org/project/wysiwyg`.

Our editor will have two buttons—a **B** button to make some text bold, and an **I** button to add italics. The editor will insert markup into the text so that the tags are visible to the user. For example, if the user types in the string **This is bold**, highlights the word "**bold**", and presses the **B** button, she or he will see the text **This is bold**.

Before we look at the code, let's take a quick look at what it should produce:

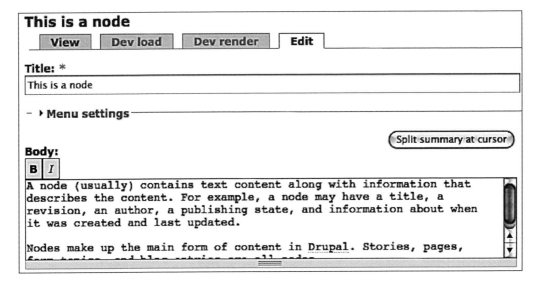

The new simple editor attaches to existing `<textarea></textarea>` elements and adds the two-button toolbar.

We want to write our code so multiple text areas on the same screen can all have editors. We also want the editor to load as soon as the page is loaded and attach to all text areas.

 If we were implementing a complete editor solution, we would probably not want the editor to attach to all text areas, since not all areas accept HTML input. But for our project, we will simplify the process by attaching the editor to all text areas.

Let's start out by looking at our `frobnitz.info` file, which will point to a new CSS file and a new JavaScript file:

```
; $Id$
name = Frobnitz
description - Table-based multi-column theme with JavaScript
enhancements.
version = 1.0
core = 6.x
base theme = bluemarine
stylesheets[all][] = frobnitz.css
stylesheets[all][] = simpleeditor.css
scripts[] = printer_tool.js
scripts[] = sticky_rotate.js
scripts[] = behaviors.js
scripts[] = simpleeditor.js
```

The two new files, highlighted in the previous code, will provide a stylesheet and a JavaScript library for our tool.

The stylesheet is very simple. Here it is:

```
.editor-button {
  border: 1px solid gray;
  padding: 3px;
  width: 1em;
  text-align: center;
  background-color: #eee;
  float: left;
}

.editor-button:hover {
  background-color: #ccc;
}

.button-bar {
  clear: both;
}
```

It simply takes the elements that make up the buttons and button bar, and makes them look and behave a little more like form buttons. Now, let's move on to the JavaScript.

Here is the `simpleeditor.js` script in its entirety. After taking a quick look at the entire file we will go through it more carefully:

```
// $Id$
/**
 * Simple text editing controls for a textarea.
 */
```

```
var SimpleEditor = SimpleEditor || {};

SimpleEditor.buttonBar =
  '<div class="button-bar">' +
  '<div class="editor-button bold"><strong>B</strong></div>' +
  '<div class="editor-button italics"><em>I</em></div>' +
  '</div>';

SimpleEditor.selection = null;
/**
 * Record changes to a select box.
 */
SimpleEditor.watchSelection = function () {
  SimpleEditor.selection = Drupal.getSelection(this);
  SimpleEditor.selection.id = $(this).attr('id');
};

/**
 * Attaches the editor toolbar.
 */
Drupal.behaviors.editor = function () {
  $('textarea:not(.editor-processed)')
    .addClass('editor-processed')
    .mouseup(SimpleEditor.watchSelection)
    .keyup(SimpleEditor.watchSelection)
    .each(function (item) {
      var txtarea = $(this);
      var txtareaID = txtarea.attr('id');
      var bar = SimpleEditor.buttonBar;

      $(bar).attr('id', 'buttons-' + txtareaID)
        .insertBefore('#' + txtareaID)
        .children('.editor-button')
        .click(function () {
          var txtareaEle = $('#' + txtareaID).get(0);
          var sel = SimpleEditor.selection;
          if (sel.id == txtareaID && sel.start != sel.end) {
            txtareaEle.value = SimpleEditor.insertTag(
              sel.start,
              sel.end,
              $(this).hasClass('bold') ? 'strong' : 'em',
              txtareaEle.value
            );
            sel.start = sel.end = -1;
          }
```

```
        });
      });
    };

    /**
     * Insert a tag.
     * @param start
     *   Location to insert start tag.
     * @param end
     *   Location to insert end tag.
     * @param tag
     *   Tag to insert.
     * @param value
     *   String to insert tag into.
     */
    SimpleEditor.insertTag = function (start, end, tag, value) {
      var front = value.substring(0, start);
      var middle = value.substring(start, end);
      var back = value.substring(end);
      return front + '<' + tag + '>' + middle +
        '</' + tag + '>' + back;
    };
```

The previous code has been organized in the order in which we will look at it below. This makes the overarching structure a little less evident. Here's a high-level description of what's going on.

The `SimpleEditor` namespace will hold most of the information pertinent to our editor. We will use a Drupal behavior for attaching and handling various events. Most of the major logic will be inside of our behavior.

Other than that, we will add a few helper function that will be part of our `SimpleEditor` namespace.

Let's look at the first several lines of code in the `simpleeditor.js` file:

```
    var SimpleEditor = SimpleEditor || {};

    SimpleEditor.buttonBar =
      '<div class="button-bar">' +
      '<div class="editor-button bold"><strong>B</strong></div>' +
      '<div class="editor-button italics"><em>I</em></div>' +
      '</div>';
```

The `SimpleEditor.buttonBar` variable holds some generic HTML that creates a basic button bar. We will use this as a template to add buttons to text areas.

Next, we will look at the new behavior. This is the most complex piece of code in our project.

The main behavior

There is one main behavior registered for our simple editor. It learns about all of the text areas in the document and then adds editor support to those areas.

This behavior illustrates the compactness that is achievable with jQuery and `drupal.js`. It also makes use of constructs that you are likely to see in Drupal code, such as nested anonymous functions.

Since it is complex, we will walk through it carefully.

Here's the behavior code:

```
Drupal.behaviors.editor = function () {
  $('textarea:not(.editor-processed)')
    .addClass('editor-processed')
    .mouseup(SimpleEditor.watchSelection)
    .keyup(SimpleEditor.watchSelection)
    .each(function (item) {
      var txtarea = $(this);
      var txtareaID = txtarea.attr('id');
      var bar = SimpleEditor.buttonBar;

      $(bar).attr('id', 'buttons-' + txtareaID)
        .insertBefore('#' + txtareaID)
        .children('.editor-button')
        .click(function () {
          var txtareaEle = $('#' + txtareaID).get(0);
          var sel = SimpleEditor.selection;
          console.log(sel.id + ' ' + txtareaID);
          if(sel.id == txtareaID && sel.start != sel.end) {
            txtareaEle.value = SimpleEditor.insertTag(
              sel.start,
              sel.end,
              $(this).hasClass('bold') ? 'strong' : 'em',
              txtareaEle.value
            );
            sel.start = sel.end = -1;
          }
        });
    });
};
```

The main part of this function is controlled by a large jQuery chain. This chain serves three purposes:

1. It finds all of the text areas that need processing.
2. It adds event handlers to those text areas.
3. It loops through each text area and attaches a button bar to the text area.

Step 1: find text areas that need processing

Here's the chain:

```
$('textarea:not(.editor-processed)')
  .addClass('editor-processed')
  .mouseup(SimpleEditor.watchSelection)
  .keyup(SimpleEditor.watchSelection)
  .each(/* more code here */);
```

Take a look at the first pair of lines.

We saw this pattern earlier in the chapter. The main query looks for text areas that have not already been processed by the behavior (`textarea:not (.editor-processed)`). To the returned list, it first adds the class that indicates that the behavior has been processed (`addClass('editor-processed')`).

Step 2: add event handlers

Once we've found the appropriate text areas and marked them as processed, we can move on to lines three and four. Here, we need to attach two event handlers:

1. `mouseup`: This event will be triggered when a mouse button is released.
2. `keyup`: This event will be triggered when a key is released.

These are the two events which might indicate that some text within the text area has just been selected.

How? Consider the case where a user is selecting text with a mouse. The user presses the mouse button down, drags the mouse to select the text, and then releases the mouse button. We want to check button releases to see if new text was selected.

The `keyup` event works the same way. The user may hold down the *shift* key while selecting text with the arrow key. It's the key release that we want to use as a clue. We should check it to see if the user selected any text.

In both cases, the same function is assigned. The `SimpleEditor.watchSelection()` function checks a text area to find out what has been selected. Let's take a look at that function before we continue examining the third part of the jQuery chain:

```
SimpleEditor.selection = null;

SimpleEditor.watchSelection = function () {
  SimpleEditor.selection = Drupal.getSelection(this);
  SimpleEditor.selection.id = $(this).attr('id');
};
```

The `SimpleEditor.watchSelection()` function does two things. First, it calls the `Drupal.getSelection()` function to find out what text (if any) is selected in the given text area. The value of `this` in the event handler function will be the element from which the event was fired. In other words, `this` will be the text area element that most recently changed.

The returned object will be stored in `SimpleEditor.selection`, where other parts of our editor can access it.

The second thing this function does is get the ID of the current text area element. Since we can have multiple text areas on the same page, we need to track which one was modified. That's what `SimpleEditor.selection.id` is used for.

 The `id` property is not a part of the object returned from `Drupal.getSelection()`. Instead, we add it on an ad hoc basis.

At this point we have handled one of the major tasks that our editor must do. We have created code that will track what is happening in the text area. Next, we will move onto the third step in the jQuery chain.

Step 3: attach the button bar

First, the jQuery chain found the text areas to process. Next, the event handlers were added. In the third step, the jQuery chain loops through each of the matching text areas with a call to the `each()` function.

Inside of the `each()` function, we define an anonymous function that will operate on each text area element. Here's that function:

```
function (item) {
  var txtarea = $(this);
  var txtareaID = txtarea.attr('id');
  var bar = SimpleEditor.buttonBar;
```

```
$(bar).attr('id', 'buttons-' + txtareaID)
  .insertBefore('#' + txtareaID)
  .children('.editor-button')
  .click(/* Event handler function */);
}
```

This function will be called once for each text area that is found on the page.

This function defines three variables. The `txtarea` variable points to a jQuery object wrapping the current text area. In order to identify the text area, we will need to get the ID of the current area. The ID gets stored in `txtareaID`. We also need a local copy of the button bar string that we created at the beginning of the script. This gets stored in the `bar` variable.

As we've seen before, jQuery can distinguish between a string that contains HTML and the one that contains a CSS selector. So when we call `$(bar)`, jQuery parses `bar` into an HTML DOM fragment. From there, we can manipulate the `bar` DOM just as we do with the main `document`.

The first thing we do is generate an ID for our button bar—an ID based on the ID of the text area that this button bar will be attached to.

We can use this ID later to distinguish one button bar from another. Again, if we have several text areas on a page, we will have several button bars too. We need to make sure that clicking on a button for one text area doesn't change text in another text area.

Now we have a copy of the button bar and we've given it a unique ID. The next thing to do is insert it into the `document`'s DOM immediately above the text area that it will be attached to. What we want to accomplish is to attach the current jQuery DOM to some point in the document's DOM. We do that with the `insertBefore()` jQuery function, which will insert the button bar above the desired text area.

Our button bar is structured like this:

```
<div class="button-bar" id="button-someID">
  <div class="editor-button bold"><strong>B</strong></div>
  <div class="editor-button italics"><em>I</em></div>
</div>
```

Our current jQuery object is pointing to the outer `<div></div>` element. But now we want to work on the two inner `div`s, each describing a button. To go from the outer element to the inner elements, we use `$().childrend('.editor-button')`.

Now the current jQuery object will wrap both—the **B** button and the **I** button.

Currently, these aren't really buttons at all. Nothing will happen when you click them. We need to add an event handler to these two so that they respond when clicked. We use jQuery's `click()` function to add an event handler for the `click` event.

The `click()` function takes a function as an argument. Once again, we define an anonymous function to handle this.

Here's the event handler function that is attached to the click event:

```
function () {
  var txtareaEle = $('#' + txtareaID).get(0);
  var sel = SimpleEditor.selection;
  if(sel.id == txtareaID && sel.start != sel.end) {
    txtareaEle.value = SimpleEditor.insertTag(
      sel.start,
      sel.end,
      $(this).hasClass('bold') ? 'strong' : 'em',
      txtareaEle.value
    );
    sel.start = sel.end = -1;
  }
}
```

Each time one of our buttons is clicked, a version of the above function will be executed.

What do I mean by *a version*?

This function, as an anonymous function, is created once per button. Furthermore, the function definition is nested within another function definition (the definition for the anonymous function inside of `each()`). Each time the function is defined in the `each()` loop, it takes with it the environment defined by its parent function. In short, it's not just a function, but also a snapshot of the environment in which the function was created.

While each version of this function does the same thing, each has access to a different environment.

For example, `txtareaID`, defined in the parent function (as we just saw), is still available inside of this function. Furthermore, the `txtareaID` for the function assigned to the first text area is different than the `txtareaID` assigned to the second text area. In spite of the fact that the variable name is the same, the scope of the variable is such that one `click` handler retains a copy, while another `click` handler retains a different copy with a different value.

For all practical purposes, we have created what is called a **closure**. We have defined a function that carries with it some values it got from its original context, but which are now *closed off* to any outside context. The function may still have access to the txtareaID that was set when the function was defined, but that txtareaID is closed off from any other parts of the program. It no longer lives in any scope outside of the anonymous function's scope. In Chapter 9, we will take another look at closures.

By using anonymous methods in this way, we have made it possible to register event handlers so that the context is carried with them. For example, there's no need to add onclick attributes in our HTML that provides the ID of the text area or some other bit of information. All of that is stored in the anonymous function as the behavior is attached.

So what does this function do? The first thing it does is define a few variables. The txtareaEle variable contains the actual text area element that this button relates to. Notice that this function uses the txtareaID variable defined by the parent to get this information.

The second variable, sel, is a copy of the SimpleEditor.selection variable. It contains information about what text area was last active, and what part of that area is selected. This SimpleEditor.selection object is maintained by the code we looked at earlier, notably the SimpleEditor.watchSelection() function.

We now have the ID of the text area that this handler is attached to, and we have information about the last text area that was active.

The next thing this click handler does is to find out whether it needs to make any changes to the text area that it is responsible for. There are two criteria for this:

- First, is the currently active text area (sel.id), the text area that this click handler is responsible for (txtareaID)? Remember, there will be one click handler for every button attached to every text area. Each click function needs to find out if the current text area target is the one that it is responsible for.

- Second, is there any text selected? Our primitive editor will only surround selected text with tags. So it will only insert tags if there is selected text to surround.

If either of these two criteria fails, the click handler will quietly return.

But if the target text area is the one this handler handles, and if there is also some selected text, then this function will go about wrapping the selected text in the appropriate tags:

```
if(sel.id == txtareaID && sel.start != sel.end) {
  txtareaEle.value = SimpleEditor.insertTag(
    sel.start,
    sel.end,
    $(this).hasClass('bold') ? 'strong' : 'em',
    txtareaEle.value
  );
  sel.start = sel.end = -1;
}
```

The highlighted code is responsible for inserting the tag. It resets the value of its text area (`txtareaEle.value`) to whatever gets returned from `SimpleEditor.insertTag()`.

In just a moment we will look at `SimpleEditor.insertTag()`. But first, let's look at the parameters that are passed in:

- The first parameter, `sel.start`, indicates where the selection starts. It's the index of the first character in the text area that is selected.

- The second parameter, `sel.end`, is the last selected character in the text area.

- The third parameter determines what tag is going to be inserted. If the button that was clicked has the class `bold`, then clicking this button should make the text bold (`strong`). Otherwise, we assume that the text should be put in italics (`em`).

- Finally, we pass in the string that contains all of the text in the text area. In this case, we simply get the `value` property of the text area element.

So this last function call in the `click` event handler will take the text in the target text area, find the selected text in that area, and surround the selected text with the appropriate HTML tag.

After the call to `SimpleEditor.insertTag()` returns, we clear out the old selection by setting `sel.start` and `sel.end` to `-1`. We clear it because the selection disappears in the browser window when a button is clicked, and also because we want to make sure that another button click doesn't insert another tag.

It's time to turn to the `SimpleEditor.insertTag` function to see how that works:

```
SimpleEditor.insertTag = function (start, end, tag, value) {
  var front = value.substring(0, start);
```

```
    var middle = value.substring(start, end);
    var back = value.substring(end);
    return front + '<' + tag + '>' + middle + '</' + tag + '>'
      + back;
};
```

We saw the four parameters that are passed to SimpleEditor.insertTag():
the position of the first selected character(start), the position of the last selected
character (end), the name of the tag to surround the selection with (tag), and the
string that contains all of the text (value).

There are a few ways we could do this, some probably more economical than this.
But this function follows a very simple path. It breaks the string into three parts: The
part before the start tag should be inserted, the part between the start and end tags,
and the part after the end tag.

For example, let's imagine the value of value to be this:

```
The cat sat on the mat.
```

Now let's imagine that the word cat has been selected. That would make the
value of start equal to 4, and the value of end equal to 7. This would result in
the following three parts:

```
var front = 'The ';
var middle = 'cat';
var back = ' sat on the mat.';
```

And if the **I** button was clicked then the value of tag is em.

Now, all the function does is glue these strings back together:

```
front + '<' + tag + '>' + middle + '</' + tag + '>'  + back;
```

This would produce the string **The cat sat on the mat**.

When SimpleEditor.insertTag() returns this value, it would replace the old
text as the value of the text area. The result, then, is that the selected text has been
wrapped with the appropriate HTML tags.

We've now created an editor capable of adding bold and italic tags to text in a text
area. We've done this with a combination of jQuery and drupal.js functions,
including a behavior and the Drupal.getSelection() utility function.

While this editor is certainly primitive, it's also less than 100 lines of code (including
comments). This should give you some idea of how powerful tools can be efficiently
built using the libraries included with Drupal 6.

Summary

In this chapter, we looked at Drupal Behaviors and the major utility functions provided by `drupal.js`.

We began with an overview of the `drupal.js` file, which provides functions for behaviors, translation, theming, as well as other utility functions. Then looked at what Drupal Behaviors are and how they work. We even saw how seemingly correct uses of behaviors can result in bugs that are difficult to diagnose.

In our first project, we used behaviors to add a sliding effect to all blocks on a page.

Then we looked at several utility functions included in `drupal.js`, learning when and how to use them. This led us to our second project, where we created a simple editor using jQuery, behaviors, and the `Drupal.getSelection()` function.

In the next chapter, we will continue our exploration of `drupal.js` by looking at JavaScript translation features. In the chapter after that, we will look at the JavaScript theming engine where we will again encounter behaviors.

5
Lost in Translations

Drupal offers some enticing JavaScript tools, one of which is jQuery. The theming and behavior capabilities provided by drupal.js are other examples. Along with those cool tools comes a feature that has had a remarkable influence on the success of Drupal, but which provides far less glitz and glamour.

This tragic hero is the **translation engine**, which will be the subject of this chapter.

Translations are important—one might even say vital—to the success of Drupal. Consequently, it is imperative that all Drupal developers become familiar with these tools. JavaScript written in Drupal 6 (and in later versions) should be translation-aware.

 Even if you don't think you need the translation functions, I advise you to read this chapter. The tools covered here play a very important role in Drupal, even providing additional security to your code.

We will move quickly in this chapter, retaining our focus on the practical. We will not spend time in closely examining the translation system.

Here are the things we will cover in this chapter:

- Get our bearings in the drupal.js library
- Enable multi-language capabilities in Drupal
- Learn the translation functions
- Build language files

For our project, we will create a small tool that takes advantage of JavaScript translation features. And to see it in action, we will create our own translation.

Translations and drupal.js

There are four main families of tools in `drupal.js`:

1. Theming functions.
2. Translation functions.
3. Utility functions.
4. Support for Drupal behaviors.

Our focus in this chapter will be on the translation functions. When we talk about translation tools, what exactly are we talking about?

Translation functions provide language translation facilities to JavaScript. Text that would normally be hardcoded into the JavaScript is translated through this system to the user's preferred language.

As is the case with the theming system, the `drupal.js` translation system is designed to provide an API similar to the server-side PHP translation system.

The translation functions are designed to be simple for the developer's use. In fact, the developer needn't even turn on Drupal's translation module to use the JavaScript libraries. The idea is to make it painless enough for the developer to use, and train the developer to habitually use the translation features.

In order to show how things work, we will not only look at the translation functions, but also at how the larger translation system is used.

Translation and languages

One of the Drupal's more distinguished points is its well-integrated support for multiple languages. Drupal has been translated into dozens of languages, and installing and enabling a translation is a simple process. For these reasons, Drupal has gained an international audience.

In earlier versions of Drupal, this language support was confined to server-side PHP code. JavaScript did not have access to the translation library. But with the release of Drupal 6, basic translation support was extended to JavaScript.

In order to see how translations work, we are going to walk through the process of enabling the translation system on the server. We will then return to the `drupal.js` library to see how it uses the system.

Translation functions are the portions of code that developers use to make it possible for code to perform translations when appropriate. The **translation system** is the part of Drupal that does the actual translation. We will start with this second part, the translation system, and then go back to the translation functions.

English is the default language for Drupal. In fact, it is the only one installed by default. But since Drupal provides a complete language translation subsystem, and Drupal code is developed to support translation, enabling multi-language support is a straightforward process.

We will begin by installing a new language.

There are three steps that must be performed the first time you install a language:

1. Multi-language support must be turned on.
2. Translation files must be downloaded and installed.
3. Drupal's translation preferences must be configured.

We will briefly walk through this process.

Turning on translation support

By default, Drupal's translation support is disabled. It is disabled for the practical reason that if it is not needed, the performance hit incurred by the translation subsystem should be avoided.

Turning it on is a matter of enabling a couple of modules. These modules are included in the Drupal core, so there's no need to download anything. All you need to do is go to **Administer | Site building | Modules**, and then check the boxes next to the **Locale** and **Content translation** modules.

Once you've done that, click on the **Save configuration** button at the bottom of the screen. That should do it.

Getting and installing translations

Dozens of translations are available in the **Translations** repository on the official Drupal.org web site. To find and download a new language, go to http://drupal.org/project/Translations and download the desired language.

Once you have the translation archive, you can install it by uncompressing the file in the same directory where Drupal is installed. For example, if Drupal is installed in /var/www/drupal (a common location for it on Linux servers), you will want to uncompress the translation file in /var/www/drupal. The language files will automatically be placed in the correct location.

The next thing to do is to let Drupal know that you have a new language installed.

Configuring languages

Once we have downloaded and unpacked the desired language(s), we need to configure Drupal's language support to determine how to handle multiple languages.

There are two steps to this process:

1. Add the new language.
2. Configure the global language settings.

In the first step, we are going to let Drupal know about the new language.

Adding the language

We've already *installed* the language, but we also need to tell Drupal that we want it to go through the process of scanning the language files and compiling a translation database. This process is called **adding a language**.

To do this, we need to go to the **Administer | Site configuration | Languages** page and click on the **Add language** tab as seen in the following screenshot:

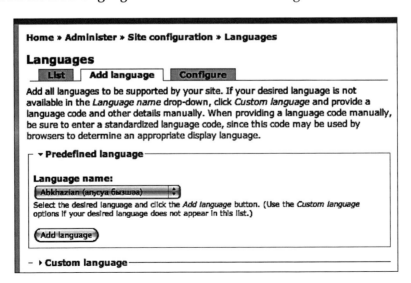

On this screen you will need to select the language from the **Language name** drop-down list. Unfortunately, this list is not limited to the languages you have already installed, so you will have to find the language in the list. Languages are indexed by their English name. Thus, you should look for **German** instead of Deutsch.

Once you've found the language, click **Add language** and sit back while Drupal parses all of the language files.

After the parsing is finished, we are ready to move on to the next step.

Configuring languages

We have multiple languages supported, now. But we need to tell Drupal how it should determine what language we want to see when we visit a page.

To configure this, we can click on the **Configure** tab on the **Administer | Site configuration | Languages** page. There is only one set of options on this page: **Language negotiation**.

> The path prefix or domain name for a language may be set by editing the **available languages**. In the absence of an appropriate match, the site is displayed in the **default language**.
>
> **Language negotiation:**
>
> ⦿ None.
>
> ⦾ Path prefix only.
>
> ⦾ Path prefix with language fallback.
>
> ⦾ Domain name only.
>
> Select the mechanism used to determine your site's presentation language. **Modifying this setting may break all incoming URLs and should be used with caution in a production environment.**
>
> (Save settings)

These settings let us configure how Drupal will determine which language to display. By default, **None** is checked. This means only the default language will be used.

Path prefix only determines which language to use based on a language identifier string present at the beginning of the URL. For example, my site is running at `http://localhost:8888/drupal/`. I have English set as the default language, and the Spanish translation is also installed.

Using these settings if I type in the previous URL, I will see the page in English (the default language). However, if I type in the URL `http://localhost:8888/drupal/ es/`, the site will be displayed in Spanish. The `es` identifier is a prefix to the Drupal portion of the URL. So if I want to view a node using the Spanish translation, the URL would look like this: `http://localhost:8888/drupal/es/node/1`.

Path translation and language prefixes

The URLs mentioned make use of Drupal's **clean URLs**. By using Apache's **mod_rewrite** module, data that would normally appear in a query string can be embedded in the URL. If you do not have clean URLs turned on, then the previous URL would look something like this: `http://localhost:8888/drupal?q=es/node/1`. With the query string clearly isolated, it's a little easier to see how `es` is treated as a prefix.

The **Path prefix with language fallback** option is similar to the previous option, except that it adds one more step.

If the path provides a language prefix, then that language is used (assuming the language has been installed and added). But if no prefix is found, Drupal then checks the language preferences that the web browser sends in its HTTP headers. These look something like this:

```
User-Agent: Mozilla/5.0 (Macintosh; U; Intel Mac OS X 10.5; en-US;
rv:1.9.0.1) Gecko/2008070206 Firefox/3.0.1
Accept: text/html,application/xhtml+xml,application/
xml;q=0.9,*/*;q=0.8
Accept-Language: es,en-us;q=0.7,en;q=0.3
Accept-Encoding: gzip,deflate
Accept-Charset: ISO-8859-1,utf-8;q=0.7,*;q=0.7
Keep-Alive: 300
Connection: keep-alive
Cache-Control: max-age=0
```

This is a subset of the HTTP headers my browser sent when requesting a page from Drupal (and I viewed the headers using Firebug).

The highlighted line shows the language preferences. Spanish (`es`) is the first language, with US English (`en-us`) and generic English (`en`) set as my second and third choices.

With **Path prefix with language fallback** enabled, when I type in `http://localhost:8888/drupal/`, I will get the page in Spanish because Drupal will inspect the **Accept-language** header and determine that it is the best language to use.

If the **Accept-language** header isn't available, or there is no language match, then Drupal will fall back to the site's default language.

Finally, the last language negotiation type is **Domain name only**. In this case, the domain name portion of the URL is used to determine language. For example, `http://es.example.com` would resolve to the Spanish language, while `http://en.example.com` would resolve to English.

For multi-language development work, I find the **Path prefix only** choice to be the easiest to work with.

 The translation feature is used to translate the strings that appear in Drupal code. This is done manually by a dedicated team of translators. Consequently, enabling translation will not affect the content you create. For example, if you write content in English, it will not be translated to Spanish for you. Only the interface (built-in menus, module descriptions, and so on) will be translated.

We now have multi-language support enabled, and you should be able to configure your Drupal installation to use more than one language. It's time to take the developer's perspective again. First, we will look at the main JavaScript translation functions. Then, we will look at a developer's tool to create translations.

Using the translation functions

Regardless of whether or not you intend to translate your module, you should always use the translation functions where applicable. There are a few reasons for this:

- By coding in a translation-friendly way, you pave the way for easy translations later. This is especially important for contributed modules, where your module may indeed be used by speakers of other languages.
- The translation functions provide additional security. This might sound counterintuitive at first. How can adding translation support *increase security*? As we will see shortly, the translation functions also perform additional escaping on text. Untrusted text is automatically escaped for display. Escaping is one way of preventing a malicious user from performing **Cross-Site Scripting** (often called **XSS**) scripting attacks or other code injection attacks.
- Using translation functions is just good coding practice. As with many other aspects of Drupal coding, the developer community encourages (and in many cases enforces) clean, well-written, and portable code. Using the translation functions is one way of conforming to Drupal's coding guidelines.

The `drupal.js` file contains a pair of functions that can make use of Drupal's multi-language support. These two functions are `Drupal.t()` and `Drupal.formatPlural()`.

If you've done any Drupal PHP coding, both of these should immediately be familiar to you. They are directly analogous to the `t()` and `formatPlural()` functions in Drupal's core PHP library. Not only do they share a name, but also the same method signature. They take the same arguments and return the same type of content.

Let's start out by looking at the `Drupal.t()` function.

 In the previous chapter, we looked at the `jQuery.extend()` function, and I mentioned that it worked like a *static function*. Many of the functions we will see in the `drupal.js` library are also used this way. There is no need to call `new Drupal()`. In fact, the `Drupal` object has no constructor, so it cannot be used to create new instances.

The Drupal.t() function

As with all of core Drupal JavaScript functions, this function uses the `Drupal` namespace. The `t()` function is a member of the `Drupal` library. This function's job is to take a string and perform any translation actions on it. Here's a simple example of this:

```
alert(Drupal.t('hello world'));
```

In this case, the translation function would check the language database for the user's preferred language and see if there was a translation available. If there is, then the function will return the translated string. If not, then **hello world** will be returned unaltered.

Shortly, we will take a closer look at how the translation happens. It is a slightly more complex process than what initially meets the eye. But before we move on in that direction, let's look at a more complex use of the `Drupal.t()` function.

The `Drupal.t()` function can take up to two arguments. They are (in order):

1. The string that should be translated.
2. An object containing name/value pairs for substitution into the string.

Here's a brief example that makes use of both:

```
var params = {
  "@siteName": "Example.Com",
  "!url": "http://example.com/"
};
var txt = Drupal.t("The URL for @siteName is !url.", params);
```

In the code, we first create the `params` object that contains a mapping of placeholders to text. What is this mapping for? Look ahead to the contents of the `Drupal.t()` function. The `Drupal.t()` function takes a string object and the `params` mapping we created.

The string looks like this: `The URL for @siteName is !url`. There are two placeholders in this string, `@siteName` and `!url`. When the `Drupal.t()` function is executed, the placeholders will be replaced by values from the `params` object.

In this case, `@siteName` will be replaced by `Example.Com`, and `!url` will be replaced by `http://example.com/`. So the English rendering of the string would be **The URL for Example.Com is http://example.com/**.

But wait! There are a couple of details to fill in. First of all, why are we using placeholders in the first place? And second, what are the `@` and `!` signs for?

In answer to the first question, placeholders should be used for any values that should not be translated. The example uses a proper name for `@siteName` and a URL for `!url`. In cases like this, translation would be unnecessary. Presumably, the site name and URL are the same in all languages.

This is a simple case where placeholders might be used. However, it's not all that common in practical cases.

A more realistic use of placeholders is to substitute it in values that are not known at translation time. To elaborate the example, consider the case where the site name and site URL are retrieved from some other object. Let's say we have an object called `SiteInfo` that contains this information (This is a fictional example. There is no such object.)

Our `params` object might look like this instead:

```
var params = {
  "@siteName": SiteInfo.name,
  "!url": SiteInfo.url
};
```

Here, the values of these variables may not be known until runtime, long after the translation has been generated. So using placeholders clearly makes sense.

> Translations are created by humans, and the process of translation is mostly handled manually. We will see this process in a few minutes. But nothing magical happens at runtime. Translated strings are simply substituted for the default (usually English-language) text.

Placeholders are then used in cases where values need to be inserted into a translated string, but where the values themselves should not be translated as part of that string.

In answer to the second question, placeholders can be demarcated by three different symbols: `@`, `%`, and `!`. Any word (alphanumeric characters surrounded by whitespace) inside a translation string that begins with one of those three characters will be treated as a placeholder.

Each of these three placeholder symbols serves a special purpose. Each indicates to `Drupal.t()` how the string should be substituted in, as explained here:

- Placeholders that begin with the `@` symbol are escaped for display in HTML. For example, if we have a `param` that looks like this: `'@tag': '<p>'`, `Drupal.t()` will convert the value to `&lt;p&gt;` before substituting it into the target string. Mostly, you should use this method of escaping to prevent security holes.

- Placeholders that begin with `!` are inserted verbatim. Drupal does not encode any of these. This should be used with care, for it could open security holes that might, for instance, allow XSS attacks.

- Finally, placeholders that begin with `%` are first encoded (like `@` placeholders), and then themed for emphasis. It means, in the default Drupal configuration, the resulting string will be placed inside the `<em></em>` tags. Using the example `'@tag': '<p>'`, the output would be `<em>&lt;p&gt;</em>`.

So what should you use and when? Most of the time, placeholders should be prefixed with `@`. That will do the encoding, but without necessarily adding any additional format (like `%` does). Placeholders should only begin with `!` when escaping content would damage the output, and when the value to be substituted is known. For example, you shouldn't take user-entered text and then use a `!` placeholder.

That's how the `Drupal.t()` function works.

When should a string be translated?

Ideally, every static piece of text in your application—labels, help text, descriptions, and so on—should be translated. Of course, there are exceptions. For example, proper nouns are usually not translated.

The Drupal.formatPlural() function

The second translation function is `Drupal.formatPlural()`. As you may have guessed from the name of the function, its job is to format a reference to singular and plural objects. This comes from the problem that in many languages (English and Spanish are good examples) single items and plural items have different suffixes. For example, we say "Johnny has 1 apple" and "Johnny has 2 apples". We also say, "Johnny has 0 apples."

So 1 is the only singular case in English (not all languages are this way, French treats 0 as singular). To handle this in a translation-friendly way (not all languages add *s* to form a plural), Drupal contains a function `Drupal.formatPlural()` that can determine whether the current case needs a singular form or a plural form.

This function takes these arguments:

- A number (If it is 1, then the singular will be used, otherwise the plural form will be used.)
- A singular string (in English)
- A plural string (in English)

Elaborating our example, we might have code that looks something like this:

```
for (i = 0; i < 6; ++i) {
  alert(
    Drupal.formatPlural(i, "Johnny has 1 apple.", "Johnny has
                        @count apples.")
  );
}
```

The formatting is a little stilted to get everything on one line, but the important part is the highlighted call to `Drupal.formatPlural()`.

When this script is run, it will loop six times and pop-up an alert message each time. Each time `Drupal.formatPlural()` is called, it will be passed `i` and the singular and plural strings.

If the value of `i` is `1` then the alert will say **Johnny has 1 apple**. In all other cases, the third parameter will be used: `Johnny has @count apples`. The `@count` placeholder is automatically replaced with the value of `i`. So for the first loop, we get **Johnny has 0 apples**. On the third loop, we get **Johnny has 2 apples**.

But this function doesn't just toggle between two strings. It uses the translation subsystem to translate the selected string too. So if the language is set to German and `i` is `0`, the output should look something like this (assuming the German translation exists): **Johnny hast 0 Äpfel**.

That's all there is to the `Drupal.formatPlural()` function. The next thing we will be look at is how to translate a string and make it available to your JavaScript.

Adding a translated string

When we create a translation for our content, we want to fulfill two goals:

1. Build a translation in such a way that the `Drupal.t()` function can make use of it.

2. Make this translation portable, so that we can use the same JavaScript on different servers. Even if we are only planning on using our JavaScript on a single site, we want it to be portable for ease of migration or rebuilding.

The easiest way to meet these two goals is to install a special module. This module is called the **Translation template extractor**. It basically analyzes our code, looking for the `Drupal.t()` calls. It then generates a template that we can easily modify to add our translation.

To get this module, go to `http://drupal.org/project/potx` and get the latest release. The release contains both a module and a command-line tool. If you like, you can use the command-line version. However, the module version is very easy to use. It is installed simply by moving the `potx/` folder in the downloaded module to your `sites/all/modules` directory, and then installing the module in the usual way by visiting **Administer | Site building | Modules**.

The main thing this module does is add a new tab to the **Administer | Site building | Translate interface** page:

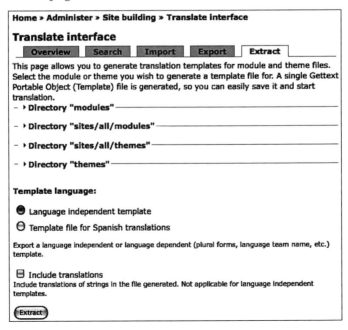

The **Extract** tab (on the far right of the list of tabs) is the one that we use to parse our files and get the strings for translation. In just a little while, we will use this interface to grab the contents from a JavaScript project that we will be creating.

This interface will generate a special file called a POT file, which maps the original untranslated text to translated strings.

 Drupal uses the **GNU gettext** system for translation. Learn more about it at `http://www.gnu.org/software/gettext/`.

Once you've gone through the process of translating strings in this POT file, it is just a matter of putting the translation file in the right place in the theme (or module) directory. Again, we will walk through that in our project.

 Translating JavaScript, translating PHP

We are focused on the JavaScript here. However, PHP translations are done in exactly the same way. There's no need to learn two translation systems—the two are fully integrated.

In fact, now that we have gone over the basics, we are ready to start our project.

Project: weekend countdown

The project that we will create in this chapter is a simple weekend countdown tool. This will display a little piece of text that indicates the current day of the week, and then says how many days are left until the weekend.

The main point of this application will be to make practical use of the translation system that we saw earlier. For that reason, we will first write some code, and then do a little translation.

 While we will consistently use the `Drupal.t()` function in this book, this is the only place where we will be writing a translation. You do not need to provide translations along with your theme or module (though if you have the ability to do the translations, it sure would be nice).

Our code is once again going to be attached to the `frobnitz` theme. The script file will be named `day.js`. Make sure you include it in the `frobnitz.info` file:

```
scripts[] = day.js
```

Here's the code:

```
var Day = Day || {};

Day.dayNames = [
  Drupal.t("Sunday"),
  Drupal.t("Monday"),
  Drupal.t("Tuesday"),
  Drupal.t("Wednesday"),
  Drupal.t("Thursday"),
  Drupal.t("Friday"),
  Drupal.t("Saturday")
];

/**
 * Create a small banner indicating the number of days until
 * the weekend.
 *
 * This will create a div element in the upper right-hand
 * corner.
 */
Day.banner = function () {
  var divProps = {
    "position": "absolute",
    "top": "5px",
    "right": "25px",
    "background-color": "black",
    "color": "white",
    "padding": "4px"
  };

  var today = (new Date()).getDay();
  var dayCount = 6 - today;
  var dayFields = {
    "@day": Day.dayNames[today],
    "@satCount": Drupal.formatPlural(dayCount,"is 1 day", "are @count
                                     days"),
    "@saturday": Day.dayNames[6]
  };

  var dayText = Drupal.t(
    "Today is @day. There @satCount until @saturday.", dayFields);
  var dayDiv = '<div id="day_div"></div>';
```

```
    $('body').append(dayDiv).children('#day_div').css(divProps)
        .text(dayText);
};


$(document).ready(Day.banner);
```

The main thing this code does is create a box in the upper-right corner of the screen that looks like this:

Today is Wednesday. There are 3 days until Saturday.

With this in mind, let's step through the code by beginning with the top portion:

```
var Day = Day || {};
Day.dayNames = [
    Drupal.t("Sunday"),
    Drupal.t("Monday"),
    Drupal.t("Tuesday"),
    Drupal.t("Wednesday"),
    Drupal.t("Thursday"),
    Drupal.t("Friday"),
    Drupal.t("Saturday")
];
```

After creating a `Day` namespace object, we create an array with seven entries, one for each day of the week. The value of the entry will be the result of a call to `Drupal.t()`. The resulting English-language version would be something like this: `["Sunday", "Monday", "Tuesday", "Wednesday", "Thursday", "Friday", "Saturday"]`.

Later we will use this array to match the numeric index of the weekday to the name of the day. This is done in the `Day.banner()` function seen here:

```
Day.banner = function () {
    var divProps = {
        "position": "absolute",
        "top": "5px",
        "right": "25px",
        "background-color": "black",
        "color": "white",
        "padding": "4px"
    };

    var today = (new Date()).getDay();
```

```
        var dayCount = 6 - today;
        var dayFields = {
          "@day": Day.dayNames[today],
          "@satCount": Drupal.formatPlural(dayCount, "is 1 day", "are
                                     @count days"),
          "@saturday": Day.dayNames[6]
        };

        var dayText = Drupal.t( "Today is @day. There @satCount until
                         @saturday.", dayFields);
        var dayDiv = '<div id="day_div"></div>';

        $('body').append(dayDiv).children('#day_div').css(divProps)
          .text(dayText);
      };
```

The first thing we do in this function is create `divProps`, which serves as a map of all of the CSS properties that we will assign later to our `<div></div>` element.

After that, we find the numeric value of the current day of the week and then calculate how many days are left until Saturday:

```
        var today = (new Date()).getDay();
        var dayCount = 6 - today;
```

Both of these values are stored for later use.

In order to create compact code, the previous code uses a shortcut. The code `(new Date()).getDay()` creates an anonymous instance of the `Date` prototype and then calls that object's `getDay()` function. The function `getDay()` returns the numeric index of the current day, where Sunday is `0` and Saturday is `6`.

This is effectively the same as writing:

```
        var myDate = Date();
        var today = myDate.getDay();
```

Our shortcut method is useful only in the case where the new `Date` instance is needed only once. By using it, we spare ourselves a line of code and an extra variable. However, there's nothing wrong with using the two-line version.

Now that we have the current date and the number of days until Saturday, we can continue.

```
        var dayFields = {
          "@day": Day.dayNames[today],
          "@satCount": Drupal.formatPlural(dayCount, "is 1 day", "are
```

```
                                  @count days"),
    "@saturday": Day.dayNames[6]
  };
  var dayText = Drupal.t("Today is @day. There @satCount until
                         @saturday.", dayFields);
```

The pattern of the previous code should look familiar because it is the setup for a `Drupal.t()` call.

First, we define our placeholders. This call is a little packed, so let's look at it closely. The `dayFields` object contains three placeholders:

- `@day`: This contains the name of the day for the current day. It uses the `Day.dayNames` array to translate the numeric day to a string. Since each item in `Day.dayNames` is already translated, the day of the week will be appropriately translated.
- `@satCount`: This placeholder is going to produce a string indicating the number of days. We use `Drupal.formatPlural()` here to handle pluralizing. It will print either `is 1 day` or `are @count days`.
- `@saturday`: This will contain the translated name of Saturday. This uses the `Day.dayNames` to get the appropriately translated name.

With the placeholders ready, the next thing the code does is run `Drupal.t()`. This will take the string `Today is @day. There @satCount until @saturday.` and substitute in the placeholders.

By the time this part of the code is run, the `dayText` variable should contain something like `Today is Wednesday. There are 3 days until Saturday.`

The last step in this function is to insert that generated text into the page. Once again, we are going to use jQuery to do this for us:

```
var dayDiv = '<div id="day_div"></div>';

$('body').append(dayDiv).children('#day_div').css(divProps)
  .text(dayText);
```

In this snippet, we first define a basic `<div></div>` element, storing it as a string in `dayDiv`. Then we use jQuery to do the following:

1. Find the `<body></body>` element and build a jQuery object that wraps it.
2. Append the contents of `dayDiv` (our `div` element) to the body.
3. Search the body element for the child with an ID `day_div` (which is the ID of the `div` we added). Essentially, what we are doing here is changing the jQuery object to point to the newly added `div` element instead of to the body element.

4. The css() function is called on the jQuery object that wraps the div element. This adds all of the items in divProps as CSS properties. In short, we are now styling the div element.

5. Finally, by using the text() function we are setting the text content of the div element.

When this long jQuery chain is executed, the HTML will contain a new div element that looks like this:

```
<div id="day_div" style="padding: 4px; position: absolute; top: 5px;
                         right: 25px; background-color: black; color:
                         white;">
      Today is Wednesday. There are 3 days until Saturday.
</div>
```

Here we've used jQuery to programmatically add a fully styled element with the information we have created.

That wraps up the Day.banner() function. Since we want this to show as soon as the page loads, we need to add one more line to our file:

```
$(document).ready(Day.banner);
```

We saw this function in the last chapter. The jQuery ready event fires as soon as the HTML is loaded and the DOM is ready for manipulation. In this case, when that event fires, the Day.banner() function is executed and the weekend countdown is displayed.

 Remember that we pass the function object (Day.banner), and not the results of the function (Day.banner()), to the ready() function.

Now we've finished the first part of this project. Regardless of what languages you have installed and your language configuration, the Day.banner() function will always return English text. Why? That's because we have not translated our tool, so every Drupal.t() lookup will fail to find translated text.

Let's fix that by creating a translation for our script.

Translating the project's strings

With our application written to take advantage of the translation system, what we want to do now is provide translations for other languages. To do this, we will use the **Translation template extractor** module discussed earlier in the chapter.

To do our translation, we will have the template extractor analyze the code in our theme and generate a translation template file. From there, we will simply add the translated text, and then add the translation file to the correct location in the file system.

The first step is to generate the translation template. This is done in **Administer | Site building | Translate interface**. We are interested in the **Extract** tab.

For our example, we are going to translate the Frobnitz theme into Spanish. This theme contains the day.js file that we have created as part of this project.

Here is what the **Extract** tab looks like:

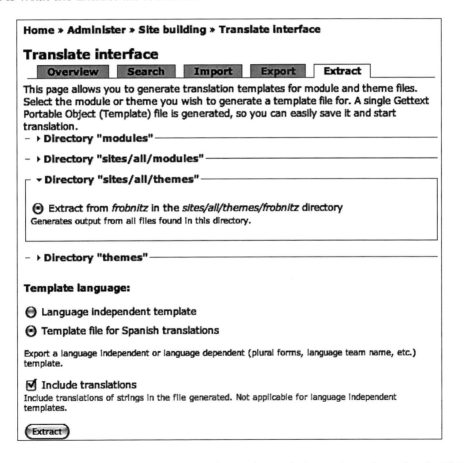

In the previous screenshot, I have already configured things for a download. All I need to do to get my translation template is press the **Extract** button.

Here's how things work.

The first thing to do is select the part of the site to be translated. I only want to work on the Frobnitz theme, so I have expanded the **Directory "sites/all/themes"** section and checked the **Extract from frobnitz in the sites/all/themes/frobnitz directory** radio button.

Next, I have selected the **Template language**. In the screenshot, there are two available options: **Language independent template** and **Template file for Spanish translation**.

The first choice provides a basic template that will work for any language. If I were translating to, say, German (which is not a currently-installed language), then I could choose this option.

Fortunately, since we already have the Spanish Drupal translation installed, we can make use of a shortcut. The second link, **Template file for Spanish translations**, allows us to generate a template that has already been tailored to our target language.

In addition to this, the last checkbox, **Include translations**, takes us a step further. It will check to see if there are any existing English-to-Spanish translations that match our own calls.

When the **Extract** button is pressed, the extractor will analyze our Frobnitz theme. It will locate the text that needs translation — the text in the `Drupal.t()` function call. Since we checked the **Include translations** box, it will also search existing translations and try to generate some translations for us.

Once all of this is done, the server will deliver a partially completed translation file.

Here's what the file looks like:

```
# $Id$
#
# LANGUAGE translation of Drupal (general)
# Copyright YEAR NAME <EMAIL@ADDRESS>
# Generated from files:
#  page.tpl.php: n/a
#  frobnitz.info: n/a
#  day.js: n/a
#  test.js: n/a
#
#, fuzzy
msgid ""
msgstr ""
"Project-Id-Version: PROJECT VERSION\n"
"POT-Creation-Date: 2008-08-28 02:47-0600\n"
```

```
"PO-Revision-Date: YYYY-mm-DD HH:MM+ZZZZ\n"
"Last-Translator: NAME <EMAIL@ADDRESS>\n"
"Language-Team: LANGUAGE <EMAIL@ADDRESS>\n"
"MIME-Version: 1.0\n"
"Content-Type: text/plain; charset=utf-8\n"
"Content-Transfer-Encoding: 8bit\n"
"Plural-Forms: nplurals=INTEGER; plural=EXPRESSION;\n"

#: page.tpl.php:20;20;21
msgid "Home"
msgstr "Inicio"

#: frobnitz.info:0
msgid "Frobnitz"
msgstr ""

#: frobnitz.info:0
msgid "Table-based multi-column theme with JavaScript enhancements."
msgstr ""

#: day.js:0
msgid "Sunday"
msgstr "Domingo"

#: day.js:0
msgid "Monday"
msgstr "Lunes"

#: day.js:0
msgid "Tuesday"
msgstr "Martes"

#: day.js:0
msgid "Wednesday"
msgstr "Miércoles"

#: day.js:0
msgid "Thursday"
msgstr "Jueves"

#: day.js:0
msgid "Friday"
msgstr "Viernes"
```

```
#: day.js:0
msgid "Saturday"
msgstr "Sábado"

#: day.js:0
msgid "Today is @day. There @satCount until @saturday."
msgstr ""

#: day.js:0
msgid "1 day"
msgid_plural "@count days"
msgstr[0] "1 día"
msgstr[1] "@count días"
```

While this file is long, it is not very complex. Let's start at the top:

```
# $Id$
#
# LANGUAGE translation of Drupal (general)
# Copyright YEAR NAME <EMAIL@ADDRESS>
# Generated from files:
#  page.tpl.php: n/a
#  frobnitz.info: n/a
#  day.js: n/a
#  test.js: n/a
#
#, fuzzy
msgid ""
msgstr ""
"Project-Id-Version: PROJECT VERSION\n"
"POT-Creation-Date: 2008-08-28 02:47-0600\n"
"PO-Revision-Date: YYYY-mm-DD HH:MM+ZZZZ\n"
"Last-Translator: NAME <EMAIL@ADDRESS>\n"
"Language-Team: LANGUAGE <EMAIL@ADDRESS>\n"
"MIME-Version: 1.0\n"
"Content-Type: text/plain; charset=utf-8\n"
"Content-Transfer-Encoding: 8bit\n"
"Plural-Forms: nplurals=INTEGER; plural=EXPRESSION;\n"
```

Lines that begin with # are comments. The comments are automatically generated and provide some useful information. But there are also a few placeholders that you might want to replace with useful information.

For example, you might want to change `Copyright YEAR NAME <EMAIL@ADDRESS>` to something like `Copyright 2008 Barbara Jenson <bjenson@example.com>`.

Next is a block of automatically generated text that provides some metadata about the translation, such as when the translation file was created. Again, you might want to change the default generated value of items, such as Language-Team, to something more accurate.

You will definitely need to set the Plural-Forms directive. This helps Drupal. formatPlural() to correctly set the plural form. The directive takes two parts. First, nplurals indicates how many plural forms the given language has. English and Spanish both have two, Slovenian has four. The second part gives the formula for selecting which of the forms to use. The singular version in our code is the first (0). Plural is in the second place (1). So we can write a simple formula for plural that looks like this: n != 1;. This tells the translator that if n!= 1, the first item (singular) should be used; otherwise, plural should be used.

So the entire Plural-Forms directive should look like this:

```
"Plural-Forms: nplurals=2; plural=(n != 1);\n"
```

 For the plural formulas of other languages, see http://drupal.org/ node/17564.

With the headers out of the way, let's look at the first translated item in the file:

```
#: page.tpl.php:20;20;21
msgid "Home"
msgstr "Inicio"
```

These three lines handle the translation of the term "Home".

The first line is an informational comment that tells us where the string appears. It can be found in page.tpl.php on lines 20 and 21.

Here's the actual code from that file (formatted for easier reading):

```
<?php if ($logo) {
 ?><a href="<?php print $front_page ?>"
title="<?php print t('Home') ?>"><img src="<?php
print $logo ?>" alt="<?php print t('Home') ?>" /></a>
 <?php
} ?>
```

Notice that both of the highlighted lines call the Drupal PHP function t(), which performs the same task for PHP as Drupal.t() does for JavaScript.

There are a few important things to note about this example:

- First, this one translation file is handling translations for both the PHP and the JavaScript translations. There is no need to generate different language files for the different technologies.

- Second, in this case the `t()` function was used twice with the same string both times. But we only have to translate the string once. This minimizes redundant work.

Looking back at that first entry in the translation file, there are two lines after the comment:

```
msgid "Home"
msgstr "Inicio"
```

A translation of any given message is broken into two parts: the original message and the translation. In the previous case, each part takes only one line (longer strings may take multiple lines).

The first line indicates the original English-language string that was passed into the `t()` function. This is called the message ID.

The second line is the translation into the file's target language—Spanish.

In this case, the translated text was automatically generated. Apparently, the template extractor found another Home message ID and that message was translated to Inicio. So here, that same translation is suggested.

In fact, as we look through the file, we will see that many of the messages we chose have already been translated. All of the day names are done for us.

In fact, the first one that needs translating is this:

```
#: day.js:0
msgid "Today is @day. There @satCount until @saturday."
msgstr "Hoy es @day. Quedan @satCount til @saturday."
```

All we need to do to complete this example is translate the string, putting the placeholders in the appropriate places:

```
Hoy es Jueves. Quedan 2 dias til Sábado.
```

That's all there is to translating a string.

If, for some reason, we needed to do a multi-line string, and the syntax is something like this:

```
msgid ""
  "Original string"
  "More text..."
msgstr ""
  "New string"
  "More text..."
```

We should note that the first string is always empty (`""`) on a multi-line translation.

Now let's take a look at a configuration for a string translated by `Drupal`. `formatPlural()`:

```
#: day.js:0
msgid "is 1 day"
msgid_plural " @count days"
msgstr[0] "1 día"
msgstr[1] "@count días"
```

Again, the extractor found existing values for us, and the translation is already complete. But the format is a little different than other entries.

The `msgid` line always points to the first string in the `Drupal.formatPlural()` call. The code that generated the previous configuration was `Drupal.formatPlural(i, "1 day", "@count days")`. That first string, `1 day`, became the message ID.

Beneath that is the original plural form:

```
msgid_plural " @count days"
```

Note that in this case, we use `msgid_plural` instead of just `msgid`.

The last two lines are the Spanish translations of these two strings:

```
msgstr[0] "1 día"
msgstr[1] "@count días"
```

Just as with `.info` files, an array-like syntax is used here. The first item, `msgstr[0]`, is the singular form. The second item is the plural form.

And that's all there is to handling the plural format translations.

Once we've translated all the strings, we are done with the translation file. Next, we just need to put it in the right place.

What if a term should remain untranslated?

Some of the terms that the extractor finds may be terms you don't want to translate. To leave these terms untranslated, just set the `msgstr` to be an empty string: `msgstr ""`.

To make the translation file available to Drupal's translation system, you should simply put the translation file in the `translations/` directory of your theme (or module). For us, the file is placed in `sites/all/themes/frobnitz/translations/`. From there, Drupal takes over and we're done.

While developing a translation, you may have to manually reload your translation in order to coerce Drupal into re-parsing the translation files. See the next section for details.

Running the code with the Spanish translation will show text that looks like this:

```
Hoy es Jueves. Quedan 2 dias til Sábado.
```

How is this working? Drupal has taken our translation file and built a new JavaScript file (located in `sites/default/files/languages/`). When the page loads and Spanish is the selected language, Drupal adds a link to that extra JavaScript file:

```
<script src="/drupal/misc/jquery.js?G" type="text/javascript">
</script>
<script src="/drupal/misc/drupal.js?G" type="text/javascript">
</script>
<script src="/drupal/sites/default/files/languages/es_fc9ac0f50be05d64
          034e46fc4de9f518.js?G" type="text/javascript">
</script>
<script src="/drupal/sites/all/themes/frobnitz/printer_tool.js?G"
type="text/javascript">
</script>
<script src="/drupal/sites/all/themes/frobnitz/sticky_rotate.js?G"
type="text/javascript">
</script>
<script src="/drupal/sites/all/themes/frobnitz/day.js?G" type="text/
javascript">
```

The highlighted section shows the inclusion of the translation JavaScript that Drupal created for us. The contents of that file look like this:

```
Drupal.locale = {
  'pluralFormula': function($n) { return Number(($n!=1)); },
  'strings': {
```

```
    "Thursday": "Jueves",
    "Friday": "Viernes",
    "Saturday": "Sábado",
    "Sunday": "Domingo",
    "Monday": "Lunes",
    "Tuesday": "Martes",
    "Wednesday": "Miércoles",
    "1 day": [ "1 día", "@count días" ],
    "Test": "carnet",
    "Today is @day. There @satCount until @saturday.":"Hoy es @day.
Quedan @satCount til @saturday."
  }
};
```

There's no need to take a detailed look at this script. The important thing to note is that it defines an object named `Drupal.locale.strings` that contains the translation pairs that our script needs.

As `Drupal.t()` and `Drupal.formatPlural()` are called, they will check the `Drupal.locale.strings` object to see if the given string or strings need translation. If they do, then the translation is performed.

Changing a translation file

There is one thing you should be aware of when developing translations for your themes and modules. Once Drupal has scanned your translation PO file once, it will not automatically scan it again. The translation database never gets automatically updated.

Practically speaking, this means that changing the translation file requires an extra step before your changes show up. You will have to manually import the modified translation file.

> If you add the new `Drupal.t()` call to you script, you can walk through the same exporting process we just did in order to create a fresh translation template at **Administer | Site building | Translation interface**. If you check the **Include translation** text box, then the translations you already created will be placed in the translation template, and you will not have to recreate any previous work.

Once you have made modifications to your translation file, you can re-import it by going to **Administer | Site building | Translation interface** and clicking on the Import tab, which will show the following screen:

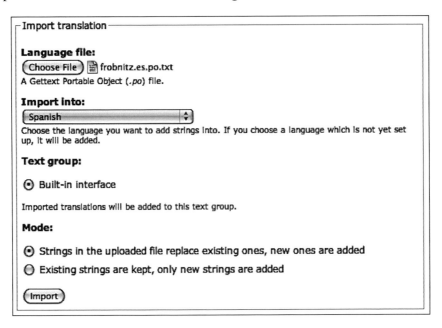

In the previous screenshot, we are re-uploading the `frobnitz.es.po.txt` file that we created before. Note that under the **Mode** section, I have selected the first option (**Strings in the uploaded file replace existing ones, new ones are added**) so that any changes I've made are given priority.

Just remember to save the updated file in your theme so that when you install the theme elsewhere, the correct version will be imported.

Summary

In this chapter, we focused on the translation system in Drupal, and the JavaScript tools that are used in conjunction with that system. We looked at installing and configuring multiple languages using the JavaScript `Drupal.t()` and `Drupal.formatPlural()` functions, and then extracting and translating the strings. In this chapter's project, we focused on using these translation functions, and then created a new translation to use for testing.

Now, we've seen an important and powerful aspect of Drupal—one that has been made accessible to JavaScript just recently (with Drupal 6). Next, we'll turn to another set of tools in the `drupal.js` file.

6
JavaScript Theming

In this chapter, we will discuss the last major component of the `drupal.js` JavaScript library. In the previous chapter we looked at the translation capabilities. Before that, in Chapter 4, we covered Drupal behaviors and utility functions. In this chapter, we will focus on the JavaScript theme system.

We will cover the following:

- The difference between theming in PHP and theming in JavaScript
- The Drupal JavaScript theming function
- Implementing custom themes in JavaScript
- Using the JavaScript theming module
- Creating a JavaScript template engine

The projects in this chapter will be focused on improving JavaScript-generated user interfaces by using the JavaScript theme system.

Theming in PHP, theming in JavaScript

In Chapter 1, we had an overview of the server-side Drupal theming system. In Chapter 2, we created the Frobnitz theme, complete with its own PHP template, a stylesheet, and some JavaScript. Since then, we've steadily added to that theme. The theme system that we have been working with runs on a server. It is written in PHP which, when executed, prepares results that are sent to a browser.

This PHP-based theme system is very powerful and complex (and, in fact, Packt Publishing has published two books on Drupal theming). However, there is a limitation to this system, namely, all of the theming must be done before the data is sent to the client.

As we have already seen, when the page is delivered and loaded, JavaScript can start doing its thing. It can rearrange the page, add new data, hide old data, and create an interactive environment in which the user's input can change what is displayed.

The server's theme engine is responsible for taking Drupal data and laying it out for display. Once loaded on the client side, JavaScript can change that display. This means even JavaScrip can become responsible for generating the look and feel of a page. Therefore, JavaScript must be able to generate and manipulate HTML and CSS.

How does JavaScript handle this task? In the past, it handled it in one of the two not-very-graceful ways.

The first way was to embed strings inside of application logic. This led to code that looked something like this:

```
function calculateSum() {
  var out = '<p>';
  var total = 0;
  if (arguments.length == 0) {
    out += 'Error: No data given.';
  }
  else if (arguments.length == 1) {
    out += 'Error: Cannot sum only one number.';
  }
  else {
    out += 'The sum is: <span '
      + 'style="color: red; font-weight: bold">';
    for(var i = 0; i < arguments.length; ++i) {
      total += arguments[i];
    }
    out += new String(total) + '</span>';
  }
  out += '</p>';
  document.getElementById('sum').innerHTML = out;
  return total;
}
```

Simply speaking, the purpose of this demonstration function is to sum all of the arguments passed to it, and then place the result inside of the element with the id sum.

Passing an arbitrary number of arguments in JavaScript

JavaScript supports passing a function, a variable number of arguments (sometimes referred to as **varargs**). Every function has access to a variable called arguments, which is an array-like object containing all of the parameters (in order) that were passed into the function.

For example, calling `calculateSum(1, 2, 3, 4)` would find the element with ID `sum`, and insert the HTML `<p>The sum is: <div style="color: red; font-weight: bold">10</div></p>`.

What we are interested in is how this function builds the information it inserts into the document.

Here, the HTML and CSS are embedded in strings, which are nested inside of the programming logic. The strings are concatenated (using the + or += operators) and the result is injected into the appropriate element.

The method exhibited here strikes many programmers as ugly. The string concatenation code is written alongside the programming logic (the actual summing of the numbers), and the result looks jumbled.

One response to this has been to get rid of the "ugly" string building code and use DOM objects. In this way, everything is essentially treated as programming logic as seen here:

```
function calculateSum2() {
    var pEle = document.createElement('p');
    var total = 0;
    if (arguments.length == 0) {
      var pcdata = document.createTextNode(
        'Error: No data given.'
      );
      pEle.appendChild(txt);
    }
    else if (arguments.length == 1) {
      var pcdata = document.createTextNode(
        'Error: Cannot sum only one number'
      );
      pEle.appendChild(txt);
    }
    else {
      var pcdata1 = document.createTextNode('The sum is:');
      var spanEle = document.createElement('span');
      spanEle.setAttribute(
        'style',
        'color: red; font-weight: bold'
      );

      for(var i = 0; i < arguments.length; ++i) {
        total += arguments[i];
      }
```

```
            var pcdata2 = document.createTextNode(' ' + total);

            pEle.appendChild(pcdata1);
            pEle.appendChild(spanEle);
            spanEle.appendChild(pcdata2);
        }

        var sumEle = document.getElementById('sum');
        sumEle.appendChild(pEle);
        return total;
    }
```

Instead of incrementally appending text and data to strings, this method uses the browser's DOM API to programmatically build up elements and then insert them into the document.

 Don't worry if this code doesn't make sense. Thanks to jQuery, we never have to write code like this again. The jQuery library provides a much more concise alternative to the DOM API.

In many ways, this second example code is more visually appealing. It just looks like a series of function calls. It all looks like serious programming logic instead of string building.

However, we're not going to use either of these methods of building a user interface. Here's why.

While there's nothing wrong with either example, they both suffer from a major drawback: The layout information is coupled with the functional aspects of the function.

A few months from now, what if somebody needs to come back and change the layout of our code? What if they want to change the `<p></p>` tags to `<div></div>` tags? In both cases, they will need to wade through the programming logic to find all of the right places to change the tags. In a sizeable JavaScript application, if all of the layout code is buried in programming logic, HTML changes can become a nightmare.

Drupal developers have already addressed the problem of separating logic and layout by developing a server-side theme system. Therefore, when they addressed the problem in JavaScript, their solution was (unsurprisingly) to implement a version of the theme system in JavaScript.

The purpose of the JavaScript theming system is to separate the display code out into separate functions, and then use a standard method of calling those functions. By separating the theming functions from the rest of the code, layout information can be isolated and easily changed. But the developers didn't stop there. Like the server-side system, the JavaScript version supports an overriding mechanism. Here, a default theme can be assigned, but another theme can be declared that overrides that default. In a moment we will see, how that works (and why it is a good thing).

The Drupal.theme() function

On the server side, the PHP theming system is remarkably sophisticated. There are PHP template files, theming functions, and preprocessing functions. There is a `.info` file and a complex system of theme inheritance.

The JavaScript side of things is considerably simpler. The `drupal.js` library in Drupal 6 only has two theme-related JavaScript functions: `Drupal.theme()` (which is a paltry seven lines of code) and `Drupal.theme.prototype.placeholder()` (with only three lines of code).

As you may have guessed, the `Drupal.theme()` function is the more important of the two. The `Drupal.theme()` function is responsible for invoking the correct theme and passing it data to be themed. Those familiar with Drupal's `theme()` PHP function should already have an accurate idea of how this works.

`Drupal.theme()` takes at least one argument—the name of the theme function that should be called. Any number of additional arguments may be passed in, too. All additional arguments will simply be passed on to the theming function as well.

An example will help clarify all of this.

There is one built-in theme that is included with Drupal 6: the placeholder theme. A few paragraphs ago, I mentioned that there were only two theme-related functions. Well, the second of these functions is the one that themes placeholders: `Drupal.theme.prototype.placeholder()`.

But we don't call that function directly. Instead, we use `Drupal.theme()` as seen here:

```
Drupal.theme('placeholder', 'Hello World');
```

The first argument, the string `placeholder`, tells Drupal to use the placeholder theme function. Any subsequent arguments are just passed into the placeholder function. It is as if we called the placeholder function like this:

```
Drupal.theme.prototype.placeholder('Hello World');
```

The placeholder theme function is responsible for formatting the passed-in string. The code would return the string `<em>Hello World</em>`.

There are two questions we might ask at this point. First, why use `Drupal.theme()` if all it does is call the longer function? Secondly, what if we don't want our placeholder text to be returned as emphasized text? (For example, what if we want it to be returned as bold text?)

These two questions are closely related, for the answer is that the `Drupal.theme()` function can do more than just call that particular function. We can define an alternate theming function to override the default behavior and themes in any way we want. And the `Drupal.theme()` function will use our overriding function instead of using the default placeholder function.

All we have to do to override the default function is create a new function in a different namespace. If the original function is `Drupal.theme.prototype.placeholder()`, we will define `Drupal.theme.placeholder()`. Then, all we do is drop the `prototype` property from the definition.

New tools are sometimes rough around the edges. Drupal's theming system misuses the `prototype` object, which has a very special purpose in the JavaScript object model. The `prototype` property should not be used as a generic namespace. Hopefully, this will be fixed in a future Drupal release.

We can easily create our own placeholder function to wrap placeholders in `<strong></strong>` tags instead of the `<em></em>` tags used by default. In fact, we can do it in a couple of ways.

Here is one way we could do it:

```
Drupal.theme.placeholder = function (str) {
   return '<strong>' + Drupal.checkPlain(str) + '</strong>';
};
```

This simply creates a new string, concatenating the strong tags to the original string. Note that we use `Drupal.checkPlain()` to do any necessary escaping on the string passed in.

The `Drupal.checkPlain()` function was discussed in Chapter 4.

We are still using the kind of string concatenation that some developers find offensively ugly. However, since we have abstracted the theme information into a separate function, at least it remains separate from the main programming logic.

Another way to write a function using jQuery that is functionally equivalent to the previous one, and perhaps a little less ugly to some programmers, is:

```
Drupal.theme.placeholder = function (str) {
   return $('<strong></strong>').text(str).parent().html();
};
```

Here, the string concatenation code has been replaced with a jQuery chain that builds a new DOM element from the `<strong></strong>` tags, and then adds `str` as its text. The jQuery `text()` function handles all of the escaping of the text. So there's no need to call `Drupal.checkPlain()` on `str`.

Getting the new element back as a string is little tricky. This is done by getting the parent element (the root of this new DOM) and then calling the `html()` function to get the HTML as a string.

The jQuery function is doing more work "under the hood," and so it will be slower. Rarely will the speed difference be noticeable. jQuery's extra work pays off. More sophisticated HTML can be built with little effort. Sometimes, jQuery will catch and clean mistakes in the HTML.

Later in this chapter, we will see how to make the most of jQuery features by moving from string concatenation to HTML templates. This will give us PHP Template like functionality from the client side.

Either of these methods will achieve the same result. Now, when `Drupal.theme('placeholder', 'Hello World')` is called, the theme function will return `<strong>Hello World</strong>`.

That's all there is to Drupal's theme system—two functions. Let's create a project where we can build something a little more interesting with the theme system.

Project: menus and blocks

We will do a few short projects in this chapter. In this first project, we will create a couple of new themes. These themes will mimic two standard Drupal layout components: blocks and menus.

The focus of this project will be to see how PHP Templates and PHP functions can be converted into JavaScript-based theme functions.

Our theming project is going to add a new menu inside of new block to a page using JavaScript. Although we will be adding these elements from JavaScript, we want them to look and perform indistinguishably from the server-generated blocks and menus.

We will put the code inside of a new file called `themes.js`. It should be included with our `frobnitz.info` file, so make sure to add a `scripts[]` entry and refresh the cache.

Adding a block with a menu in it

The new menu and block will be added as soon as the document is loaded. This means we can start with the now familiar jQuery `ready` event handler:

```
$(document).ready(function () {
  var links = [
    {name: 'Drupal.org', link:'http://drupal.org'},
    {name: 'jQuery', link:'http://jquery.com'},
    {name: 'No Link'}
  ];

  var text = Drupal.theme('shallow_menu', links);

  var blockInfo = {
    title: 'JavaScript Menu',
    content: text
  };
  var block = Drupal.theme('block', blockInfo);

  $('.block:first').before(block);
});
```

This call creates a new array of `links`, themes them, adds them to a block named **JavaScript Menu**, and then themes the entire block. Finally, the new content is added directly above the first block on the page.

The array of links is actually an array of objects, each with a `name` property. The first two also have URLs in the `link` property. The third does not:

```
var links = [
  {name: 'Drupal.org', link:'http://drupal.org'},
  {name: 'jQuery', link:'http://jquery.com'},
  {name: 'No Link'}
];
```

This list gets passed to the `Drupal.theme()` function:

```
var text = Drupal.theme('shallow_menu', links);
```

This will attempt to theme the links object using a function called `shallow_menu()`. We will create that function soon.

The input we give the `shallow_menu()` function is the `links` array—an array of objects. We will get back a single string object that contains our links marked up in HTML.

This string is stored in `text`, which is then used as part of a new object:

```
var blockInfo = {
   title: 'JavaScript Menu',
   content: text
};
```

This new object defines the two pieces of content we are already used to seeing in blocks: a `title` and some `content`.

To get from our object to a string of HTML that represents a block, we have to take another step. We need to theme the block:

```
var block = Drupal.theme('block', blockInfo);
```

This will look for a `block()` function somewhere in the `Drupal.theme` namespace and use that to theme our new block.

The resulting block, as an HTML string, will be stored in `block`. This block is inserted into the DOM using jQuery:

```
$('.block:first').before(block);
```

This query will find the first block that appears on the page, and then insert our newly minted block just before it.

One thing to note here is the order of theming. If you were to scan through the PHP source code of Drupal's server-side, you would notice that theming happens incrementally. First, one piece of information is prepared for display, and then it is combined with other data and themed into a larger chunk. This continues until one large document has been constructed. The document is then sent to the client.

 On the server side, Drupal uses both theming functions and PHP Template files to apply themes to data. But both are applied in this incremental fashion.

We are following the same pattern here. Once we have the link objects all built and stored in an array, we theme them. After all, we know they are ready for display.

That piece of information is then combined with more information to create a block object, which can then be themed. Now we have a larger chunk of HTML.

We can stop there since we don't have to rebuild the entire document. Instead, we insert the fully composed fragment into the existing document.

My choice of theming methods — theme the menu first, then add it to a block — isn't a trumped-up structure that I invented to make a point. In fact, I took the structure straight from the PHP system. There are existing PHP theming tools for menus and blocks, and I simply re-implemented them in JavaScript.

In the previous example, we called `Drupal.theme()` twice. First, we called it for `'shallow_menu'`, and the second time we called it for `'block'`. These two calls have corresponding JavaScript functions that we need to create.

In the next two subsections, we will look at each of the two themes, beginning with `Drupal.theme.prototype.block()`, and see how they compare to their server-side counterparts.

Theming a block

When we looked at the jQuery ready handler in the previous section, we saw how the menu was themed first, and then the resulting string was used as one of the components for building a block.

We are going to look at the theming functions in reverse. The reason for this is simplicity. Block theming in both PHP and JavaScript is simple. Theming a menu is considerably more complex. So we will build up from easy to harder.

In the Bluemarine theme, which is the base for our Frobnitz theme, blocks are themed using a template. You can find this template under Drupal's installation directory at `/themes/bluemarine/block.tpl.php`. Here's what the PHP Template looks like:

```php
<?php
// $Id: block.tpl.php,v 1.3 2007/08/07 08:39:36 goba Exp $
?>
  <div class="block block-<?php print $block->module; ?>"
    id="block-<?php print $block->module; ?>-<?php
      print $block->delta; ?>">
    <h2 class="title"><?php print $block->subject; ?></h2>
    <div class="content"><?php print $block->content; ?></div>
  </div>
```

That's the entire thing. It is a short snippet of HTML with a few embedded PHP statements (`<?php ... ?>`).

 We looked at another template, `page.tpl.php`, in Chapter 2. This one is even simpler than the one we saw there.

When this template is rendered, it will generate a piece of HTML that looks something like this:

```
<div class="block block-mymodule" id="block-mymodule-1">
  <h2 class="title">The Title</h2>
  <div class="content">The Content</div>
</div>
```

How does it get from the earlier template to this output? Each of the PHP statements is executed, and the results are added into the HTML. `<?php print $block->module; ?>` prints the name of the module that created the block (`$block->module`). A `print` statement tells PHP that the text should be added into the document.

Each piece of PHP code is simply printing parts of the block into the HTML. So if the block's content (`$block->content`) is `The Content`, then you might wonder what happens with code like this:

```
<div class="content"><?php print $block->content; ?></div>
```

The value of `$block->content` is inserted between the `<div class="content">` and `</div>` tags. So the output becomes:

```
<div class="content">The Content</div>
```

Of course, as you have no doubt noticed already, the `<?php` and `?>` as well as everything between them is left out of the rendered document. Only the HTML remains in the document that is sent to the client.

In order to re-implement this template as a JavaScript function, we need to find out what data gets placed into the template. Here's the information that gets pulled from the `$block` object into the template:

- `$block->module`: This is the name of the module that generated the block. We have the luxury of getting to hardcode this in our function.
- `$block->delta`: This is a numeric value that augments the module name, giving us a delta number for this module's block. If a module includes only one block on the page, that block's delta will be `0`. The next block generated by that module will be `1`, and so on. The key is to make the module name and delta number combination unique.

- $block->subject: This is the title of the block.
- $block->content: This is the content of the block.

These four pieces of information are all that is used to populate the template.

Now that we can interpret the PHP Template, the next step is to transform that into JavaScript.

As we saw before, JavaScript has no template system, and the Drupal theming system does not add one. Therefore, we will be turning the template into a JavaScript function that builds a string of HTML.

While this might not be the prettiest solution, it is the de facto way of doing things using the Drupal JavaScript theme system.

Here's our function for theming a block:

```
/**
 * Theme a block object.
 * This matches the bluemarine block.tpl.php.
 *
 * @param block
 *    A block object. Like the PHP version, it is expected to
 *    have a title and content. It may also have an id.
 * @return
 *    Returns a string formated as a block.
 */
Drupal.theme.prototype.block = function (block) {
  if (!block.id) {
    block.id = "frobnitz-" + Math.floor(Math.random() * 9999);
  }

  var text = '<div class="block block-frobnitz" id="block-' +
    block.id +
    '">' +
    '<h2 class="title">' +
    block.title +
    '</h2><div class="content">' +
    block.content +
    '</div></div>';

  return text;
};
```

The function Drupal.theme.prototype.block() will be get called when we call Drupal.theme('block', blockObject).

Earlier, when we looked at the jQuery `ready` handler, we saw that there are two properties to the `block` object that gets passed into this function: `title` and `content`. These correspond to two of the values we saw before.

The first thing the previous function does is check to see if the `block` object also has an `id` property. We want to set an ID attribute on our block. It is a requirement of HTML that ID attributes have to be unique within a document.

If the block doesn't have an ID attribute, we generate one based on a random number.

That is the only additional piece of information we need. Instead of using a module name (the code isn't generated from a module, and hence does not have a module name), we are just hardcoding in the name `frobnitz`. So there is no need to get the fourth piece of information that the PHP Template used.

From here, all that is left is to build up a string containing the HTML and return that string. This is done in one big string concatenation operation:

```
var text = '<div class="block block-frobnitz" id="block-' +
  block.id +
  '">' +
  '<h2 class="title">' +
  block.title +
  '</h2><div class="content">' +
  block.content +
  '</div></div>';
return text;
```

The string that this returns should be in the same form as the PHP Template's output that we just saw. It might look something like this:

```
<div id="block-frobnitz-3931" class="block block-frobnitz">
  <h2 class="title">Title Goes Here</h2>
  <div class="content">
    Content Goes Here
  </div>
</div>
```

As you can see, with a simple PHP Template, not much work is involved in translating it to JavaScript.

 Since the HTML is generated by JavaScript, the newly added HTML will not show up when you view the source. However, you can use the HTML inspector in Firebug. This works because Firebug shows the HTML as it currently is, not as it was when the page was loaded.

The next one we will look at is going to be a little different.

Theming a menu

Menus are a familiar fixture in Drupal. In fact, once Drupal is installed, one of the first things we do is use the menu. It looks like this:

If you quickly scan through the templates included in Bluemarine (or Garland, or any of the default themes), you won't find the template that generates this menu. Why not? That's because it comes from a set of theming functions buried deep in Drupal's `includes/menu.inc` file.

The main menu function is `menu_tree_output()`, which is not actually a theming function, technically speaking. While we're not going to dwell on it, here's how that function looks:

```
function menu_tree_output($tree) {
  $output = '';
  $items = array();
  foreach ($tree as $data) {
    if (!$data['link']['hidden']) {
      $items[] = $data;
    }
  }
  $num_items = count($items);
  foreach ($items as $i => $data) {
    $extra_class = NULL;
    if ($i == 0) {
      $extra_class = 'first';
    }
    if ($i == $num_items - 1) {
      $extra_class = 'last';
    }
    $link = theme('menu_item_link', $data['link']);
    if ($data['below']) {
```

```
        $output .= theme('menu_item', $link, $data['link']['has_
children'], menu_tree_output($data['below']), $data['link']['in_
active_trail'], $extra_class);
      }
      else {
        $output .= theme('menu_item', $link, $data['link']['has_
children'], '', $data['link']['in_active_trail'], $extra_class);
      }
    }
  }
  return $output ? theme('menu_tree', $output) : '';
}
```

The basic idea of the previous function is to traverse a menu tree and theme it so that it is ready for display. Each call to the `theme()` function (the PHP equivalent of the `Drupal.theme()` JavaScript function) is highlighted. There are four `theme()` calls to three different theming functions: `menu_item_link()`, `menu_item()`, and `menu_tree()`.

 The three theming functions are much less daunting and also bear some resemblance to the block function we just created. Feel free to look at them. They are all in `/includes/menu.inc`.

If we were to reproduce this in JavaScript, we would need to write at least four functions (assuming none of the themes would call something else).

Now we should ask ourselves some questions: What are we trying to implement in our JavaScript theme function? Do we need the complex logic present above? We could create a JavaScript equivalent, but do we need to?

All we really want to do, in our example at hand, is create a simple menu containing links. We don't need to support an elaborate tree structure at all. We don't really need to break out the theming of menu items and menu item links, or even of the menu as a whole and each of the menu items.

The most important thing is getting our code to look like the menu generated from `menu_tree_output()`. The fastest way of finding out how to generate our theme will not be analyzing the code. It's going to be analyzing the generated HTML.

In fact, let's take a look at the HTML source for the menu we saw in a screenshot a few pages back. Here's what that looks like:

```
<ul class="menu">
  <li class="leaf first">
   <a href="/drupal/user/1">My account</a>
  </li>
```

```
  <li class="collapsed">
   <a href="/drupal/node/add">Create content</a>
  </li>
  <li class="collapsed">
   <a href="/drupal/admin">Administer</a>
  </li>
  <li class="leaf last">
   <a href="/drupal/logout">Log out</a>
  </li>
</ul>
```

Ah, that's much better. We can generalize a little more to see the structure of a menu in its simplest form like this:

```
<ul class='menu'>
  <li class='leaf'>
    <a href='link'>name</a>
  </li>
</ul>
```

Also, from the example before, we can see that the `<li></li>` for the first node in a menu has the additional class `first`. Similarly, the last one has the `last` class.

We're now ready to code this up in JavaScript. This time, we will use the jQuery-based method for building:

```
/**
 * Build a single (non-colapsed) menu list.
 * Mimics the complex menu logic in menus.inc.
 * @param items
 *   An array of objects that have a name and a link property.
 * @returns
 *   String representation of a link list.
 */
Drupal.theme.prototype.shallow_menu = function (items) {
  var list = $('<ul class="menu"></ul>');

  for (var i = 0; i < items.length; ++i) {
    var item = items[i];

    // Get text for menu item
    var menuText = null;
    if (item.link) {
      menuText = item.name.link(item.link);
    }
    else {
      menuText = item.name;
    }
```

```
    // Create item
    var li = $('<li class="leaf"></li>');

    // figure out if this is first or last
    if (i == 0) {
      li.addClass('first');
    }
    else if (i == items.length - 1) {
      li.addClass('last');
    }

    // Add item to list
    li.html(menuText).appendTo(list);
  }

  return list.parent().html();
};
```

Don't let the size of this function distract you. It's actually not very complex.

This function takes a list of objects that represent links. We saw this list in the jQuery `ready` handler we created earlier:

```
var links = [
  {name: 'Drupal.org', link:'http://drupal.org'},
  {name: 'jQuery', link: 'http://jquery.org'},
  {name: 'No Link'}
];
```

This is the object that is passed into our `Drupal.theme.prototype.shallow_menu()` function.

 Our theme is named `shallow_menu()` because it does not take the deep tree-structured menu data that its PHP counterpart did. Instead, this function only creates shallow menus.

We start out by creating a `list` object, which is our list element wrapped inside of a jQuery object. Once again, we are taking advantage of jQuery's flexible constructor to pass it an HTML fragment instead of a CSS selector.

Once our list container is ready, all we need to do is loop through each object in the list of links, formatting and adding it to the `list` as we go.

The loop starts out like this:

```
for (var i = 0; i < items.length; ++i) {
  var item = items[i];

  // Get text for menu item
  var menuText = null;
  if (item.link) {
    menuText = item.name.link(item.link);
  }
  else {
    menuText = item.name;
  }
  /* More here... */
};
```

The first thing we do in the `for` loop is store the current item in the `item` variable.
We know that each `item` will have a `name`, but we don't know if it will have a
`link` property.

If it has a link, we want to create a piece of HTML that looks like this: `<a`
`href='link'>name</a>`. But if it doesn't, we want HTML that looks like this: `name`.

This is all done within that first `if`/`else` conditional.

Easy linking
A useful JavaScript function that is used surprisingly infrequently is
the string method `link()`. Any string can be turned into a link by
calling this method and passing in a URL like this: `'a string'`.
`link('http://example.com')`. This little snippet of code will
generate an HTML looking like this: `<a href="http://example.`
`com">a string</a>`.

The next part of the `for` loop looks like this:

```
for (i = 0; i < items.length; ++i) {
  var item = items[i];

  // Get text for menu item
  var menuText = null;
  if (item.link) {
    menuText = item.name.link(item.link);
  }
  else {
    menuText = item.name;
  }

  // Create item
```

```
    var li = $('<li class="leaf"></li>');

    // figure out if this is first or last
    if (i == 0) {
      li.addClass('first');
    }
    else if (i == items.length - 1) {
      li.addClass('last');
    }

    // Add item to list
    li.html(menuText).appendTo(list);
  }
```

The highlighted portion is the new code.

First, we create a jQuery-wrapped list element:

```
    var li = $('<li class="leaf"></li>');
```

Once we have the `li` object we check it to see if it is either the first or last menu item. If it's the first, we add the `first` class. And if it is last, we add the `last` class. All others will have only the `leaf` class.

Now that we have our list item element (`li`) ready, we add content and then append the entire thing to the `list` object:

```
    li.html(menuText).appendTo(list);
```

By the time the `for` loop is done, a new `li` object will have been added to the `list` for each item that was in the original array of links.

Finally, after the `for` loop we have one last line. We bring things together with a last jQuery chain:

```
    return list.parent().html();
```

A theme function needs to return a string, so we grab a string representation of the main `<ul></ul>` element (together with its contents) using `parent().html()`.

When all of this is put together, we should get a menu embedded in a block. The entire thing should look something like this:

We've finished our project. We created two themes—one based on a PHP Template file and one based on a very complex function. But when we put everything together, our JavaScript themes look just like their PHP-generated counterparts.

The JavaScript theming module

In the project we just created, we built a couple of simple themes that implemented existing Drupal functionality. On the JavaScript side, we recreated some features already present on the server side. The only theme function that ships with the Drupal 6 core is the placeholder function. Unfortunately, this means that doing this kind of basic re-implementation work is necessary when you want to recreate the look and feel.

Fortunately, there are Drupal modules that provide features that Drupal itself lacks. In this case, there is a module that provides some much-needed general purpose theming functions. This module is called the **JavaScript theming** module, and is available at `http://www.drupal.org/project/js_theming`.

 The JavaScript theming module makes use of some of the newer features of the JavaScript language. Not all of the features will work on older or less-supported browsers.

Installing the JavaScript theming module is as simple as downloading the module from the URL given above, unpacking it in the `/sites/all/modules` directory of your Drupal installation, and enabling it from **Administer | Site building | Modules**. Once the module is enabled, the JavaScript tools will be available to you on all pages.

This module provides themes for the following common user interface components:

- Tables
- Nested lists
- Notification messages
- Images

In addition to these themes, it also provides some basic utility functions that make working with Drupal easier (and for the PHP developer, more familiar). Two important functions are `Drupal.l()` and `Drupal.url()`, both of which are used to construct URLs.

Let's take a look at a few of these.

Theming tables

Tables provide a great way of visually presenting certain forms of data. Unfortunately, the HTML used to create them is verbose; a lot of tags are required to properly build a table. For that reason, tables make a perfect candidate for theming.

It should come as no surprise that this common user interface component is one of the themes that JavaScript theming provides. It is used like this:

```
Drupal.theme('table', headers, rows);
```

Here, `headers` is an array of column headings, and `rows` is an array of rows, where each row is an array. Let's take a look at a fragment of JavaScript code:

```
var headers = ['Library', 'Purpose'];
var rows = [
  ['jquery.js', 'Document manipulation'],
  ['drupal.js', 'Drupal interaction'],
  ['js_theming.js', 'Provide additional themes']
];
var table = Drupal.theme('table',headers, rows);
```

The `headers` array contains two column headers, `Library` and `Purpose`. Underneath that is the `rows` array, which contains three rows of data. Each row is, in turn, an array, and each item in that array represents a cell.

We have three rows of data, each with two cells (one for the `Library` column and one for the `Purpose` column).

 In code that was used for something more than an example. We would surround each of these strings with `Drupal.t()` to allow the translation subsystem to translate them when necessary.

At the end of this fragment, if we were to dump the contents of the `table` variable, it would look like this:

```
<table class="sticky-enabled">
 <thead>
  <tr>
    <th>Library</th>
    <th>Purpose</th>
  </tr>
 </thead>
 <tbody>
  <tr class="odd">
    <td>jquery.js</td>
    <td>Document manipulation</td>
```

```
    </tr>
    <tr class=»even»>
      <td>drupal.js</td>
      <td>Drupal interaction</td>
    </tr>
    <tr class=»odd»>
      <td>js_theming.js</td>
      <td>Provide additional themes</td>
    </tr>
  </tbody>
</table>
```

Our headers are now encapsulated in the `<thead></thead>` section, and each row of the row table is now a `<tr></tr>` element containing each of its items in `<td></td>` tags.

If we took a look at this in a browser window, it would look something like this:

Library	Purpose
jquery.js	Document manipulation
drupal.js	Drupal interaction
js_theming.js	Provide additional themes

The table uses standard Drupal CSS class names. Therefore, it is styled by the existing Drupal theme's stylesheets (in this case, the Bluemarine CSS that Frobnitz inherits).

This is a simple use of the table theme. It supports more complex table formatting by taking objects in addition to strings. For example, if we wanted to add an additional class to each `<td></td>` tag, we could do something like this:

```
var headers = ['Library', 'Purpose'];
var cell1 = {data: 'jQuery.js', 'class':'myClass'};
var cell2 = {data: 'Document manipulation', 'class':'myClass'};
var rows = [
  [cell1, cell2]
];
var attrs = {'width': '100%'};
var caption = "Drupal JS Libraries";
var table = Drupal.theme(
  'table', headers, rows, attrs, caption
);
```

In this example, I have shortened the table down to one row to make it a little clearer.

> The `class` is enclosed in single quotes because the bare literal is a JavaScript-reserved word. Using `class` without quotes will cause errors.

This time, the two cells in the row have been moved out to their own variables: `cell1` and `cell2`. Each of these is an object with two properties: `data` (the element data) and `class` (the CSS class to add).

The object notation for cells works in the following manner: a property named `data` holds the table's data. All other properties will be assumed to be the name of an HTML attribute, and will be converted to attribute/value pairs. Here, `class:'myClass'` will become `class='myClass'`. We could likewise use `id:'myID'` to add an attribute like `id='myID'`.

We have also added an `attrs` object, which holds the attributes for the table tag, and a `caption` element that will hold the caption for the table. Both of these are passed as additional parameters to `Drupal.theme()` on the last few lines of the previous code.

When the results of this code are displayed, they will look something like this:

Drupal JS Libraries	
Library	**Purpose**
jQuery.js	Document manipulation

Notice this time the table is wider and there is a caption above the table. If we were to look at the underlying HTML, we would see the additional CSS classes we added to each table cell:

```
<table width="100%" class="sticky-enabled">
  <caption>Drupal JS Libraries</caption>
  <thead>
    <tr>
      <th>Library</th>
      <th>Purpose</th>
    </tr>
  </thead>
  <tbody>
    <tr class="odd">
      <td class="myClass">jQuery.js</td>
      <td class="myClass">Document manipulation</td>
    </tr>
```

```
      </tbody>
   </table>
```

Looking at the highlighted lines, we can see the effect of turning our cells into objects.

The table has more features, including support for server-driven, sortable columns (which require a little bit of server-side coding). But we will continue to look at a few other features of the JavaScript theming library.

Sending notifications to the user

What happens when an error occurs and our code needs to inform the user of this? What if something succeeds and we want to let the user know? What if we just need to provide a little information for the user, and provide it in a standard way that is easy to identify?

On the server side there is a standard procedure for handling these three situations. There is a PHP function, `drupal_set_message()`, which can be used to inform users about errors, warnings, or additional information.

This is another useful feature that the JavaScript theming module provides.

This function is called like this:

```
Drupal.messages.set(text, level);
```

Here, `text` is the text of the message, and `level` is one of three predefined levels: `'warning'`, `'error'`, or `'status'`. (Note that each of these is a string and must be passed into the function in quotation marks.)

Here's how we might use it to display an error message:

```
Drupal.messages.set("An error occurred.", "error");
```

When this executes, it will display a red box near the top of the user's page (just under the page's header section) with the error message:

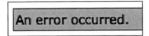

This message will be displayed for several seconds, and will then disappear. (The time is configurable through the module's administration interface.)

The other two message levels function similarly, but `warning` will create a yellow box and `status` will create a grey box (colors, of course, are determined by the CSS).

If you are using this module, the `Drupal.messages.set()` function is a good tool for providing user notifications.

Adding links

There are many useful functions in the JavaScript theming library, but to save space (and cover more ground regarding theming), we will cover only one more. This function is `Drupal.l()`, and it is the main function used for creating links.

Those familiar with PHP programming for Drupal, will find it unsurprising that `Drupal.l()` provides the same functionality as the Drupal PHP `l()` function. It is typically called in this way:

```
Drupal.l(text, url);
```

Here, `text` is the text that will be linked and `url` is the relative URL of a Drupal resource. For example, we could create a link to the fifth node in our system like this:

```
Drupal.l('Node 5', 'node/5');
```

This would return a string of HTML that looked like this:

```
<a href="/drupal/node/5" class="active">Node 5</a>
```

Note that the link for the base path on my system has been adjusted. It has turned `node/5` into `/drupal/node/5`.

There is an optional third parameter which can contain additional options. These options are all documented at `http://api.drupal.org/api/function/l/6`. For example, if we wanted to use an absolute URL, instead of a relative one, we could set the `absolute` property to `true`:

```
Drupal.l('Drupal', 'http://drupal.org', {'absolute':true});
```

This would result in a link pointing to `http://drupal.org`, instead of a relative link to our own server.

The JavaScript theming module provides some useful tools for extending the JavaScript capabilities of your Drupal 6 system.

Next up, we are going to work on another project. In this project, we will implement a simple template system.

Project: templates for JavaScript

So far we've seen a few ways in which a theming function can format text. One method is to build up a string by appending HTML fragments and variables. Our first string building example looked like this:

```
Drupal.theme.placeholder = function (str) {
   return '<strong>' + Drupal.checkPlain(str) + '</strong>';
};
```

In the previous project, we used this method to implement `Drupal.theme.prototype.block()`. In this method, an HTML fragment is created by appending strings together. We also saw another method that relied upon jQuery to handle the HTML. We re-implemented the previous function using the jQuery method:

```
Drupal.theme.placeholder = function (str) {
   return $('<strong></strong>').text(str).parent().html();
};
```

In this case, the HTML is composed at the DOM level, and is then converted back into a string at the end. Although it incurs more overhead, it looks more elegant, can improve error checking, and can also provide additional features.

 There is one possible advantage in using the string-based method. In some hard-to-debug cases, Internet Explorer does not correctly handle the manipulation of elements until after they are added to the parent document. This seems to occur when working with <object/> tags. However, these are rare cases, and most of the time the jQuery builder method works fine.

One of our original goals was to separate the logical workings of a program from the layout of the program. The `Drupal.theme()` function is a step in the right direction, to be sure. However, on the server side, the PHP Template system makes an even cleaner separation. Template files are easier to edit than strings embedded in functions. Also, for all its compact functionality, if what you are interested in is merely changing minor layout details, jQuery is probably even harder to edit.

It would be nice to have a template language for Drupal JavaScript. In this project, we are going to write one.

We want a simple template system where the HTML is separated from the JavaScript code as much as possible. We want to make it very easy for a themer to edit the look and feel of our JavaScript-themed code. This means getting the markup out of functions. Ideally, one should be able to change the layout without ever having to see a line of JavaScript code.

Oh, and we also want to do this without making any changes at all to the PHP code that drives Drupal.

Here are our design goals:

- Taking a cue from the PHP Template system, let's make it possible for each template to be stored in its own style.

- We don't want to reinvent the entire theme system. Therefore, we want to make this mesh with the existing `Drupal.theme()` function, and as much of the rest of the subsystem, as is possible.

- We already have some powerful tools in the `drupal.js` and jQuery libraries. Let's try to minimize the amount of code we generate. (We will not introduce any new dependencies either).

- Finally, we want to make our new template language simple enough for themers and developers to pick it up quickly.

The last point implies that we will be writing a new template language. Why not just re-use PHP Templates in JavaScript? What makes PHP Templates a winner for Drupal is how it balances performance and simplicity. It is trivially easy for a PHP developer to learn, and it executes quickly because it is only made up of PHP.

However, JavaScript is a different language than PHP. If we try to use PHP Templates in JavaScript, we will have a lot of work to make it possible for our scripts to be able to parse the PHP files. Since we don't want to implement all of PHP just to make a few templates, we are stuck in the situation of having to document exactly how our templates differed from standard PHP Templates.

However, maybe we can look for the same balancing point on the client side that Drupal server developers found in PHP Templates. If PHP is fast on the server, what is a browser good at parsing and interpreting? HTML, CSS, and JavaScript all come to mind. It just so happens that web developers tend to be well-versed in at least the first two of these technologies.

We now have a candidate for a template language. Let's now see if we can build a template language that primarily uses HTML and CSS for markup.

The node template

For this project, let's build some code that will add a new node to the list of nodes we see on the home page. In the previous project, we built code for adding blocks on the fly. This time, we'll add nodes on the fly.

Again, the place to start with is the normal `node.tpl.php` file that is included with Bluemarine:

```php
<?php
// $Id: node.tpl.php,v 1.7 2007/08/07 08:39:36 goba Exp $
?>
  <div class="node<?php if ($sticky) { print " sticky"; } ?>
    <?php if (!$status) { print " node-unpublished"; } ?>">
    <?php if ($picture) {
      print $picture;
    }?>
    <?php if ($page == 0) { ?><h2 class="title">
    <a href="<?php print $node_url?>"><?php
      print $title?></a></h2><?php }; ?>
    <span class="submitted"><?php print $submitted?></span>
    <div class="taxonomy"><?php print $terms?></div>
    <div class="content"><?php print $content?></div>
    <?php if ($links) {
      ?><div class="links">&raquo; <?php print $links?></div>
      <?php
    }; ?>
  </div>
```

As usual with the PHP Template files, this is made up of a mixture of HTML and very simple PHP code. There are a couple of `if` statements to conditionally add CSS classes, display pictures, and include links. There are plenty of `print` statements, which inject strings into the HTML. However, there is no complex logic, or unusual functions, used in this template.

Let's remove all of the PHP and see what the underlying HTML basically looks like:

```html
<div class="node">
  <h2 class="title"><a href="#"></a></h2>
  <span class="submitted"></span>
  <div class="taxonomy"></div>
  <div class="content"></div>
  <div class="links"></div>
</div>
```

Based on the CSS class names, we can take a glance at this fragment and get a pretty good idea about what each piece of the fragment ought to do. In fact, the class names provide enough information so we can even computationally fill it out. Where should the title go? How about inside the link in the tag with `class='title'`! We can find locations like that using a jQuery CSS selector: `$('.title a')`.

We might want to flag a node as unpublished using the element with class `submitted`. If we have taxonomy terms, we can put them in the element with the `taxonomy` class. Similarly, content and links go inside of the `div` tags with the appropriate class names.

It looks like we have the information we need. Let's make this pure HTML fragment our template.

Following a naming convention similar to the PHP Template names, let's store the previous code inside of our theme with the name `node.tpl.html`. Notice that the last part of this filename is `.html`, not `.php`. We don't want this file to be executed on the server side (it would be a waste of time and would make this template look like a PHP Template).

From a template to a system: what next?

We have now devised a template language that fills some requirements. It should be easy for any experienced HTML author to create templates in our system. After all, they're just HTML fragments. Of course, we would want to make sure they used the correct CSS classes, but no new language will need to be learned.

We have also stored our template in its own file. That should make it easier to edit as well.

But wait. What do we do with these templates? How can we use them from JavaScript? After all, the templates are on the server, and unless the browser requests them, they will not be sent to the client.

Furthermore, templates on the server side are composed into a single HTML document before they are transmitted to the client. However, a client-side template is obviously not going to work that way. The JavaScript template engine won't even have started until a pre-built document has been sent.

What we need is a way to get the template from JavaScript, use that template for theming, and then inject the results into the existing document (the one built on the server). This might initially seem like a tall order, but we are going to borrow a little technology from the next chapter and create an engine that will do just what I have described.

 The strategy used here could be generalized with a little bit more code to provide template services to any Drupal JavaScript application. However, to keep our code concise, we will create a specific application to meet our needs.

We will continue adding code to the `themes.js` file that we created for the last project. From here, we are going to proceed as follows:

1. We will create a simple template layer that sets up the environment we will need for templating.
2. We will employ the existing Drupal theming system, using it as a frontend to our template system.

Let's look at the first step.

A template system

We now have HTML templates on the server and a theming system on the client. The first step toward linking these two is to fetch the templates from the server.

To do this, we are going to create a new namespace object named `TplHtml`. We don't want to put our custom code inside of the `Drupal` namespace as this code is not the official Drupal code.

This new namespace will house our main template function, in addition to all of the templates that we load from the server.

Here's what the code for our complete template system looks like:

```
var TplHtml = {template: {}};

TplHtml.loadTemplate = function (name, uri) {
  var url = Drupal.settings.basePath + uri;

  jQuery.get(url, function (txt) {
    TplHtml.template[name] = txt;
  });
};

$(document).ready(function () {
  TplHtml.loadTemplate('node',
    '/sites/all/themes/frobnitz/node.tpl.html');
});
```

The first line creates the new `TplHtml` namespace that adds an empty `template` object. `TplHtml.template` is where the templates we get from the server will be stored.

Next is the `TplHtml.loadTemplate()` function. This is the key piece of our template system. It takes a template `name` and a URL fragment (`uri`) that will be used to find the template on the server.

The `name` parameter should be a short name for our template. For example, our node template would probably have the name `node`. Later, we will use it as a keyword for referring to our template. It must be made up of alphanumeric characters only, and contain no spaces.

The `uri` parameter should be the relative path of the template within the theming system. In a few moments, we will see this used to point to the `node.tpl.html` file we just created just before.

The `TplHtml.loadTemplate()` function has only four lines of code. The first line takes the `uri` parameter and prepends it with the base path to the server:

```
var url = Drupal.settings.basePath + uri;
```

In Chapter 2, we discussed how the `Drupal.settings.basePath` variable will always point to absolute server path where Drupal is installed. By constructing the URL this way, we don't have to know anything about where on the server Drupal is installed. Instead, we can just build a relative path from Drupal's base to our specific template file.

The next three lines are responsible for fetching the file from the server:

```
jQuery.get(url, function (txt) {
  TplHtml.template[name] = txt;
});
```

Here we are using a jQuery function that is new to us: `jQuery.get()`. In a nutshell, this function makes it possible to fetch a file from the server, and then manipulate it locally. It's part of jQuery's powerful **AJAX (Asynchronous JavaScript and XML)** library, which we will take a closer look at this function in the next chapter.

 Chapter 7 will cover AJAX in detail. There, we will cover jQuery's AJAX features and do projects that involve retrieving XML and JSON data from the Drupal server.

For now, we will just take a quick look at what it does for us in this context.

We pass it two arguments: the URL that we just constructed (`url`) and an anonymous function. jQuery will request the URL from the server. When the server responds, jQuery will execute the anonymous function, passing the server's response as the first parameter to this function. Therefore, `txt` will contain a string representation of the document we requested.

Since we will be requesting templates, `txt` will hold a complete template. We want to take that template and cache it somewhere convenient. We have already created that place: the `TplHtml.template` object.

Taking advantage of JavaScript's array-like object reference syntax, we can add this new template to the `TplHtml.template` object in this way:

```
TplHtml.template[name] = txt;
```

If we add a template with the name block, we could then access this template as a JavaScript object:

```
alert(TplHtml.template.block);
```

That's all there is to our template retrieval function. This gives us a tool for fetching as many templates as we need from the server.

Next, we will look at the simple jQuery `ready` handler:

```
$(document).ready(function () {
  TplHtml.loadTemplate('node',
    '/sites/all/themes/frobnitz/node.tpl.html');
});
```

With this snippet of code, we move from general to specific. When the document is ready, we load a very specific template file using our `TplHtml.loadTemplate()` function. This will fetch our template file, which is located at `/sites/all/themes/frobnitz/node.tpl.html` (the relative path from Drupal's base to our custom theme). Once retrieved, the template will be stored in `TplHtml.template.node`, since `node` is the name passed into `TplHtml.loadTemplate()`.

With this chunk of code, within moments of the main document loading, we should also have the `node` template available to us. If we were to look at the contents of `TplHtml.template.node`, we would see a string that looked like this:

```
<div class="node">
  <h2 class="title"><a href="#"></a></h2>
  <span class="submitted"></span>
  <div class="taxonomy"></div>
  <div class="content"></div>
  <div class="links"></div>
</div>
```

Does this look familiar? It should since it's the template we created at the beginning of this project.

The next step is to build theme functions that can make use of this template system.

Theming with templates

The last part of our template system is a theme function that can make use of the template.

Based on the jQuery `ready` handler we just wrote, we now have a template stored in `TplHtml.template.node`. Here, we need to provide a function that will take that template and then populate it with data.

To do this, we will once again use jQuery since it provides powerful tools for navigating HTML and modifying the document's structure. Here's our new function:

```
Drupal.theme.node = function (node) {
  var out = '';
  if (TplHtml.template.node) {
    var tpl = $(TplHtml.template.node);

    // Is it sticky?
    if (node.sticky) {
      tpl.parent().find('.node').addClass('sticky');
    }

    // Do title and title's link at the same time.
    if (!node.nodeUrl) node.nodeUrl = '#';
    tpl.find('.title a').text(node.title)
      .attr('href', node.nodeUrl);

    // These are the things we are going to place in
    // the template.
    // Fortunately for us, class names match 1-to-1 with
    // the names of the node properties.
    var values = ['content','submitted','taxonomy','links'];
    for (var i = 0; i < values.length; ++i) {
      var value = values[i];
      if (node[value]) {
        tpl.find('.' + value).html(node[value]);
      }
      else {
        tpl.find('.' + value).hide();
      }
    }

    // Now we dump the template to a string.
    out = tpl.parent().html();
  }
  return out;
};
```

Though this function is large, it doesn't use any new functions or techniques. In fact, all it is doing is taking the node data and the `TplHtml.template.node` template, and merging the data into the template.

To get through this large function, let's look at it in smaller chunks:

```
Drupal.theme.node = function (node) {
```

The theme function takes one parameter: node. This parameter is expected to be an object and may have any of the following properties:

- `node.title`: The title of the node. This is the only required item.
- `node.nodeUrl`: The relative URL of the node.
- `node.sticky`: A flag indicating whether this node should be treated as sticky at the top of the page. (The default is `false`.)
- `node.content`: The content of the node.
- `node.submitted`: Information about the date and submitter of the node.
- `node.taxonomy`: A string containing hyperlinks to taxonomy terms.
- `node.links`: A string containing additional links (like to comments).

As we build up the layout, we will put each bit of node information into its appropriate place in the template.

Let's take a look at the next section of the function:

```
Drupal.theme.node = function (node) {
  var out = '';
  if (TplHtml.template.node) {
    var tpl = $(TplHtml.template.node);

    // Is it sticky?
    if (node.sticky) {
      tpl.parent().find('.node').addClass('sticky');
    }

    // Do title and title's link at the same time.
    if (!node.nodeUrl) node.nodeUrl = '#';
    tpl.find('.title a').text(node.title)
      .attr('href', node.nodeUrl)

    // More here...
  }
  return out;
}
```

The out variable is going to hold the string that we return.

The first thing we do after declaring our out variable is check to see whether the template exists. If it does, we continue with the formatting. If not, we return an empty string.

> Returning an empty string like this is fine for demonstration purposes, but it isn't a great way of doing things on a production system. Since the template is being fetched from a remote server, it is possible that the template couldn't be loaded. It might be a better solution to add some default theming in cases where the template cannot be loaded.

Inside the conditional, we create a new jQuery object to wrap the node template. The tpl variable will refer to our template jQuery object. We can now conveniently manipulate the HTML DOM for our template.

Next, we begin modifying the template. We check to see if node.sticky is set and true. If it is, we then want to add a sticky CSS class to any element with the node class. This is done with a simple jQuery string: tpl.parent().find ('.node').addClass('sticky'). This starts from the top of the template DOM (tpl.parent()), and then finds all elements with the node class. Each of those nodes gets the sticky class added.

From here, we move on to the node title and URL. The HTML template we created had a title section that looked like this:

```
<h2 class="title"><a href="#"></a></h2>
```

We want to find that section and add both a title and a URL. We can do this with one long jQuery chain:

```
tpl.find('.title a').text(node.title)
  .attr('href', node.nodeUrl)
```

This finds the link element inside the title section, sets its text to node.title, and then re-targets the link to node.nodeUrl.

The following chunk of code makes it easy enough for us to accomplish several content-filling tasks in a compact loop:

```
Drupal.theme.node = function (node) {
  var out = '';
  if (TplHtml.template.node) {
    var tpl = $(TplHtml.template.node);

    // Is it sticky?
```

```
    if (node.sticky) {
      tpl.parent().find('.node').addClass('sticky');
    }

    // Do title and title's link at the same time.
    if (!node.nodeUrl) node.nodeUrl = '#';
    tpl.find('.title a').text(node.title)
      .attr('href', node.nodeUrl)

    // These are the things we are going to place in
    // the template.
    // Fortunately for us, class names match 1-to-1 with
    // the names of the node properties.
    var values = ['content','submitted','taxonomy','links'];
    for (var i = 0; i < values.length; ++i) {
      var value = values[i];
      if (node[value]) {
        tpl.find('.' + value).html(node[value]);
      }
      else {
        tpl.find('.' + value).hide();
      }
    }

    // Now we dump the template to a string.
    out = tpl.parent().html();
  }
  return out;
};
```

The first thing we do in this highlighted section is define a new array:

```
var values = ['content','submitted','taxonomy','links'];
```

We have four CSS classes defined in the document that we need to fill in: content, submitted, taxonomy, and links. We potentially have four attributes on our node object that need to be slotted in these spots: node.content, node.submitted, node. taxonomy, and node.links.

Fortunately for us, the names match up! We can loop through the values array and drop the contents of our node properties into the correct location in the template:

```
for (var i = 0; i < values.length; ++i) {
  var value = values[i];
  if (node[value]) {
```

```
      tpl.find('.' + value).html(node[value]);
  }
  else {
    tpl.find('.' + value).hide();
  }
}
```

We can make use of the fact that JavaScript allows array-like access to object properties to check whether or not each of the items in the values array exists. For example, if the `node.submitted` exists, then `node['submitted']` will be evaluated as `true`. So we look through the values array and check for each property in the node object. If it exists (`if (node[value])`), then we insert the value. If it doesn't exist, we hide the relevant part of the template so an empty container is not displayed.

The highlighted line in the previous code is responsible for adding the content into the template:

```
tpl.find('.' + value).html(node[value]);
```

This jQuery chain begins with the template and finds all elements whose class is the current value. During first iteration, it will look for is `content`, then `submitted`, and so on until all of the items in the values array have been inserted. With any match, it will simply add the appropriate `node` property's content.

We will see an example of this in a moment.

Finally, there's one more thing this function does before returning the themed content:

```
Drupal.theme.node = function (node) {
  var out = '';
  if (TplHtml.template.node) {
    var tpl = $(TplHtml.template.node);

    // Is it sticky?
    if (node.sticky) {
      tpl.parent().find('.node').addClass('sticky');
    }

    // Do title and title's link at the same time.
    if (!node.nodeUrl) node.nodeUrl = '#';
    tpl.find('.title a').text(node.title)
      .attr('href', node.nodeUrl)

    // These are the things we are going to place in
    // the template.
    // Fortunately for us, class names match 1-to-1 with
    // the names of the node properties.
```

```
      var values = ['content','submitted','taxonomy','links'];
      for (var i = 0; i < values.length; ++i) {
        var value = values[i];
        if (node[value]) {
          tpl.find('.' + value).html(node[value]);
        }
        else {
          tpl.find('.' + value).hide();
        }
      }

      // Now we dump the template to a string.
      out = tpl.parent().html();
    }
    return out;
  }
```

The template has now been populated. However, like all theme functions, this must return the results neither as a jQuery object, nor as HTML elements, but as a string. To do this, we call `tpl.parent().html()`. This goes to the very root of the template and retrieves the HTML as a string. At the end of this function, the string is returned.

Using the template system

We now have a basic template system. We can very quickly mock up a new function to test out our template-based theme:

```
function addNode() {
  var node = {
    title: "New Node",
    content: "JavaScript created this node!",
    nodeUrl: 'http://drupal.org'
  };
  $('.node:last').after(Drupal.theme('node', node));
  Drupal.attachBehaviors();
}
```

The `addNode()` function creates a new `node` object with a `title`, `content`, and a `nodeUrl`. It then finds the node section and adds the new node to the end of the existing list of nodes. For example, on the front page, it would add it at the bottom of the page.

Notice that we call `Drupal.theme('node', node)` to invoke the `Drupal.theme. prototype.node()` function that we just defined, and pass it our new `node` object.

Finally, since we have just altered the DOM, we need to run the `Drupal. attachBehaviors()` function to make sure any new elements get evaluated by the behaviors system.

To make it possible to call our new function, we might also want to add a link somewhere in the document. One easy way of doing this, for testing purposes, is to add another jQuery ready function that adds a link to the pure JavaScript menu we created earlier in the chapter:

```
$(document).ready(function () {
  $('.block:first')
  .append('<a href="#">Add node</a>')
  .children('a:last').click(addNode);
}
```

This simply adds a new **Add node** link which, when clicked, runs our demo addNode() function.

What happens when we click this new link running the addNode() function? The node is themed and the results of that theming look like this:

```
<div class="node">
  <h2 class="title"><a href="http://drupal.org">New Node</a></h2>
  <span style="display: none;" class="submitted"></span>
  <div style="display: none;" class="taxonomy"></div>
  <div class="content">JavaScript created this node!</div>
  <div style="display: none;" class="links"></div>
</div>
```

Note that several elements are marked display: none. They are hidden because the node object had no corresponding property, so we know they shouldn't be displayed.

Next, the now-populated HTML template is injected into the existing document. The results look something like this:

Note that under the already existing **This is a node** node (which was created in Chapter 1), there is another node called **New Node**. This is the node we just created with our JavaScript template tool.

A word of warning

The code we generated to retrieve templates from the server does come with a caveat. It takes time for the browser to get the template from the client. Sometimes, it may take a second or two, and at times even more.

How do we handle the case where we want to theme something and the template hasn't yet completely loaded?

There are two options:

1. Implement a default local theme that can be used when the server hasn't sent a template back.

2. Use a timer (`setTimeout()`), callback, or another similar mechanism to delay and give the server time to respond.

In the next chapter, when we look at AJAX in more detail, we will see some additional jQuery functionality that could be used to make the `loadTemplate()` function more robust. Rewriting that function might eliminate the need for precautions like this. We might also consider rewriting the template feature to use synchronous, rather than asynchronous, requests for templates. However, this could become a performance bottleneck.

Both of these options can be used in conjunction. Here's the sample function that illustrates how we might use both:

```
var max_wait = 3000; // 3 seconds
var attempt = 0;
function addNode() {
  var wait = 200;
  var node = {
    title: "New Node",
    content: "JavaScript created this node!",
    nodeUrl: 'http://drupal.org'
  };

  if (TplHtml.template.node) {
    var txt = Drupal.theme('node', node);
    $('.node:last').after(txt);
    Drupal.attachBehaviors();
  }
  else if (attempt * wait < max_wait) {
    ++attempt;
    setTimeout(addNode, wait);
    console.log("delaying");
  }
```

```
    else {
      var txt = Drupal.theme('defaultNode', node);
      $('.node:last').after(txt);
      Drupal.attachBehaviors();
    }
  }
```

This is a variation of the `addNode()` testing function we looked at before. There are two new variables, `max_wait` and `attempt`, which are in a broader scope than the function and will persist across function calls. The first one—`max_wait`—sets the maximum amount of time that this script will wait for the server to load the template. The second one—`attempt`—is a counter that will record the number of attempts made to use the template.

These will make more sense in a moment.

The important code is the big `if/else-if/else` conditional. Here's how it works.

It first checks to see if the `TplHtml.template.node` template exists. If it does, then we know that the template must have been loaded already. We can then go on and do our theming by using the function we created earlier.

If the template does not exist, we check the `else if` condition:

```
    else if (attempt * wait < max_wait) {
      ++attempt;
      setTimeout(addNode, wait);
      console.log("delaying");
    }
```

Here, we check to make sure that we still have time to check for the template. The `wait` variable, set early in the `addNode()` function, is the amount of time between checks. We can multiply `attempt` and `wait` to see how long we've been trying to use the template. Of course, the first time this is run, it will be `0`. We haven't delayed at all as of now.

 Using this method, we can account for cases when the remote server is unavailable. If the server takes too long to respond, a default template is used. One drawback of using a callback (an alternative to this method) is that there is no way to gracefully handle server failures.

If we make it to the inside of the `else if` condition, we know that the template isn't loaded and we still have time to wait for it to be loaded. So here's what we do:

- Increment the attempt counter: `++attempt`.

- Register a timeout function (`setTimeout(addNode, wait)`). This tells the JavaScript runtime to wait for `wait` milliseconds (200 in our case) and then call the `addNode()` method. Essentially, this function is registering itself as the callback.
- For debugging purposes (this is a test function, after all), we are logging this to the Firebug console so we can tell that it is in a waiting state.

If this condition takes effect, the application will wait before trying to theme and display the content.

 If we expect long delays and need to notify the user, we may use a throbber as a visual device to indicate the waiting state. We will discuss this in Chapter 8.

However, if the server hasn't retrieved our template by `max_wait`, then the `else` block of the conditional will be executed. In this case, a different theming function will be called:

```
var txt = Drupal.theme('defaultNode', node);
```

This fictional theme (we haven't written a function for it) would hold a default theme implementation for a node theme. This would be an implementation that doesn't rely on a template retrieved from the server.

The example here illustrates one way of working around timing issues with our AJAX-based template system.

At this point we have finished our last project, and also the chapter.

Summary

The focus of this chapter was on the JavaScript theming system. We began by looking at the tools included in the `drupal.js` library. We then moved on and built our own themes. From there, we looked at the JavaScript theming module, examining some of the themes and user interface tools that it provides. Finally, we implemented our own template system, which was based on HTML, CSS, and JavaScript.

This chapter rounds out our look at `drupal.js`. In the remaining chapters of the book, we will make frequent use of the features we covered in this, and the previous two chapters. The next chapter will cover AJAX using jQuery and Drupal. There, we will see how much we can gain by adding more client-server interaction to our scripts.

7
AJAX and Drupal Web Services

In the first chapter, I mentioned two key technologies that contributed to JavaScript's rise from a toy language to an application language. So far, we have made use of dynamic page reflowing (the ability to change what the page looks like without reloading the page), which is the first key technology.

We will now focus on the: JavaScript's ability to pull data from the server, which is the second key technology.

For better or worse, this methodology is usually called **AJAX**, (**Asynchronous JavaScript And XML**). We will talk about the family of tools typically grouped under the AJAX title and see how these tools can be used in Drupal.

In this chapter we will:

- Introduce the AJAX family of tools
- Use jQuery's built-in AJAX support to get content from Drupal
- Fetch existing XML content from Drupal
- Use additional Drupal modules to expose more data to AJAX
- Use JSON (JavaScript Object Notation) as a JavaScript-friendly way of sending data from Drupal

As you may have noticed, our earlier chapters were heavy on explanation. Projects were used to simply illustrated the main points. Gradually, projects have gotten bigger, and the explanatory text has taken up a secondary role. In this chapter, we will spend most of the time looking at code and creating projects. First, we will have a quick overview of AJAX and how it fits into the Drupal landscape.

AJAX, JSON, XHR, AHAH, and Web 2.0

Among the many glorious improvements the Web has brought to our lives, it has created an entirely new vocabulary consisting almost entirely of acronyms. First, it was just HTML and HTTP. Then came XML and CSS, followed by RDF (Resource Description Framework). Enterprise computing brought us WSDL (Web Services Description Language), XML-RPC, and SOAP (Simple Object Access Protocol). Then along came RSS and Atom, two syndication formats that led to a plethora of orange "button" images.

However, the acronym that has contributed the most hype to recent web development is AJAX.

AJAX officially describes the practice of using JavaScript for requesting data from a remote server in a way which does not interrupt the user's browsing experience. No page refreshes take place, no plug-ins need to be loaded, and no "Do you really want to do this?" dialogs are displayed. In fact, well-constructed AJAX is completely unobtrusive. A user need not even know it is happening behind the scenes.

But, as the name suggests, AJAX was about JavaScript and XML. The assumption was that all of the data passed back and forth, between JavaScript and the server, would be some flavor of XML.

While the general idea of passing data in the background with JavaScript has gained tremendous traction, XML isn't the only data format being used. JavaScript, HTML, plain text, and other forms of structured content have all become "formats" for AJAX-style data transfer.

Therefore, if we aren't passing XML, are we still doing AJAX? The more pedantically inclined have argued that we are not. But that catchy term AJAX has become entrenched as a general catch-all for any similar JavaScript-centred, behind-the-scenes data passing.

Web application and Web 2.0

AJAX, and related technologies, have given web developers a new degree of freedom. Data can be crunched in the background while users continue doing their thing. Network latency, which is quite visible during a full-page refresh, suddenly seems less evident. Smaller amounts of data are passed from the client to the server, and the user may not even be aware of the exchange.

When AJAX came to the attention of developers, a cascade of changes followed. Suddenly, web pages could be more responsive while, at the same time, doing much more. Developers realized that web pages can act more like desktop applications. Clunky, old page-by-page web tools were rewritten to take advantage of AJAX, and a new class of web applications was born.

These applications, which were more efficient than their predecessors, were grouped under the amorphous umbrella term **Web 2.0**. If you ask a dozen experienced web developers what Web 2.0 is, you will likely get twelve different answers. While many disagree on specifics, it seems most agree that Web 2.0 refers to a big change in the way web tools are structured.

The browser is no longer treated only as a display device for server-generated content. HTML isn't treated as just a formatting language. Servers no longer handle all of the application logic. Instead, the task of assembling data into meaningful information is handled by many different programs, perhaps running, in many different locations. In short, the Web has become more distributed.

From this description of Web 2.0, it is easy to understand how mashups have become the poster child for this new generation of tools. A **mashup** is a web tool created by combining two or more web services in a novel way.

At this point, we could drift into a discussion of the so-called **semantic web**. In this, the "meaning" of web content is gleaned from individual pages, and then used by web services to provide tools driven by meaning instead of by structure. But this is outside of our present scope. Instead, we will return to one of the other Web 2.0 stars—AJAX.

The position of AJAX in Web 2.0

The role of AJAX in Web 2.0 is to delegate some of the distributed application logic to the client. Phrased simply, AJAX turns JavaScript into a major component in a web application. Instead of becoming just a display device by translating markup into a visual representation, browsers now take on some of the data-crunching responsibility. The programming language that makes all of this possible is JavaScript.

To an extent, we have been using JavaScript in this way already. By using its ability to dynamically alter the DOM, we have added and removed elements from the user's view. We have altered the look and feel of a page. We have made it easier for the user to do certain tasks. Also, we have made the user interface more responsive.

However, AJAX grants one additional capability. Not only can we change the way the page looks, but by fetching new content from the server, we can also exchange data. We can send data back to the server for processing. The server can then deliver raw results (perhaps encoded as XML) and the client-side JavaScript will determine how that information is displayed.

In the Web 2.0 landscape, it is AJAX that gives the browser the power to make use of all of those web services.

Now that we have a feel for the current web landscape, and we've seen how JavaScript and AJAX play a role in Web 2.0. It's time to dive deeper into the technical aspects of AJAX and the related technologies.

Getting technical

How does AJAX work? At the core of the technique is a built-in browser component called the **XMLHttpRequest** object. Initially included in Microsoft Internet Explorer as an ActiveX object, XMLHttpRequest became famous only after the Mozilla family of browsers (including Firefox) began including it as a standard JavaScript object.

The idea behind the XMLHttpRequest object (**XHR**) was simple. It provided JavaScript scripts with the ability to open a new HTTP connection to the remote server and then retrieve an XML document. It was assumed that the returned page would be XML. In practice, there are no restraints on the type of data returned.

 Practically speaking, what's the difference between HTML and XML? Not much. To an untrained eye they look the same. It's the interpretation that makes the difference. HTML tags already have a well-defined meaning. XML, on the other hand, provides the syntax, but leaves the meaning up to developers. The structure of the data can then be crystallized into XML.

However, the rationale for XHR was that servers could send updated data to the client, essentially allowing the client-side scripts to refresh data on the screen without requiring a page or frame reload.

 As the story goes, Microsoft developed XHR so the Exchange web client could behave more like the Exchange desktop client. Making web applications as responsive as desktop applications is one of the hallmarks of Web 2.0.

Before XHR, if a JavaScript developer needed to transfer information in the background, the only way to accomplish this was in hidden frames. But that method was clumsy, difficult to debug, and fraught with browser compatibility issues. Not just from vendor to vendor, but also from browser version to browser version.

XHR made it easy to retrieve and parse data. Though it had its own cross-browser compatibility issues, such issues could usually be resolved with just a few lines of code.

The basic workflow, regardless of browser, was something like this:

1. Create a new XHR object.
2. Request a piece of XML from the remote server.
3. Wait for a response.
4. When the response arrives, parse the returned XML.
5. Use the new data to do something.

That third step, waiting for a response, could be done one of two ways. First, either the browser could hold all operations until the server returned (synchronous). Second, it could go about its business and check back periodically to see if the server responded (asynchronous). Using the latter method, scripts could continue to respond to user input while the XHR object worked in the background.

Unsurprisingly, the 'asynchronous' part of Asynchronous JavaScript and XML comes from this second method.

Each of these steps (even the waiting) required some boilerplate coding for each script. But it didn't take long for savvy web developers to realize the process was general, and that a library could be written to meet the requirements of web application development. A plethora of AJAX libraries burst onto the scene. These days, you have a choice of hundreds of libraries.

We won't have to go far to find our library. As we saw in the previous chapter, jQuery provides AJAX capabilities. In fact, it provides a robust set of tools designed to make simple AJAX calls trivially easy, yet still make it possible to craft advanced AJAX applications should you need to do something fancier.

Move over, XML

XML has enjoyed tremendous success in the online world. Every major programming language has at least one XML parser available. PHP 5 comes with several XML tools out of the box, including a DOM. This DOM provides an interface almost identical to the JavaScript DOM API.

But the DOM-XML combination isn't a panacea. Some problems (even problems involving data formatting) are better solved by other tools. In addition, the "X" in AJAX hasn't always right for the job.

Sometimes, instead of getting XML, it is more convenient to get fragments of HTML. This makes sense when it is more desirable to simply insert some extra content into the present document. In the previous chapter, we saw another case where HTML was the desired format. There, we used HTML fragments as templates for other information.

On other occasions, the data transmitted needs to contain programming logic, namely, JavaScript. This method has been used to create JavaScript "loaders" that fetched additional libraries as needed.

Since the XHR object was suitably flexible, HTML and JavaScript could both be handled this way.

For a while, the conventional wisdom on XHR data transfer went something like this:

- Use XML if you are transferring structured data
- Use HTML if you are transferring marked up data intended for user display
- Send Javascript if you are transferring programming logic

Then along came another format that challenged the role of XML.

XML has its weaknesses. One weakness is that it is relatively bulky. To send a transmission containing only a title, I would need to create, at minimum, an XML document like this:

```
<?xml version="1.0"?>
<title>My Title</title>
```

That's the absolute bare minimum. Mostly, even more information is needed in order to display a title. What else could we possibly be missing? In the ideal XML world, the above should have a character set declaration, a namespace definition, and a schema (or DTD) to define the document's structure. We're talking a dozen lines of code to transmit a title!

XML has a second drawback. The parsing routine is sophisticated, and can be time-consuming.

XML's challenger came in the form of a lightweight format that was easy to parse, more concise, and already familiar to web developers. The new format was called **JSON** (JavaScript Object Notation).

As the name implies, JSON is a data format based on JavaScript. It uses the literal forms of JavaScript arrays and objects, along with JavaScript's main types, to create a straightforward data form.

Using our previous example, if we wanted to transmit our title in JSON format, it would look like this:

```
{'title': 'My Title'}
```

This format should look familiar. It is equivalent to a JavaScript object declaration. In fact, we've already used this type of structure a number of times in this book.

We will take a look at both JSON and XML later in this book. The fact that we are looking at both should lead to a clear implication. There is room for both JSON and XML in the AJAX world. While you, the developer, may have one more decision to make (whether to use JSON or XML for this application), both formats are widely adopted and supported. That means you can make the choice based on the best fit, and not just based on the availability of tools.

Before moving on to our first project, let's take a quick look at the seven jQuery AJAX functions. These functions deal directly with AJAX transactions which are made to a remote server. All of these functions, except `jQuery.ajax()`, take the same three arguments: a **URL**, some **data** (optional), and a **callback function** object. (`jQuery.getScript()` does not ever use the optional data.) A couple of methods, such as `jQuery.get()` and `jQuery.post()`, take an optional fourth parameter that indicates what type of data should be returned, for example JSON, XML, JavaScript, HTML, and so on.

- `jQuery.get()`: This function is the most generic of jQuery tools. It does a simple HTTP GET request from the server. The data that is passed into the callback function is in the form of a string. We used this function in the previous chapter and we will use it in the next project we do. There is a variation of this function, `jQuery.getIfModified()`, that does the same thing, but only invokes the callback if the returned document has changed since it was last loaded by this script.

- `jQuery.getJSON()`: This function works like jQuery.get() with one difference. The returned data is treated like JSON data and is parsed into JavaScript objects. If you try to get XML content with this function, it will generate an error.

- `jQuery.getScript()`: This function also works like `jQuery.get()`, except that it expects that the returned data will be JavaScript. The script is loaded and interpreted as soon as the AJAX request completes.

- `jQuery.post()`: This function does an HTTP POST, instead of using an HTTP GET. This function is good for posting form data, or sending messages that would result in changes on the server. From the programmer's perspective, it works like `jQuery.get()`.

- `jQuery.ajax()`: The other functions are "high level." Simply call the function, and it takes care of all of the details of an AJAX transaction. Sometimes, you may want greater control over the details. This function gives you access to more of the details of the AJAX call, including access to the `XMLHttpRequest` object. Our code here is simple, so we will not be using this function. However, it is fully documented at `http://jQuery.com`.

- `$(o).load()`: This function provides even more functionality than the others. It retrieves HTML content from a remote server, and then injects it right into the DOM for you. The other jQuery methods are called from the main jQuery object. This one requires an instance of a jQuery object to know where to insert the content. For example, to insert content into the first paragraph of the document, we could do something like this: `$('p:first').load(myUrl)`. There is also a variation of this function, `$(o).loadIfModified()`, which does the same thing only if the remote document has been modified since the last time this function was called.

> After reading this chapter, you may find it useful to go back to the code in the previous chapter and see how `$().get()` was used to load templates for our simple template engine.

In addition to these, there are nearly a dozen helper functions. Some of them allow you to interact with every step of the (normally behind-the-scenes) AJAX workflow, while others simply provide utilities for making AJAX programming easier.

In this chapter, we will only use a handful of AJAX functions. However, the other tools can come in handy when writing AJAX-enabled web applications. jQuery is a well-document toolkit. To learn more about its AJAX features, visit `http://jQuery.com`.

> *"Learning jQuery"*, *Packt Publishing, 978-1847192509*, provides an in-depth coverage of the entire jQuery library, including the AJAX functions.

That's it for the theory portion of this chapter. We are now ready to dive into our first project.

Project: web clips with RSS and AJAX

We want to begin with a simple tool, one that we can quickly sink our teeth into. To that end, it would be nice to start with an existing XML source and focus just on the JavaScript needed to work with that source.

Wouldn't it be nice if Drupal provided such an XML source out of the box?

Actually, it does. It provides an RSS feed, and RSS is an XML format.

Really Simple Syndication (RSS)

Really Simple Syndication (RSS) was devised as a way of sharing news with other websites. Initially, it was envisioned as a thin web service, where some remote site could simply access a URL and get back an XML-formatted list of the latest articles.

It became an attractive offering for two reasons. First, the XML format is simple, which makes a programmer's life easier. Second, the idea of getting an up-to-the-minute news feed has a wide appeal. RSS readers and aggregation services quickly appeared on the scene. Now, RSS is employed all around the Web.

Due to its widespread adoption, and diversity of ways in which it has been used, RSS represents a Web 2.0 success story.

Since RSS is an XML format (and a simple one at that) it makes a great candidate for an AJAX project. Since Drupal 6 provides an RSS feed out of the box, we won't have to do any additional server-side setup.

Before we dive into the JavaScript code, let's take a look at an RSS XML file.

My local Drupal instance is running at `http://localhost:8888/drupal`. This feed came from `http://localhost:8888/drupal/rss.xml`. I just added the `rss.xml` part to my base URL to access the feed. Clicking the orange feed button, along the bottom of Drupal's default home page, will also get you to the feed.

Here's what the feed looks like. This file is an abbreviated version of the one Drupal provides by default. (The original had more than one entry.)

```
<?xml version="1.0" encoding="utf-8"?>
<rss version="2.0" xml:base="http://localhost:8888/drupal"
  xmlns:dc="http://purl.org/dc/elements/1.1/">
<channel>
 <title>Frobnitz Central</title>
 <link>http://localhost:8888/drupal</link>
 <description></description>
 <language>en</language>
<item>
 <title>A Sticky Node</title>
 <link>http://localhost:8888/drupal/node/5</link>
 <description>
  &lt;p&gt;This node should always be displayed
  near the top of the home page.&lt;/p&gt;
```

```
    </description>
    <comments>
     http://localhost:8888/drupal/node/5#comments
    </comments>
    <pubDate>Sun, 10 Aug 2008 22:10:48 +0000</pubDate>
    <dc:creator>mbutcher</dc:creator>
    <guid isPermaLink=»false»>
     5 at http://localhost:8888/drupal
    </guid>
    </item>
    </channel>
    </rss>
```

An RSS file is composed of a main container (the `<rss></rss>` tags), which contains a channel (`<channel></channel>`). A channel contains one or more items (`<item></item>`).

A **channel** describes the contents of the feed. Typically, it will include a title, a description, some language information, and a link back to the website that this feed describes. You can see in the channel definition how `<title></title>`, `<link></link>`, `<description></description>`, and `<language></language>` are used to convey this information.

There are pointers inside of a channel to individual pieces of content from the website. These are stored in **items**. An item typically includes a title, link, description, publication date, and a GUID (globally unique identifier).

There are many other possible fields that can go inside of an item. Also, there are entries for the content creator (`<dc:creator></dc:creator>`), and a link to comment about the item (`<comments></comments>`). More sophisticated feeds may have enclosures, links to audio files (a **podcast**), and video (a **vodcast** or **video podcast**), or other legal XML content.

When it comes down to it, that's all there is to an RSS feed. It's just a container with a channel that contains a list of items; and it's all XML.

The project goals

In this project, we are going to make use of that RSS feed to add a web clips region to our pages. We will allocate a small portion of the page layout to display a random item from our XML feed. This is similar to what Google does in Gmail. By showing a random item from our RSS feed on every page, we might entice site visitors to spend more time clicking around on the site.

To accomplish our project goals, we are going to use some of the tools we have already encountered. To name a few, we will be using JavaScript themes, behaviors, and jQuery. However, our focus will be on using jQuery AJAX.

Creating the web clips tool

In this project, we will create our web clips tool in `webclips.js`. As we have done in previous chapters, this file will be added to `frobnitz.info` using a directive like this: `scripts[] = webclips.js`.

We will begin by taking a quick look at the code in its entirety. We will then look at it more closely. One thing that should be immediately noticeable is our use of several tools introduced in earlier chapters:

```
// $Id$
/**
 * Create a web clips tool for displaying random RSS items.
 * @file
 */
var WebClips = WebClips || {settings:{}};
WebClips.settings.feed = 'rss.xml';

Drupal.behaviors.webclips = function (cxt) {
  // Return early if this has already been
  // attached.
  if ($('#main.webclips-processed').size() > 0) {
    return false;
  }

  var feedUrl = WebClips.settings.feed;
  if (
    feedUrl.indexOf('http://') != 0
    && feedUrl.indexOf('https://') != 0
    && feedUrl.indexOf('/') != 0
  ) {
    // The path is relative.
    feedUrl = Drupal.settings.basePath + feedUrl;
  }

  // Get the feed:
  jQuery.get(feedUrl, function (data, res) {
    if (res == 'success') {
      WebClips.items = $(data).find('item');

      var clip = Drupal.theme('webclipArea', 'webclips');

      $('#main').addClass('webclips-processed').prepend(clip);
      $('.webclip-area').css({
```

```
            "background-color":"#eef",
            "width":"100%"
        }).prepend(
            $('<span>[+]</span>').click(WebClips.showItem)
        );
        WebClips.showItem();
    }
  });
};

WebClips.showItem = function () {
  var items = WebClips.items;
  var theOne = Math.floor(Math.random() * items.length);
  var item = $(items.get(theOne));
  var theLink = Drupal.theme(
    "webclip",
    item.find('title'),
    item.find('link')
  );

  $('#webclips').html(theLink);
};

Drupal.theme.prototype.webclip = function (title, href) {
  return '&rarr; ' + title.text().link(href.text());
};

Drupal.theme.prototype.webclipArea = function (id) {
  var tpl = '<div class="webclip-area"><span id="' +
    id +
    '"></span></div>';
  return tpl;
};
```

This code adds a new web clips area at the top of the main content container. It then uses Drupal's RSS feed to insert a random item into this new container. As you can see, to achieve these goals, we will use behaviors, themes, and jQuery.

Let's take a closer look at the first few lines:

```
var WebClips = WebClips || {settings:{}};
WebClips.settings.feed = 'rss.xml';
```

The WebClips namespace will be used for our custom objects and functions. We don't want to run the risk of interfering with Drupal, or other modules, by putting features inside of the Drupal namespace in unexpected places.

Drupal.behaviors and Drupal.themes are namespaces that are set aside for custom functions. We do risk name collisions with other modules when we use those areas. But in other areas of Drupal, where functionality is not dependent on using the Drupal namespace, it is always best to avoid adding things inside the Drupal object.

On the second line of the code, we define WebClips.settings.feed, which holds a URI for our RSS feed. By default, we want to point this to the relative path rss.xml. Our code, as we shall see shortly, will expand this to point to the default rss.xml file inside our Drupal installation. If you are not using Drupal's "Clean URLs", you will need to adjust this path to point to ?q=rss.xml. It is recommended that you use Clean URLs while doing the examples in this chapter.

This variable is in the WebClips.settings object (which is visible globally). Therefore, it is easy to customize this code, setting it to use a different feed simply by assigning a new value. For example, some other bit of JavaScript could set this using:

```
WebClips.settings.feed = 'anotherFeed.xml';
```

We want it to use the default Drupal RSS feed, rss.xml.

Next, let's move on to the first function in our library.

The WebClips behavior

We took a detailed look at behaviors in Chapter 4. There, we saw how behaviors are executed when the document is ready for manipulation and any other time Drupal. attachBehaviors() is called.

By defining a behavior, we are indicating that this function should be run when the page is loaded and ready.

Since this function is a little large, we will break it down into three smaller chunks, and look at each in detail:

```
Drupal.behaviors.webclips = function (cxt) {

  // Return early if this has already been
  // attached.
  if ($('#main.webclips-processed').size() > 0) {
    return false;
  }

  // The rest of the function...
}
```

This is the first part of the behavior that we will examine. While every behavior function is passed a context (cxt in the code), we don't need to use the context for since we know exactly which part of the document we are concerned with.

The first part of this function is a conditional:

```
if ($('#main.webclips-processed').size() > 0) {
  return false;
}
```

We have seen conditionals such as this in other behaviors we have written, but it has a twist. Remember that a behavior can be executed more than once. All registered behaviors will be executed when the page first loads. Then, anytime Drupal. attachBehaviors() is called, they will be executed again. Behaviors need to be written in such a way that they can safely be called multiple times without, for example, attaching duplicate content.

In the past, we have avoided this problem by using a construct like this:

```
if ($('#main:not(webclips-processed')) {
  // Do main behavior here...
}
```

The code inside the conditional is only executed if the behavior has not already been processed. This is fine for short behaviors.

But our behavior is a long one, and using this pattern would result in our wrapping a large block of code inside a conditional. It is considered a good programming practice (especially in object-oriented languages) to avoid this kind of nesting. There are two good reasons for this:

- Catching an "undesirable" case (where there is nothing to do) is best done early in a function because it is easier to read. We read functions from top to bottom. It is convenient (and easier to debug) to have these cases caught at the beginning, rather than at the end of the function.

- Nested code is harder to read. The further the indentation goes, the harder it is for a programmer to determine how the function works. Every layer of nesting requires the programmer to remember more context. Reducing the burden on the programmer also reduces the likelihood of bugs creeping in.

So, instead of using something like if ($('#main:not(webclips-processed)) {}, we take the opposite approach. We check to see if the element has been processed, and if it has, we return early.

A rule of thumb

How do we determine when we should catch undesirable cases and return early? Generally, if the body of the conditional is longer than a dozen lines, catch the undesirable case first and return early.

With that bit of checking out of the way, we know we can proceed with the function while knowing that this is the first time the behavior has been executed. Let's now look at the second part that makes up this behavior:

```
Drupal.behaviors.webclips = function (cxt) {

  // Return early if this has already been
  // attached.
  if ($('#main.webclips-processed').size() > 0) {
    return false;
  }

  var feedUrl = WebClips.settings.feed;
  if (
    feedUrl.indexOf('http://') != 0
    && feedUrl.indexOf('https://') != 0
    && feedUrl.indexOf('/') != 0
  ) {
    // The path is relative.
    feedUrl = Drupal.settings.basePath + feedUrl;
  }

  // More code here...
};
```

The highlighted block is the second of the three parts that make up this behavior. This is a deceptively simple piece of code. Before we can fetch the feed using AJAX, we need to prepare the URL. If the URL is a relative path (one that does not start with a slash), we need to prepend the Drupal path. But in other cases, it is better for us to not attempt to alter the URL.

This code is not necessarily designed to increase security. Its purpose is to ensure the URL is correctly formed. The XMLHttpRequest object has some security features built in. One of these is that the XHR object will not contact any domain other than the one that served the current page.

The first thing we do is copy the URL from WebClips.settings.feed into a local copy named feedUrl. Having copied the variable, we can now modify the copy without changing the original.

In some cases (three, in fact), we don't want to change the URL. But in other cases, we will want to prepend the `Drupal.settings.basePath` to the beginning of the path so the RSS file will be located correctly.

This piece of code checks to make sure that the URL doesn't fit the pattern of a URL that should remain unaltered. We don't want to alter the following three URL patterns:

1. A URL that begins with `http://`. This is a fully qualified URL, and adding Drupal's base path to it would cause a failure.

2. A URL that begins with `https://`. We don't prepend path information to this for the same reason that we do not prepend it to an `http://` URL.

3. An absolute path beginning with `/`. If a path begins with a slash, we should assume that the author intended this to be a path that begins with the server's root. By making this assumption, we have allowed the author to specify another feed on the same server, even if that feed is not part of Drupal.

If the `feedUrl` does not match any of these three patterns, we assume that `feedUrl` contains a relative path. Thus, we need to prepend the `Drupal.settings.basePath` to this variable:

```
feedUrl = Drupal.settings.basePath + feedUrl;
```

We now have a complete path to the RSS feed. The next thing we need to do is fetch the content of the feed. This is done in the last part of the behavior:

```
Drupal.behaviors.webclips = function (cxt) {

  // Return early if this has already been
  // attached.
  if ($('#main.webclips-processed').size() > 0) {
    return false;
  }
  var feedUrl = WebClips.settings.feed;
  if (
    feedUrl.indexOf('http://') != 0
    && feedUrl.indexOf('https://') != 0
    && feedUrl.indexOf('/') != 0
  ) {
    // The path is relative.
```

```
    feedUrl = Drupal.settings.basePath + feedUrl;
  }
  // Get the feed:
  jQuery.get(feedUrl, function (data, res) {
    if (res == 'success') {
      WebClips.items = $(data).find('item');
      var clip = Drupal.theme('webclipArea', 'webclips');
      $('#main').addClass('webclips-processed').prepend(clip);
      $('.webclip-area').css({
        "background-color":"#eef",
        "width":"100%"
      }).prepend(
        $('<span>[+]</span>').click(WebClips.showItem)
      );
      WebClips.showItem();
    }
  });
};
```

The highlighted section handles the AJAX call. More specifically, it handles two
different stages of an AJAX transaction. It begins to send a request and defines the
function that should be called when the browser receives the AJAX response from
the server.

All of this is done with a single function, `jQuery.get()`. This function is called with
two parameters:

- `feedUrl`: the URL that this object should contact to get the RSS feed data
- An anonymous function that is executed when the data is returned

The function passed in here doesn't have to be an anonymous one. However, (as we
have seen many times in this book) since the function is called only once, the jQuery
approach is to create an inline anonymous function.

The job of the anonymous function is to take the returned information and do
something useful with it. When jQuery invokes this function, it passes two pieces
of information:

- The data returned from the server. It will be a single string.
- The result message from the server. This is also a string. In the case where
  the request succeeds, the message will be `success`. In error conditions, it will
  be a message indicating what error occurred. For example, if it is the request
  time out, this will be `timeout`. If the data returned could not properly be
  parsed, this will return `parsererror`. In other cases, it may just return `error`.

Let's look carefully at the following anonymous callback function defined in the previously highlighted section:

```
function (data, res) {
  if (res == 'success') {
    WebClips.items = $(data).find('item');
    var clip = Drupal.theme('webclipArea', 'webclips');
    $('#main').addClass('webclips-processed').prepend(clip);
    $('.webclip-area').css({
      "background-color":"#eef",
      "width":"100%"
    }).prepend(
      $('<span>[+]</span>').click(WebClips.showItem)
    );
    WebClips.showItem();
  }
};
```

When this function is called by jQuery's AJAX system, the data (`data`) and the result message (`res`) will both be passed in.

The first thing we do is check the result message to see if our transaction was successful. If the message is `success`, then we proceed with our handling. In any other case, we do nothing. The web clips section is simply not added to the page.

Why no error?

We could give some sort of error message in cases where the result is not `success`. While this might be useful for debugging, it would not be good for the user experience. Site functionality would not be significantly degraded by the absence of web clips, so there is no reason to generate an error message.

The rest of the code in this function is only executed when we have a successful result.

The data returned should be an RSS XML document captured in a string. We need to parse that string into a DOM, and begin extracting information. Once again, this is a quick one-liner in jQuery:

```
WebClips.items = $(data).find('item');
```

When the XML string is passed into the jQuery builder, it will parse the string into a new DOM, and wrap the results in a jQuery object.

Since we just want the items from the feed, we can use the jQuery `find()` function, which takes a CSS selector to query the DOM. The query that we just saw, will return all of the `<item></item>` elements. `WebClips.items`, a variable that belongs to our main `WebClips` object, is a jQuery object wrapping a list of the `<item></item>` elements.

Why do we store the items in `WebClips.items`? We do that since we want this list to be accessible to other `WebClips` functions. Here, we will make the list globally available. Other functions will retrieve data from this list of items.

Next, we begin building the display for our web clips area:

```
var clip = Drupal.theme('webclipArea', 'webclips');
$('#main').addClass('webclips-processed').prepend(clip);
```

First, we use `Drupal.theme()` to create the web clips area. This function, which we will look at in just a moment, takes one argument. The argument is the ID (`webclips`) for the web clips area. We will use that later to find the area and exchange the clip (the RSS feed item) displayed in that area.

Before moving on to the rest of this function, let's take a quick look at the `Drupal.theme.prototype.webclipArea()` theming function. This function is responsible for defining the region where the web clips will be displayed. However, individual web clips will be themed separately as seen here:

```
Drupal.theme.prototype.webclipArea = function (id) {
  var tpl = '<div class="webclip-area"><span id="' +
    id +
    '"></span></div>';
  return tpl;
};
```

This function simply builds some HTML that looks like this:

```
<div class="webclip-area"><span id="ID"></span></div>';
```

There is a `<div></div>` with the class `webclip-area`. Inside of this is an empty `<span></span>` tag. Above, I've used `ID` as a placeholder for the ID that is passed into the theming function. Ours will have the ID `webclips`.

The theme is executed in the behavior and the results are stored in `clip`.

Once we have a themed the `clip` area, we insert that into the DOM at the top of the main content area (the element with the ID `main`). To make sure the behavior doesn't run again, we need to add the `webclips-processed` class to the element with the `main` ID. Then, using the `prepend()` jQuery function, we add the web clip section directly inside the `main` section before any other content.

The `prepend()` function is similar to the `append()` jQuery function. While `append()` adds the content to the very end of an element's contents, the `prepend()` function adds it to the very beginning.

At this point, we have a newly created section on our page that is allocated for displaying web clips. We will now do a little bit of work to prepare this area for displaying an individual clip:

```
$('.webclip-area').css({
  "background-color":"#eef",
  "width":"100%"
}).prepend(
  $('<span>[+]</span>').click(WebClips.showItem)
);
```

This jQuery chain first finds the element(s) with the class `webclip-area`. Glancing back at the output from the theming function we just looked at, we can see the main `<div></div>` tag will match this. Next, this chain will add some CSS to the `<div></div>` element. It sets a gray-blue background, and then sets the element's width to `100%`.

The final part of this chain adds some new content to the `div`, again using the `prepend()` function. Referring back to the output of the theme function, this will place the content inside of the `div`, before the existing `<span></span>` element.

What do we add with this `prepend()` function? Here's the code:

```
$('<span>[+]</span>').click(WebClips.showItem)
```

This adds the: `<span>[+]</span>`, and then assigns a click event handler to this. Whenever this span is clicked the `WebClips.showItem()` function will be executed. The `[+]` text will function as a mechanism for displaying another random web clip. Whenever a user clicks this symbol, a new web clip will be displayed.

We're now down to the final line of the behavior: `WebClips.showItem()`. We just assigned this function to a click handler, and now, on the last line of the behavior, we explicitly call it. This function will grab an item and display it in the region we just created. In essence, it displays the initial value for our web clips region.

Let's look at the `WebClips.showItem()` function.

The WebClips.showItem() function

The `Drupal.behaviors.webclips()` behavior we looked at earlier was complex, performing several steps to set up the area where our web clips will be displayed. At the very end, it calls `WebClips.showItem()` to display an item. The present function is much simpler:

```
WebClips.showItem = function () {
  var items = WebClips.items;
  var theOne = Math.floor(Math.random() * items.length);
  var item = items.eq(theOne);
  var theLink = Drupal.theme(
    "webclip",
    item.find('title'),
    item.find('link')
  );

  $('#webclips').html(theLink);
};
```

This function takes no parameters. The first thing it does is make a local copy of the `WebClips.items` jQuery object. This is only done for the sake of readability.

Next, we get a random integer corresponding to a valid index in our `items` list. For example, if our list has three items, we want an integer between 0 and 2. We get this with `Math.floor(Math.random() * items.length)`.

To limit the matched items from a jQuery object to just one specific index number, we use the jQuery `eq()` method.

Now that we have an item, we are ready to theme it, and insert it into the web clips area on the page. Here's the theming call:

```
var theLink = Drupal.theme(
  "webclip",
  item.find('title'),
  item.find('link')
);
```

This uses the `Drupal.theme.prototype.webclip()` function, to which it passes: the `title` of the RSS feed item, and the `link` from the RSS feed item. The `link`, you may recall, points back to the original article that this feed item is describing:

```
Drupal.theme.prototype.webclip = function (title, href) {
  return '&rarr; ' + title.text().link(href.text());
};
```

This theme function takes two parameters: `title` and `href` (where `href` is a link). We're not doing anything fancy here. We just return code that looks like this:

```
&rarr;<a href='HREF'>TITLE</a>
```

Here, `HREF` would be replaced with the value passed in as `href`, and `TITLE` would be replaced by the `title`. The `&rarr;` HTML entity resolves to a right arrow (→). We're just using it as a decoration.

When the theme function returns, we have a formatted link. All we need to do now is insert that link into the web clips area. This is done by the last line of `WebClips.showItem()`:

```
$('#webclips').html(theLink);
```

This finds the element with the `webclips` ID, and inserts the new link into that area. The result looks something like this:

[+]→ A Sticky Node

The previous screenshot is the result of the `Drupal.behaviors.webclips()` function being called during page loading. If we click on the **[+]**, it will show a new web clip:

[+]→ This is a node

The clip is changed because we attached the `click` handler to the `<span>[+]</span>` at the end of the `Drupal.behaviors.webclips()` function. Every time the **[+]** is clicked, `WebClip.showItem()` is called, which changes the contents of the web clip region.

We have now finished our first AJAX project. As with the other projects in this book, there are many ways we could extend this project to do other, perhaps more interesting, things. For example, periodically refreshing the item instead of waiting for the user to click something.

However, instead of continuing to tinker with this project, let's move onto another one. In the next project, we will see another way of using AJAX to share data between server-side Drupal and the client-side JavaScript. But this time, we will do something more sophisticated on the server side.

Project: real-time comment notifications

In the previous project, we created a web clips feature that retrieved an RSS feed and displayed random items along the top of the content area of a page. We took an existing piece of XML content and made use of it in JavaScript.

But more often, we'll find that Drupal doesn't provide exactly the data we want in an AJAX-friendly format. So how can we get that information?

One way would be to write some custom PHP code to retrieve the content we want. This is the approach I took in my book *"Learning Drupal 6 Module Development"*, *Packt Publishing*, *978-1847194442*. However, doing this requires considerable PHP knowledge.

A second option would be to find other ways of extracting content from Drupal and converting it to an AJAX-friendly format such as XML or JSON. That's what we are going to do here.

Displaying comments as notifications

The goal of this project is to create a **comments notification tool**. This tool will alert the user every time a new comment is posted to the site. As with popular instant messaging clients, when a new comment is posted, our tool will raise a notification box in the browser's lower righthand corner. It will display the new comment for a few seconds and then disappear. Notifications will appear as new comments are posted. With a little AJAX, this tool will unobtrusively maintain contact with the Drupal server while we browser around the site.

To accomplish our goal, we will need a little more than JavaScript. Using a pair of popular add-on modules, we will add some functionality to the Drupal server. These modules will allow us to do two things:

- Run a query to retrieve some specific content from the server
- Format that content into JSON and make it accessible at its own URL

Once we have this data source available, we can use JavaScript and jQuery to grab the information and display it in our theme.

A project like this presents many possibilities and complexities. One such complexity is the issue of determining how many comments we need to show. Should we send an alert for every single comment? If a user goes offline for a while, should we try to "catch up" when the user logs back on, sending a list of all of the comments? How often should the server check for new messages? If several new messages are posted between checks, should we show them all, or only the most recent?

The complexity of the tool (and length of our code) can vary widely depending on how we answer these questions. We're going to go with a simple configuration in this project. We will check every ten seconds for the newest comment. Our tool will only display the comment if it is newer than the last comment we displayed. This means some comments may get skipped if more than one is posted in the ten second interval. But for our purposes, simple code is the more valuable goal.

The first step in building our new tool is to install the: **Views** and **Views Datasource** modules. Then we will build a data source for later use.

Installing Views and Views Datasource

One of the most frequently used add-on modules for Drupal is the **Views** module. This module provides Drupal developers and administrators the ability to build up a dynamic view of content by composing a query and determining how the results will be displayed.

Want to show all nodes created before July 1, 2008 in a block? Want to display all Page nodes created by mbutcher? Want to create an RSS feed containing a list of all Story nodes with the taxonomy term important? Views is the most popular tool for providing such functionality.

 Along with CCK, Views is a tool that any serious Drupal developer must know. Learn more about views at http://drupal.org/project/ views. In this chapter, we are using the version Views 2.0-RC1.

Views provides a back-end engine for creating, storing, and executing queries. It also provides a user interface, complete with a visual query builder. This can be used to create new views from the comfort of the Drupal administration interface.

To install Views, download the module (from the URL we just saw), unpack it in the /sites/all/modules directory under your Drupal installation. Next, go to **Administer | Site building | Modules** and enable **Views** and **Views UI**. This will give you the Views engine as well as the user interface for building queries.

The Views module is very powerful. Like Drupal, one of the things that makes Views so powerful is the fact that it can easily be extended. By default, Views allows data to be formatted as HTML snippets for insertion into parts of a Drupal page (like a block or a node).

But we want to create a data source that can be retrieved on its own, and that contains JSON content. To do this, we need a helper module that adds more functionality to Views. The module we will use for this is **Views Datasource**.

Views Datasource provides a suite of formatters for Views, which includes JSON, RDF XML, XHTML microformats, and a handful of other XML formats (like Atom, another syndication format).

> The Views Datasource project page can be found at http://drupal. org/project/views_datasource. From there, you can read more about the other formats this module supports.

To install Views Datasource, download it from the URL, put it in /sites/all/ modules, and then go to **Administer | Site building | Modules**. This module provides several submodules. You may install as many of those as you like but we will only be using the **Views JSON** module though. Make sure you enable it.

Creating a JSON view

The Views module comes with a very sophisticated builder interface for creating your own views. If this book were on using Drupal modules, we would certainly spend several pages (at least) describing the details of the **Views UI**. But for our immediate purposes, we will constrain our discussion to building just one simple view.

> **Views UI** is a module that is included with Views. This module contains the user interface for building custom views.

We want to track new comments as they are created on our website. We then want to make that information, available in the JSON format, and assign it to a URL so our JavaScript can retrieve and parse the information.

We want the following information:

- We only want the newest comment.
- For that comment, we want the author and the body of the comment. We also want the comment ID.
- We want to know the node that this comment refers to. (Remember, a comment is a comment on a node.)
- We want the title of that node and the node ID.
- We want JSON data returned.
- We want to be able to access this JSON data feed at its own URL.

This is all of the information we need to create the new view.

If the Views UI module is enabled, then we can create a new view by going to **Administer | Site building | Views** and clicking the **Add** tab.

We will name our new view **NewestComment (with no spaces in the name)**.

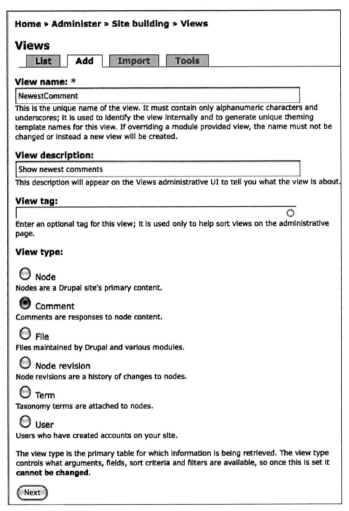

In the previous screenshot, we set the **View type** to **Comment** since we are primarily interested in comments for our view.

Clicking the **Next** button at the bottom of the page will take us to the main view editor. The complex UI on this screen makes it possible to edit all major aspects of a view from one screen. We will just look at the options we need to configure to create our feed.

Here is a labeled screenshot showing how we need to configure our view:

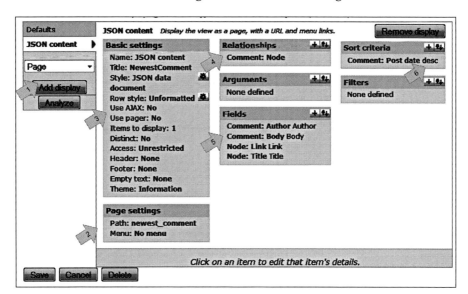

We will go through the arrows in the previous screenshot, starting with the arrow labeled **1**. Note that when you change a setting in views, the changed value has a different background color (pale yellow, by default) than unchanged values. In our grayscale image, this does not show up well.

1. Choose **Page** from the drop-down list and click on the **Add display** button. This tells the Views builder that we are building a new page, not a block, feed, or something else. When you first do this, your page will be labeled **Page**, not **JSON Content**.

2. A page needs a path. Click on the **Path** item in **Page Settings** and set the path to `newest_comment`. This assigns a relative path that we will use to construct a URL.

3. Next, we have several things to set in the **Basic Settings** area. **Name (JSON Content)** will help us distinguish this display from others. **Style** needs to be set to **JSON data document** to indicate that we want JSON data for the entire document, and **Row style** should be **Unformatted**. This is used when styling tables or lists and JSON doesn't need styling. In the screenshot, I set the **Title** property, though it has no impact on JSON data. Finally, set **Items to display** to **1**, since we only want one comment.

4. By default, we are working with comment objects. We also want information about related nodes, so we click the **+** (plus) icon in **Relationships** and add **Comment: Node**. This will make information about related nodes available to us.

5.   Next, we click on the **+** (plus) sign in the **Fields** area and add all of the fields we want access to including **Comment: Author**, **Comment: Body**, **Node: Link**, and **Node: Title**. Note that the ID fields for the comment and the related node are automatically included in the results.

6.   Finally, we need to set the **Sort criteria** to only give us the newest comment. This is done by setting **Comment: Post date** with **Desc** (descending) ordering.

We now have created a new view. Make sure you click the **Save** button once you have completed all of the fields above.

Once it is saved, you can click the **Preview** button to see the output. Or, since we registered it to a path, we can construct a URL. Beginning with our base path, we can appending the value of Path (`newest_comment`) in the view we just created. On my server, that gives me `http://localhost:8888/drupal/newest_comment`.

If I enter that URL in my browser, it returns data which looks something like this:

```
[
  {
    "cid": "12",
    "comments_name": "mbutcher",
    "comments_uid": "1",
    "comments_homepage": "",
    "comments_comment": "Lorem ipsum dolor sit amet, consectetur
adipisicing elit, sed do eiusmod tempor incididunt ut labore et dolore
magna aliqua.",
    "comments_format": "1",
    "node_comments_nid": "5",
    «node_comments_title»: «A Sticky Node»,
    «comments_timestamp»: «1223830766»
  }
]
```

How do we make sense of this? Actually, for the JavaScript programmer, reading the above output should be fairly straightforward.

 The JSON data is also available in the view building **Preview** section. However, the JSON results are all displayed on a single line. This does not make for easy reading.

Look at the resulting JSON document as a JavaScript object. JSON is essentially a serialization format that uses JavaScript constructs. Square brackets (`[]`) are used for arrays, so the code above is an array with one item in it.

Curly braces ({ }) are used for object literals. So the first (and only) item in the array above is an object.

Inside the object, nine properties are declared, each following the form `"name"` : `"value"`. If the value is a number, or a Boolean value (`true` or `false`), quotation marks are not needed around the value.

JSON data and trailing commas

Developers used to working with Drupal PHP often add a trailing comma at the end of array declarations (`[1, 2, 3,]`). This is incorrect in JavaScript and will (correctly) result in errors on some browsers. Similarly, object literals cannot end with an extra comma.

The following fields are returned as a part of our JSON feed:

- `cid`: The comment ID number
- `comments_name`: The name of the person who posted the comment
- `comments_uid`: The user ID of the person who posted the comment
- `comments_homepage`: A placeholder for a link to the comment
- `comments_comment`: The body of the comment
- `comments_format`: The formatter that should be used when outputting the code
- `node_comments_nid`: This is the node ID of the node that the comment refers to
- `node_comments_title`: The title of the node that the comment refers to
- `comments_timestamp`: The time that the comment was posted

There are two questions that you might be asking when viewing this.

First, why doesn't the data encoded in JSON match the data we requested when we constructed the view? For instance, why do we have `comments_format` (which we didn't ask for) but lack the comments link, which we did ask for?

A short answer is that Views returns the information to construct all of the requested information, along with some extra utility information (such as `comments_format`). But the output generator (in this case, Views Datasource) is responsible for combining some of that information. JSON content is returned almost unaltered. We must do some of the data building ourselves.

Secondly, why are the names so long? We asked for the title and got `node_comments_title`. Why not just `title`?

Views is capable of creating very complex queries against the Drupal database. It does the heavy lifting automatically, without requiring you to (for example) write the SQL to retrieve information from the database. Part of this automation process requires the generation of field names that are unlikely to conflict with other fields in the returned results. Therefore, it uses a rather complex naming convention to assign field names.

We now have our view constructed. We will now turn to the JavaScript code that will run on the client.

The comment watcher

We have just configured the server to give us the information we need in order to find out what the latest comment is, using AJAX and JSON. In this section, we will develop a JavaScript tool that will use this information in order to generate comment notifications.

The script will watch the JSON feed for changes. When a new comment appears in the JSON feed, the comment watcher will notify the user.

To create our script, we are going to draw on our existing toolkit, using behaviors, theming, and jQuery to build the comment watcher.

Let's first take a glance at the code in its entirety. We will then take a closer look at each section. This code is from the script `commentwatcher.js`, which is loaded into our theme using a `scripts[] = commentwatcher.js` directive in the info file:

```
// $Id$

/**
 * Watch for new comments and display a message when a comment
 * is posted.
 *
 * @file
 */
var CommentWatcher = CommentWatcher || {settings: {}};

CommentWatcher.settings.path = 'newest_comment';
CommentWatcher.settings.maxLength = 128;
CommentWatcher.settings.showSeconds = 7;
CommentWatcher.settings.checkSeconds = 10;

Drupal.behaviors.commentWatcher = function () {
  if ($('#comment_watcher').length == 0) {
    $('body').append('<div id="comment_watcher"></div>');
```

```
      CommentWatcher.check();
      var checkInterval = CommentWatcher.settings.checkSeconds *
        1000;
      setInterval(CommentWatcher.check, checkInterval);
  }
};

CommentWatcher.check = function () {
  var url = Drupal.settings.basePath +
    CommentWatcher.settings.path;

  jQuery.getJSON(url, function (data, result) {
    if (result != 'success') {
      return;
    }
    var comment = data[0];
    if (comment.cid > CommentWatcher.getLastID()) {
      CommentWatcher.setLastID(comment.cid);
      var content = Drupal.theme('commentArea', comment);
      var hideInterval = CommentWatcher.settings.showSeconds *
        1000;

      $('#comment_watcher').append(content).show('slow');

      setTimeout(function () {
        $('#comment_watcher').hide('slow', function () {
          $(this).find('#' + comment.cid).remove();
        });
      }, hideInterval);
    }

  });
};


CommentWatcher.setLastID = function (lastCommentID) {
  var oneDay = 1000 * 60 * 60 * 24;
  var expireTime = (new Date).getTime() + oneDay;
  var expire = new Date(expireTime).toGMTString();
  var myCookie = 'last_comment_id=' + lastCommentID +
    '; expires=' + expire + '; path=' +
    Drupal.settings.basePath;
  document.cookie = myCookie;
};
```

```
CommentWatcher.getLastID = function() {
  var found =
    document.cookie.match(/last_comment_id=([\d]+);/);
  if (!found || found.length < 2) {
    return 0;
  }
  return new Number(found[1]);
};

CommentWatcher.formatComment = function (text) {
  text = Drupal.checkPlain(text);
  if (text.length > CommentWatcher.settings.maxLength) {
    text = text.substring(
      0,
      CommentWatcher.settings.maxLength
    );
    var lastSpace = text.lastIndexOf(' ');
    if (lastSpace > 0) {
      text = text.substring(0, lastSpace);
    }
    text += '...';
  }
  return text;
};

Drupal.theme.prototype.commentArea = function (comment) {
  var text =
    CommentWatcher.formatComment(comment.comments_comment);
  var node_url = Drupal.settings.basePath + '/node/' +
    comment.node_comments_nid;
  var title_link =
    Drupal.checkPlain(comment.node_comments_title);
  title_link = title_link.link(node_url);
  var author = Drupal.checkPlain(comment.comments_name) +
   Drupal.t(' said...');
  var tpl = '<div class=»new_comment»></div>';

  var out = $(tpl).attr('id', comment.cid)
    .append('<div class=»node_title»>' + title_link  +
      '</div>')
    .append('<span class=»author»>' + author +'</span>')
    .append('<blockquote>' + text + '</blockquote>')
    .parent().html();

  return out;
};
```

There are six functions in this code. The behavior is executed when the document is loaded. It initiates the watching process. Periodically (every ten seconds, to be precise), the application checks the server for a new comment. If one is found, the theming function is used to format the data, and it is displayed on the page for seven seconds. After that time, it is hidden.

Information about the current comment is stored in a cookie. This ensures that as the user navigates throughout the site, a comment notification is only generated when a new comment is posted. Otherwise, the user would be notified anew on each page load, even if he or she had already seen the comment.

Let's take a quick glance at the settings for this application. We will then move on to the behavior. Here are the settings:

```
var CommentWatcher = CommentWatcher || {settings: {}};
CommentWatcher.settings.path = 'newest_comment';
CommentWatcher.settings.maxLength = 128;
CommentWatcher.settings.showSeconds = 7;
CommentWatcher.settings.checkSeconds = 10;
```

The namespace we will use is `CommentWatcher`. Inside the `settings` object, we have four parameters. The `CommentWatcher.settings.path` points to the path for the view. This is the same value we put in the **Path** field when constructing the view in the previous section. If you are not using Drupal's "Clean URLs" feature, you will need to adjust this to use the `?q=newest_comment` syntax.

Next, we set `CommentWatcher.settings.maxLength` to `128`. This is the maximum number of characters from the comment body that will be shown in the body of a notification.

Then we set a few time values:

```
CommentWatcher.settings.showSeconds = 7;
CommentWatcher.settings.checkSeconds = 10;
```

This is how long a notification will be shown (seven seconds) and how long the tool will wait between AJAX checks to the server (ten seconds). These are all declared as settings making them easy for behaviors, or other scripts, to modify.

Next, let's look at the main behavior.

The comment watcher behavior

Our behavior is going to initialize the comment watcher, and then prepare it for its task of periodically checking the server:

```
Drupal.behaviors.commentWatcher = function () {
  if ($('#comment_watcher').length == 0) {
    $('body').append('<div id="comment_watcher"></div>');
    CommentWatcher.check();
    var checkInterval = CommentWatcher.settings.checkSeconds *
      1000;
    setInterval(CommentWatcher.check, checkInterval);
  }
};
```

The first thing it does is check for an element with the ID `comment_watcher`. If there is one, we know that this behavior has already been run and we don't do anything.

If there is not a `comment_watcher` element, we know that we need to set up our comment watcher.

To set it up, we first insert the main area where notifications will be displayed. It should come as no surprise (given the check that we just did) that this element will have the ID `comment_watcher`. This is appended to the body of the HTML document. It will be styled by a `commentwatcher.css` stylesheet that looks like this:

```
#comment_watcher {
  position: fixed;
  right: 25px;
  bottom: 0px;
  background-color: white;
  display: none;
  border: 2px solid #eee;
  font-size: 10px;
  width: 200px;
  padding: 3px;
}

.new_comment blockquote{
  font-size: 12px;
  padding-left: 10px;
  margin-left: 2px;
}
```

As can be seen from this stylesheet, the comment area will be located in the lower-right corner of the browser's viewport.

The next task of the behavior is to display the first comment (if there is one). Then, the behavior registers a callback function that will be periodically executed to see if a new notification needs to be displayed.

This is done in three lines:

```
CommentWatcher.check();
var checkInterval = CommentWatcher.settings.checkSeconds *
  1000;
setInterval(CommentWatcher.check, checkInterval);
```

The `CommentWatcher.check()` function, which we will look at next, checks the remote server, and then displaying notifications. It is immediately called to show the newest comment. Then, using `setInterval()`, we tell the JavaScript interpreter to re-run the `CommentWatcher.check()` function every ten seconds.

The `setInterval()` function takes a function object as the first parameter, and an interval (in milliseconds) as the second parameter. The interpreter will wait the prescribed interval of time and then execute the function. It will continue to wait and execute until the interval is cleared (with `clearInterval()`), or the script is terminated.

Let's now turn to the `CommentWatcher.check()` function and see what happens when it is called.

The CommentWatcher.check() function

The `CommentWatcher.check()` function plays the most important role in our tool. It polls the server and creates a notification when a new comment is posted.

However, with such a large toolkit available to us, even this function is not terribly complex. Let's take a look:

```
CommentWatcher.check = function () {
  var url = Drupal.settings.basePath +
    CommentWatcher.settings.path;

  jQuery.getJSON(url, function (data, result) {
    if (result != 'success') {
      return;
    }
    var comment = data[0];
    if (comment.cid > CommentWatcher.getLastID()) {
      CommentWatcher.setLastID(comment.cid);
```

```
      var content = Drupal.theme('commentArea', comment);
      var hideInterval = CommentWatcher.settings.showSeconds *
        1000;

      $('#comment_watcher').append(content).show('slow');

      setTimeout(function () {
        $('#comment_watcher').hide('slow', function () {
          $(this).find('#' + comment.cid).remove();
        });
      }, hideInterval);
    }

  });
};
```

On the first line, we construct a relative URI to the server by appending the
`CommentWatcher.settings.path` to the Drupal base path. This will be passed in as
the URL parameter to the `jQuery.getJSON()` function.

Along with the URL, we pass an anonymous function `jQuery.getJSON()`. That
function will be executed when the JSON data has been retrieved from the remote
server. Let's look closely at this anonymous function:

```
function (data, result) {
  if (result != 'success') {
    return;
  }
  var comment = data[0];
  if (comment.cid > CommentWatcher.getLastID()) {
    CommentWatcher.setLastID(comment.cid);
    var content = Drupal.theme('commentArea', comment);
    var hideInterval = CommentWatcher.settings.showSeconds *
      1000;

    $('#comment_watcher').append(content).show('slow');

    setTimeout(function () {
      $('#comment_watcher').hide('slow', function () {
        $(this).find('#' + comment.cid).remove();
      });
    }, hideInterval);
  }

});
```

As usual, the first thing we do in the anonymous function is check to make sure the results were fetched successfully. If the network transfer was successful, and the content could be parsed as JSON, the `result` is set to `success`.

Therefore, if the result is not `success`, we simply return without doing anything.

The `jQuery.getJSON()` function not only fetches the data from the remote server, it also parses it using the JSON parsing rules. Therefore, if the `result` is `success`, we know that `data` will be a JavaScript object decoded from the JSON data.

Earlier, we took a look at what that data looks like as it is returned from the view. It is something like this:

```
[
  {
    "cid": "12",
    "comments_name": "mbutcher",
    "comments_uid": "1",
    "comments_homepage": "",
    "comments_comment": "Lorem ipsum dolor sit amet, consectetur
adipisicing elit, sed do eiusmod tempor incididunt ut labore et dolore
magna aliqua.",
    "comments_format": "1",
    "node_comments_nid": "5",
    «node_comments_title»: «A Sticky Node»,
    «comments_timestamp»: «1223830766»
  }
]
```

So, `data` is an array with one item. That one item is an object describing the newest comment. Since we will directly reference that object several times, we assign `data[0]` to `comment`.

Next, we check to see if the comment just retrieved from the server is newer than the last comment we looked at:

```
if (comment.cid > CommentWatcher.getLastID()) {
  CommentWatcher.setLastID(comment.cid);
  var content = Drupal.theme('commentArea', comment);
  var hideInterval = CommentWatcher.settings.showSeconds *
    1000;

  $('#comment_watcher').append(content).show('slow');

  setTimeout(function () {
```

```
    $('#comment_watcher').hide('slow', function () {
      $(this).find('#' + comment.cid).remove();
    });
  }, hideInterval);
}
```

Later, we will see how `CommentWatcher.getLastID()` and `CommentWatcher.setLastID()` work. For now, we can just say that the first is used for determining what the last new comment ID was, and the second one sets the newest content ID.

If the comment ID (`comment.cid`) is newer than the latest comment ID the tool has seen, then a new comment has been posted. In this case, we do several things:

1. We set the last comment ID using `CommentWatcher.setLastID()`.

2. Next, we use a theming function, `commentArea`, to turn the comment object into formatted HTML.

3. That data is then appended to the contents of the `comment_watcher` element, and then (using the `$().show()` function) the new element is gradually displayed on the screen.

4. Finally, since we only want the new comment to be shown for a few seconds, we use JavaScript's `setTimeout()` function to tell JavaScript to run a function after a given number of milliseconds: (`CommentWatcher.settings.showSeconds * 1000`).

The function passed to `setInterval()` is an anonymous function:

```
function () {
  $('#comment_watcher').hide('slow', function () {
    $(this).find('#' + comment.cid).remove();
  });
}
```

This function finds the element with the ID `comment_watcher` and then gradually hides it (using `$().hide('slow')`). Once the element is hidden, the `$().hide()` function will execute the anonymous function we pass in, which simply removes the comment from the `comment_watcher` element.

When a new comment is added, and the `CommentWatcher.check()` function runs, a new notification will expand from the lower righthand corner of the browser's viewport as seen here.

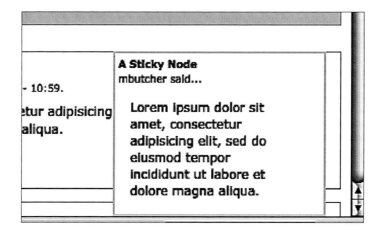

The jQuery `show` and `hide` effects will cause the notification to expand out from the corner, and after seven seconds have elapsed, collapse back down into the corner.

Now that we have an idea of how the notification looks, let's examine the theming function.

Theming the comment notification

There are two functions involved in theming the content. The first is our custom theming function, `Drupal.theme.prototype.commentArea()` which we see here:

```
Drupal.theme.prototype.commentArea = function (comment) {
  var text =
    CommentWatcher.formatComment(comment.comments_comment);
  var node_url = Drupal.settings.basePath + '/node/' +
    comment.node_comments_nid;
  var title_link =
    Drupal.checkPlain(comment.node_comments_title);
  title_link = title_link.link(node_url);
  var author = Drupal.checkPlain(comment.comments_name) +
   Drupal.t(' said...');
  var tpl = '<div class="new_comment"></div>';

  var out = $(tpl).attr('id', comment.cid)
    .append('<div class="node_title">' + title_link +
      '</div>')
```

```
    .append('<span class="author">' + author +'</span>')
    .append('<blockquote>' + text + '</blockquote>')
    .parent().html();

  return out;
};
```

This code is straightforward. As with the other theme functions we have seen throughout this book, the job of this function is to build up a string containing formatted content.

The first thing this does is format the main comment content. This is done with `CommentWatcher.formatContent()`, which we will look at in just a moment.

From there, it builds up several smaller pieces of content including a URL, which is then transformed into a link, the string "AUTHOR said...", and then the primary `<div></div>` tag , which is used as a wrapper for our comment content.

 When retrieving content over AJAX, especially when the content isn't embedded in XML, you should use `Drupal.checkPlain()`, or another encoding tool, to prevent HTML tags from being injected. This is especially important when the content comes from users, as is the case with comments.

Once that is out of the way, we use one long jQuery chain to incrementally build up the contents of the comment. At the end of the chain, we get the HTML contents of the jQuery object and return those.

Let's look at the `CommentWatcher.formatContent()` function:

```
CommentWatcher.formatComment = function (text) {
  text = Drupal.checkPlain(text);
  if (text.length > CommentWatcher.settings.maxLength) {
    text = text.substring(
      0,
      CommentWatcher.settings.maxLength
    );
    var lastSpace = text.lastIndexOf(' ');
    if (lastSpace > 0) {
      text = text.substring(0, lastSpace);
    }
    text += '...';
  }
  return text;
};
```

The job of this function is to make sure the content of the comment is appropriately formatted for the notification box. This involves a few things. First, we want to use `Drupal.checkPlain()` to make sure no HTML is inserted.

The second thing we want to do is make sure the content fits in the small notification area. Earlier, we set `CommentWatcher.settings.maxLength` to `128`. This is the maximum length we will allow the text to be before we begin the process of truncating it.

If the text is longer, we go about the process of shortening it. First, we do this by getting a substring of the text from the beginning through the 128th character. However, just doing that could be ugly. We may chop off part of a word.

So the next thing we do is search backward in the string for the last space character. Once there, we can be certain that we have not split a word. After the last space character in the string has been found, we shorten the string again and then add ellipsis (...) to let the reader know there is more to the comment.

Using this algorithm, it is possible for a string to end up being 131-characters long because of the appending of the ellipsis to the end. For our purposes, this doesn't really matter. However, if the length of the string is very important, it is a good idea to account for these three characters when doing the initial truncation.

The escaped, shortened string is then returned.

Managing cookies

There are still two more functions in our `CommentWatcher` tool. These are `CommentWatcher.getLastID()` and `CommentWatcher.setLastID()`.

These two functions provide a mechanism for tracking the last comment ID. This is necessary if we want our tool to "only" show new comments.

We could store this information in a local variable. In that case, for any given page view, the user would see a comment no more than once. Let's think about a situation we would like to avoid. No new comments are posted, but the user quickly travels from page to page inside of our site. Each time the user visits a page, she or he is notified repeatedly of the last comment. The same comment is being displayed on each page load.

Instead of subjecting our users to repeated notifcations, we only want the user to see comments when they are new to the user.

There are two ways of doing this. First, we could write code on the server that would track the comments the user has viewed. This method would require some PHP coding.

A second option would be to use cookies to store the information and have JavaScript handle the reading and writing of those cookies. Since cookies are stored over a longer term, they would work well for our situation. While there are occasional users who turn off cookie support in their browser (which will leave those users in the position of receiving repeat notifications), the vast majority of web users have cookies enabled in their browsers. In a production environment, we might want to go to greater lengths in order to detect whether the user has cookies turned off. But for our demonstration tool, we will assume that cookies are enabled.

 Cookies have been around for a long time. With AJAX technologies and web applications, cookies can be very useful. Keep cookies in mind as a way to store small pieces of data between page loads. Just remember, sensitive information should not be stored in a cookie unless it is encrypted.

We are going to use the second option. Here are the two functions that take care of this:

```
CommentWatcher.setLastID = function (lastCommentID) {
  var oneDay = 1000 * 60 * 60 * 24;
  var expireTime = (new Date).getTime() + oneDay;
  var expire = new Date(expireTime).toGMTString();
  var myCookie = 'last_comment_id=' + lastCommentID +
    '; expires=' + expire + '; path=' +
    Drupal.settings.basePath;
  document.cookie = myCookie;
};

CommentWatcher.getLastID = function() {
  var found =
    document.cookie.match(/ last_comment_id=([\d]+);/);
  if (!found || found.length < 2) {
    return 0;
  }
  return new Number(found[1]);
};
```

The first function builds a cookie of the form `last_comment_id=COMMENTID; expires=DATE; path=DRUPAL_PATH`.

The cookie format is very specific. The first value is a name/value pair which is separated by an equal sign, and terminated by a semicolon and a space (yes, that space is important). The second value is the expiration date, beginning with `expires=`. The date must then be in a format like this (the POSIX date format):

```
Tue, 14 Jan 2008 02:29:20 GMT
```

Fortunately, JavaScript `Date` object instances have a `toGMTDate()` function that returns a date string in that format. The expiration string is also terminated by a semicolon and space.

The last item in our cookie is the path. This tells the browser when to send the cookie to the remote server. It will only send the cookie if the path component of the requested URI is within that path. We set it to the `Drupal.settings.basePath` value, which means that this cookie will only be sent to our Drupal instance, and not to other apps on the same server.

To set a cookie, we simply "assign" it to `document.cookie`. However, this isn't really a straight assignment. The `document.cookie` object is a wrapper for more complex underlying code. The code that does a `document.cookie = myCookie` is actually validating the cookie format, and assigning the value to an internal array of cookies.

If we were to read back the `document.cookie` variable, we would not simply get our cookie back. Instead, we would get a list of available cookie name/value pairs (without the date stamp or path) concatenated together like this:

```
last_comment_id=12; SESSd210eb21e=aa65da901b5d0c8; has_js=1
```

This string has three cookie pairs in it: the `last_comment_id` string we set, a session ID generated by PHP, and the `has_js` cookie generated by Drupal.

Our second function, `CommentWatcher.getLastID()`, deals with the long string returned by `document.cookie`. All we need to find is a very specific value, and so we use a regular expression to find it:

```
var found =
    document.cookie.match(/last_comment_id=([\d]+);/);
```

The regular expression, `/last_comment_id=([\d]+);/`, looks for the cookie named `last_comment_id`, and then captures its value (using the parentheses).

If this pattern is found, the variable found will contain an array with two items:

```
[
  'last_comment_id=13',
  '13',
]
```

The first item is the entire match. The second item is just the matched portion from within the parentheses. In this case, it is 13, the comment ID for the last comment.

Note that at the end of the `CommentWatcher.getLastID()` function, we convert the resulting value into a `Number`. We do this explicitly so the arithmetic comparison with the other IDs is successful. It also takes care of any additional trailing spaces (which are dropped during a conversion), which would otherwise throw off an equality check.

Using this pair of functions, we can store the comment ID inside of a cookie. Our small tool will be able to "remember", from page to page, what the last comment ID was. Therefore, the user will only see a new notification when a new comment is posted.

Summary

In this chapter, we focused on the AJAX family of tools. After a short introduction to AJAX, we worked on two projects.

First, we used Drupal's RSS feed as an XML source for an AJAX query. We retrieved that data and used it to display web clips.

In the second project, we installed the Views and Views Datasource modules to give us additional functionality on the server. We then built a view that outputs information (in the JSON format) about the last comment posted.

On the client side, we used JavaScript and AJAX to create a notification tool that polls the server, and notifies the user whenever a new comment is posted.

Drupal and jQuery both contain some powerful tools which make developing AJAX applications quick and easy. By taking the redundant, and complex aspects of AJAX, and wrapping those in library functions, these tools provide simple functions for access and manipulating data.

In the next chapter, we are going to change tracks. Up until this point in the book, our projects were focused on theming. In the next chapter, we are going to learn how to develop JavaScript modules. This will take some PHP code (at least a couple of lines), but you won't need serious PHP knowledge to understand the basics of module creation.

8
Building a Module

In the previous chapter, we used the AJAX features in jQuery and Drupal to add some new tools to our Frobnitz theme. But what if we wanted to add those tools to another theme, such as Bluemarine or Garland? Would we need to create new subthemes for those just to add a few JavaScript files?

That would certainly be one way of doing it. A better way would be to take our JavaScript tools and package them as standalone components that could be added independently. This is done through Drupal modules. In this chapter, we will learn how to create modules and use them for adding JavaScript features.

In this chapter, we will:

- Understand how modules work
- Create a bare-bones module
- Add JavaScript to a module
- Make our JavaScript available to other modules

In previous chapters, almost all of our code has been in JavaScript. In this chapter, we will use a little PHP. Don't worry, if you can write a PHP Template, you will be able to follow the simple code that we are going to write.

How modules work

In the previous six chapters, we have been creating JavaScript tools and adding them to our site using the info file for a theme. Themes are designed to take Drupal data and prepare it for presentation. Often, it serves us quite well to attach JavaScript to a theme.

But many of the tools we have written so far could just as easily be used with any theme. Why build our tool into a theme when it could be used more broadly? In this chapter, we are going to use modules as a way of packaging JavaScript into a component that can be used independently of a theme.

Modules provide a way for developers to add functional components to Drupal without having to modify the existing Drupal code.

For example, instead of opening a Drupal file and adding our own features, we can create a module to provide these features. This has several advantages:

- Since we haven't changed Drupal itself, we can continue upgrading Drupal without having to carefully patch in our own changes.
- We can enable and disable our module with a few mouse clicks. This additional functionality is easy to on and turn off.
- We can share the module with others who might also make use of it.

Also, as we did in the previous chapter, we can get modules that others have developed—such as Views and Views Datasource—and use them to build our own site.

In a nutshell, modules turn a good, general-purpose CMS, into a highly customizable and infinitely extendible web platform.

Modules are mostly written in PHP. In fact, one of the two required module files must always be written in PHP. But modules can provide JavaScript services as well. In fact, that is what we will be doing in this chapter. We will create modules that make our JavaScript tools available across Drupal, regardless of the theme.

The module structure

Drupal developers have gone to great lengths to make module writing easy. In fact, the process of creating a module is only four steps long:

1. Create a directory for your module.
2. Add a .info file to the module directory.
3. Add a few configuration directives to the .info file.
4. Add a .module file to your module directory.

After following these four steps, you will have a module that can be administered from within Drupal, though it won't do anything.

Let's briefly cover the pieces used in these steps: the directory, .info file, and .module file.

The directory

Each module must be placed in a directory. Most often, a module has its own directory. For example, if we want to create a module called `my_module`, it will be housed in the `my_module/` directory.

On occasion, several similar modules will be grouped into a package. A **package** is simply a collection of related modules, all stored in the same directory. For example, we could create a `my_tools` module with modules named `my_first_tool` and `my_other_tool`. These would both be stored in the `my_tools/` directory.

We will be creating simple modules, and each will be stored in its own directory.

The .info file

In Chapter 2, we created our first theme's `.info` file. That file is used by the Drupal theming system to glean information about the theme.

Modules also have a `.info` file. In fact, it looks very similar to a theme's `.info` file. In our case, it will be easier to create a module's `.info` file than it was to create a theme's `.info` file.

Just as a theme's `.info` file goes in the theme's directory, so a module's `.info` file goes in the module's directory.

The .module file

Drupal needs to know where the module's executable code is located. How does it do that? It looks in the module's directory for a file that ends with the `.module` extension. When it finds such a file, it loads it as a PHP script.

Writing PHP code for Drupal is just about as simple as creating the module file and writing some PHP functions.

Those are the three parts of a Drupal module.

Where do modules go?

Like themes, modules are stored in directories located in pre-defined locations beneath your site's Drupal directory.

Themes go in `/themes` (for built-in themes), `/sites/all/themes`, `/sites/default/themes`, and (if you are hosting multiple sites) `/sites/SITENAME/themes`.

Modules are similarly organized:

- Modules included as part of the Drupal Core go in the `/modules` directory under the Drupal root

- Modules used across the installation go in `/sites/all/modules`

- Modules used only by the default site go in `/sites/default/modules` (usually you would only put modules here if you are hosting multiple sites)

- Modules used only by other sites, on a multisite Drupal installation, go in `/sites/SITENAME/modules`, where `SITENAME` is replaced by the actual name of the site

Drupal has the ability to run multiple sites with only one copy of the Drupal Core. For example, if you wanted to run `my.example.com` and `your.example.com` on the same website, you could configure Drupal to manage both domains (each with its own database) without having to run two Drupal instances. For more information, see `http://drupal.org/getting-started/6/install/multi-site`.

In this book, we will always put our modules in `/sites/all/modules`.

We have now seen the three parts of a module, and we know where to put the module files. In the spirit of our project-based method, it's time for us to dive right in and create a module.

How tough will this first module be? Here's a hint: the entire `.module` file is only 27-lines long, and 10 of those are comment lines. No rocket science here!

Project: creating a JavaScript loader module

When working with themes, we added JavaScript to our site by adding a line to the theme's `.info` file like this:

```
scripts[] = my_script.js
```

Like themes, modules also have `.info` files. The format of the module's `.info` file is the same, but the directives available in module `.info` files are different from those available in theme `.info` files.

The `scripts[]` directive is an example. It is unused by module `.info` files. If you put such an entry in your module's `.info` file, it will simply be ignored.

We are going to change this. In this project, we will build a JavaScript autoloader which reads all of the scripts from a module's `.info` file, and includes them in the HTML delivered back to the client.

Why doesn't Drupal do this already?

The main reason why Drupal doesn't already do this is, in a word, performance. We are going to make it possible for one module to include its own script files. But what if we added scripts from all of the modules? Just checking all of the modules would add overhead to Drupal's page-rendering process. In the future, this could change if some clever developers figure an expedient way of doing this.

Our module is only going to read its own `.info` file. We could expand its scope to check all modules for scripts, but that would add significant complexity to the module and would have a significant performance impact.

We are going to build our module in the following order:

1. Create the module directory.
2. Add a sample JavaScript file for testing.
3. Add the module's `.info` file.
4. Write the short `.module` file.

There are two major things that I wish to convey as we walk through this project. First, this project should illustrate the process of creating a simple module. Second, we will see the primary tool for interacting with JavaScript from a module: the `drupal_add_js()` function.

Creating the module directory

The first step in developing a new module is creating a place for it to be stored. For basic modules, the directory should have the module's machine-readable name. Our module will be called `jsloader`, so we will create a directory with that name.

As mentioned in the previous section, custom Drupal modules go under the `sites/` directory. Specifically, ours will go in `sites/all/modules/jsloader/` as seen here:

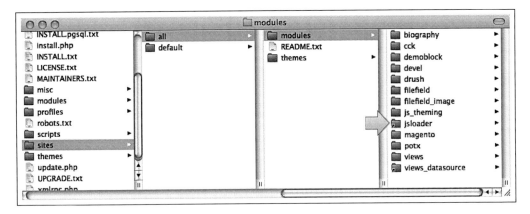

In the previous screenshot, from the Finder in Mac OS X, the base Drupal directory is on the far left. Inside of `sites/all/modules`, we have created a new directory called `jsloader`. I have included an arrow to point to the exact location of the `jsloader` directory in this screenshot.

 You might notice the `views` and `views_datasource` modules in the same directory. We installed these two modules in the previous chapter. We used the `potx` module in Chapter 5, and `js_theming` was covered in Chapter 6.

Next, we will add a simple file to that directory.

A JavaScript sample

We want a simple script to test. This is certainly not the type of thing we would use on a public web site. But it will let us know whether or not our loader is working.

We will put this script in the `jsloader/` directory we just created, and we'll name it `jsloader.js`. Here are the contents of that file:

```
// $Id$
/**
 * Verify that the autoloader is working.
 * @file
 */
jQuery(document).ready(function() {
  alert("JS Loader is ready.");
});
```

This script is going to have the annoying characteristic of opening a new alert dialog box every time a page is loaded on our site. For our purposes, it does exactly what we want. It lets us know when the script is being loaded, and we don't even have to check the HTML source.

So far, we have only one file in our `jsloader/` directory, the test script. As things stand, Drupal won't even recognize this as a module yet. First, we need to create a `.info` file.

The module's .info file

The purpose of the `.info` file is to provide Drupal with some basic information about our module. An info file is always named with the module's name, so ours will be `jsloader.info`. Also, it must be stored inside of our module's directory.

Here's a very basic `.info` file for our new module:

```
; $Id$
name = JS Loader
description = "Load JavaScript files"
core = 6.x
```

This file only has four lines.

The first line is a comment (note the leading semicolon (`;`)) with the `$Id$` tag we discussed in Chapter 2. It serves the same purpose here as it does in a theme's `.info` file. It is a placeholder for CVS versioning information that will be inserted when code is checked into the CVS repository at `Drupal.org`.

Next is the `name` directive, whose value is a human-readable name for this module. This field is used to display the module's name in the administration interface.

The third line is the `description` directive, which contains a short description about what the module does. The one above is enclosed in quotation marks. The quotation marks are not required if the description fits on one line. Only when values require more than one line of text do you need quotation marks.

The final line, `core`, indicates the minimum version of Drupal required by this module. `6.x` indicates that this module should run on any Drupal 6 system.

There are a handful of other directives that can be added to a `.info` file. Some of these are discussed in my book *"Learning Drupal 6 Module Development"*, *Packt Publishing, 978-1847194442*, and all are documented in the release notes for Drupal 6.

A custom addition

We will add one more line to our basic `.info` file. This line won't be used by Drupal, but will be used by our new module:

```
scripts[] = jsloader.js
```

This fifth line indicates that our module should include the `jsloader.js` file as a script sent to the client. In a few moments, we'll see how this is used. For now, it is only important to note that this is not a standard directive for a `.info` file. Drupal will simply ignore it.

We now have the test script and the `.info` file. The last file to create is the `.module` file.

The .module file

In the same directory where we put our other two files, we will now create the `.module` file. As with the `.info` file, the `.module` file must be named after the module. For the `jsloader` module, the file name must be `jsloader.module`.

 This file will contain PHP code. However, it does not have the `.php` extension. If you are using an IDE to edit your code, you may need to manually set it to use PHP syntax on the `.module` files.

While the file is only 27-lines long, we will dwell on it for a while, explaining various aspects of Drupal's behavior as we go.

Here is the `.module` file in its entirety:

```php
<?php
// $Id$
/**
 * A module to load JS files.
 */
/**
 * Implementation of hook_help().
 */
function jsloader_help($path, $args) {
  if ($path == 'admin/help#jsloader') {
    return t('JS Loader loads JavaScript files based on the
            contents of the .info file.');
  }
}
/**
 * Implementation of hook_init().
```

```
  */
function jsloader_init() {
  $path = drupal_get_path('module', 'jsloader');
  $info = drupal_parse_info_file($path . '/jsloader.info');
  foreach ($info['scripts'] as $script) {
    drupal_add_js($path . '/' . $script);
  }
}
```

Taking a quick look at this file. We can see the following:

- It begins with a `<?php` tag to indicate that this is a PHP file.

- Next comes a comment (`//`) to hold the `$Id$` CVS keyword.

- After that is the main documentation block for the file.

- There are two functions in this file: `jsloader_help()` and `jsloader_init()`, each has its own documentation block.

 Although the file begins with a `<?php`, it does not end with the customary `?>` tag. Why? For library files such as this, the closing tag is optional and can actually lead to application-breaking mistakes. Drupal conventions recommend omitting the closing tag for this reason.

In Chapter 2, we discussed coding standards, which included spacing, commenting, and the general structure of code. We will not repeat that discussion, but there are two things to note about the way PHP code is generally structured in Drupal.

First, most Drupal PHP code is procedural, not object-oriented. Functions are defined in the global namespace and are not usually assigned to objects. This will change in Drupal 7, which will be object-oriented to a greater extent.

Second, function names and variable names are always lowercase, with words separated by underscores. Camel case (`myVariable`) is never used in Drupal's procedural code.

With these few notes addressed, we are ready to look at the first function, `jsloader_help()`.

The jsloader_help() function

The purpose of this first function, `jsloader_help()`, is to provide some content for the Drupal built-in help system. Always provide a help function for your module, even if it does no more than provide basic information about what the module does. A little help is better than no help.

Admonitions aside, let's explore the code, starting with the comment. Believe it or not, this one line comment opens the door for a discussion of Drupal's most powerful feature:

```
/**
 * Implementation of hook_help().
 */
function jsloader_help($path, $args) {
  if ($path == 'admin/help#jsloader') {
    return t('JS Loader loads JavaScript files based on the
             contents of the .info file.');
  }
}
```

This comment says `Implementation of hook_help()`. What does it mean?

Drupal uses a very powerful system, called the **hook system**, to give custom modules the ability to strategically interact with the Drupal Core system. Here's how it works. When a client requests a page, Drupal begins processing the request by walking through a long series of steps. It begins by loading the necessary code, and ends with the sending of HTML (and other files) to the client.

At specific points during this process, Drupal checks to see if any modules need to "hook into" Drupal and do some processing of their own. If Drupal finds any modules that respond to the current state, it will call them and temporarily hand over control to them. These modules do what they need to do (even modify Drupal's data) and then return control to Drupal.

This whole procedure is so fundamental to Drupal, that even foundational pieces of Drupal, such as the node, user, and comment systems, are implemented using modules and hooks.

That's a high-level explanation. Here's how it works in practice. Drupal defines certain callback points. These are points where it will turn over control to modules. When one of these points is reached, a **hook** is called. A hook is simply a pre-defined pattern for a function name. Usually, these are represented with a function call such as `hook_help()`. In actuality, Drupal checks each module for a function that follows a pattern. It looks for a function of the form `<modulename>_help()`, where `<modulename>` is replaced with the name of the module. If it finds such a function, it executes it.

For example, when the help page is loaded, Drupal goes through each module looking for a `hook_help()` implementation. In the `node` module, it looks for `node_help()`. In comment, it looks for `comment_help()`, and in `jsloader` it will look for `jsloader_help()`.

There are dozens of hooks defined in the Drupal 6 Core. Module developers can create their own hooks, effectively passing control off to different modules! As you may guess, the module system provides potentially infinite extensibility.

 Hooks for all of the core modules are documented at
http://api.drupal.org/api/group/hooks/6.

With the hook system in mind, we can take another look at how modules function. Essentially, a module implements hook functions—it defines functions that follow hook patterns, and so will be called by Drupal. Therefore, a module can be very specific, containing only the code necessary to add the desired features at the desired places.

That is why we can create our module in only a few dozen lines of code. We are implementing two hooks, and each will be called only at the desired time in the life cycle of a Drupal request.

Hooks are the very heart of Drupal PHP programming. They make it easy to write simple, yet functional code.

Why aren't hooks used in Drupal JavaScript?

If hooks are so powerful, one might ask why they aren't used in the JavaScript libraries. In fact, the same strategy is used in JavaScript (though we often use anonymous functions instead of writing hook functions). The JavaScript event model, and even the Drupal theme and behavior systems, use callback-driven logic. However, because JavaScript is object-oriented, much of the pattern-based method invocation can be omitted. We can simply pass in objects that implement certain patterns (or as we do with behaviors and themes, attach functions to already existing objects). Drupal will then call these at the appropriate time.

Like user interface programming, Drupal hooks work on an event-like model. Certain conditions arise, and hooks are called. For example, when a user loads a help page, the `hook_help()` implementations are called. Each module is then expected to determine (based on context) whether or not it should return help information:

```
function jsloader_help($path, $args) {
  if ($path == 'admin/help#jsloader') {
    return t('JS Loader loads JavaScript files based on the
            contents of the .info file.');
  }
}
```

A `hook_help()` implementation will be passed two arguments: `$path` and `$args`. The first contains the path that was requested by the user, and the second contains an array corresponding to the components in the path. Imagine it as the results of splitting the `$path` at each slash (/) character.

For our help function, we only want to handle the case where a general overview of the module is requested. The path for general help will always be of the form `admin/help#<modulename>`.

This function will only return help text when the path is `admin/help#jsloader`. While our help text can be as long as we need, our demonstration module will just get a simple string description:

```
return t('JS Loader loads JavaScript files based on the
          contents of the .info file.');
```

Normally, the code above would all be on one line, without the backslash.

Notice that our help text is passed through the `t()` function. This is the PHP equivalent of the `Drupal.t()` translation function we saw a few chapters ago. It will translate the string when necessary.

That's all there is to the function. If help text is requested for our module, this simple description will be returned. If we enable the module in **Administer | Site building | Modules**, then go to **Administer | Help**, and then click on **JS Loader**, we should see something like this:

Home » Administer » Help

JS Loader
JS Loader loads JavaScript files based on the contents of the .info file.

We have now successfully implemented our first hook. Our module only needs one more before we finish.

The jsloader_init() function

The first hook we implemented printed the help text. This second one will do the rest of the work for our module. It will read the module's `.info` file and load any JavaScript files specified in the `scripts[]` directive. For example, when we created our `jsloader.info` file, we added a line to the bottom that looked like this:

```
scripts[] = jsloader.js
```

Drupal will simply ignore this directive when it parses the .info file. However, we can make use of it.

To do so, we are going to implement another hook: hook_init(). This hook is executed near the beginning of a page request, after Drupal has loaded all of the core libraries, and then loaded the modules. However, it is called before any HTML is sent back to the client.

We want to hook into the Drupal request cycle early. This allows us to add the JavaScript files to the HTML's head section (inside the <head></head> tags).

The hook_init() hook is easy to implement. It takes no arguments and nothing needs to be returned. To implement the hook_init() function, we simply create jsloader_init(), a function that follows the hook naming convention:

```
/**
 * Implementation of hook_init().
 */
function jsloader_init() {
  $path = drupal_get_path('module', 'jsloader');
  $info = drupal_parse_info_file($path . '/jsloader.info');
  foreach ($info['scripts'] as $script) {
    drupal_add_js($path . '/' . $script);
  }
}
```

This function reads the .info file, and then load all of the scripts that the info file points to. Both of these functions will require us to know the path to the module. Fortunately, Drupal can compute this for us.

On the first line, we retrieve the path to our module and then assign this information to the variable $path. The drupal_get_path() function takes two arguments. The first is the type of path we want to get. The string module indicates that we are interested in a module directory. In contrast, to get a theme path, we would use the string theme.

The second parameter is the module whose path we want. We are interested in our own module's path, so we pass jsloader to the function.

Now that we have the base path to our module, we can load the .info file. Again, this is a simple task because Drupal provides a function for reading and parsing this file.

The drupal_parse_info_file() takes the full path to the .info file as its parameter. We build this by concatenating the $path and '/jsloader.info'. Drupal will then read the file, parse it, and return an array.

> **PHP arrays**
>
> In JavaScript, we made frequent use of arrays and object literals. PHP's array-type functions are a combination of these two. That is, it may contain a list of values with numeric indexes or key/value pairs.

The array returned is an associative array that, if done in JavaScript, would look something like this:

```
{
  'name'  :   'JS Loader',
  'description': 'Load JavaScript files',
  'core': '6.x',
  'scripts': ['jsloader.js']
}
```

Items in the `.info` file, that have square brackets in the name, are converted to arrays. Thus, `scripts[]` is transformed into a key, `scripts`, and it has an array for a value. Each time the `scripts[]` directive is parsed, its contents are appended to the array. If we had two `scripts[]` directives, the scripts entry would look like this:

```
'scripts': ['jsloader.js', 'other.js']
```

The results of the parsed `.info` file are stored in the `$info` variable. We know that the `scripts[]` entries are now stored in the `$info` array as the name scripts and an array of script file names. What we want to do next is loop through `$info['scripts']` and tell Drupal to add each script to the output.

In PHP, this can be done conveniently with a `foreach` loop, which will iterate through each item in an array, temporarily assigning each item to a variable.

A `foreach` loop follows the pattern `foreach ($array as $array_item) {}`. In each iteration, the `$array_item` will contain the value of the current item in the array:

```
foreach ($info['scripts'] as $script) {
  drupal_add_js($path . '/' . $script);
}
```

For each `script[]` item added in the `.info` file, this will use the `drupal_add_js()` function to add that JavaScript file.

The `drupal_add_js()` function is multifunctional. It can be used three ways:

1. To add a JavaScript file to the head of the generated HTML.

2. To add inline JavaScript to the output, inside of `<script></script>` tags. This will also go in the HTML head.

3. To add an individual setting to the `Drupal.settings` array. We have seen the `Drupal.settings.basePath` variable in previous chapters. This extends that same object.

Unfortunately, the arguments are different in each case and therefore mean different things. Here, we have used the simplest case as we are simply adding a file. The syntax for doing this from within a module is `drupal_add_js($filename)`. As we can see, the `drupal_add_js()` function needs to know the path to the filename.

In the above code snippet, this loads each script file.

In the next project, we will see how `drupal_add_js()` can be used to add settings.

 The three uses of this function are documented in the Drupal API at `http://api.drupal.org/api/function/drupal_add_js/6`.

That is all there is to our loader. Now, every script that we add to the `.info` file using the `scripts[]` directive will automatically be loaded on every page request. At the beginning of this project, we created a module that fired an `alert()` every time a page loaded. Now that our module is complete, we should be able to test the loader by loading a page on our site. Here's a screenshot of what that should look like:

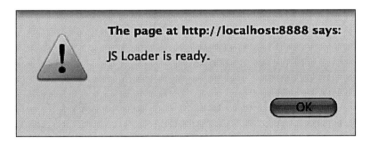

The page at http://localhost:8888 says:

JS Loader is ready.

OK

If the alert box pops up, we know that our script is being loaded.

The module we just created provides a way for integrating JavaScript files into Drupal, without relying on a theme, and without requiring any additional code. With this single module, we could add all of the scripts created since Chapter 3. The one in Chapter 2 relied a little too heavily on a template file to be used outside of a theme. No additional PHP would be necessary.

On the other hand, this module doesn't exploit the possibility of using PHP code to inform JavaScript. In the next project, we will see how we can use PHP code in modules to pass information on to a JavaScript tool.

Project: the editor revisited

In the previous project, we created a simple module to automatically load any JavaScript files indicated in the .info file. In this project, we are going to create a module that provides features for a specific JavaScript tool.

This project will improve the Simple Editor project we did in Chapter 4. Here, we will package an editor as a module, making it easy to use in many themes. We'll also make a little more use of PHP as a way of passing configuration options from the server to the client.

The goal of this project is to illustrate server-side PHP code can be used to generate JavaScript for the client. Here's a theme you may notice as we go: There is more than one way to write code like this, and in some cases, it's hard to tell which is preferable. We will run into two specific cases during our coding where we will need to make decisions about how something ought to be done.

We are going to make some improvements on the Simple Editor, add a few features, and rewrite some parts in light of what we now know. We will call our new editor **Better Editor**.

When we wrote our Simple Editor back in Chapter 4, we had not yet learned about themes. Instead of using theme functions to edit our code, we simply built strings where needed. Here, we are going to progress to theme functions.

Also, Simple Editor had only a few buttons, and adding more buttons required laborious re-writing of the code. Several things needed to be changed for each new button.

In Better Editor, we are going to change the way buttons are created. We will make it possible for the server to dictate what buttons get created. This means we will be writing a little extra PHP code for this section. Once again, it is simple code. Even if you are new to PHP, this code should be easy to follow.

Now, let's create our module.

First step: creating the module

Just as with the previous module, we will begin by creating a module directory, `bettereditor`, in `sites/all/modules/`. We will create two files: the .info file and the .module file.

Here's what `bettereditor.info` looks like:

```
; $Id$
name = Better Editor
description = Provide a simple editor for HTML.
core = 6.x
php = 5.2
```

One again, we set a `name` and `description`. We have also indicate the version of Drupal Core that this module is designed to work with. We also add one new directive, `php = 5.2`, at the end. This directive tells Drupal that the module will only work on servers running PHP 5.2 or later.

While Drupal 6 still runs on PHP 4, it is not advised to run anything on PHP 4. It is now unsupported and is no longer maintained. Instead, PHP 5.2 or later should be used on any server. In fact, Drupal 7 will require at least PHP 5.2.

Our module will make use of a function introduced in PHP 5.2. Therefore, we added this last directive to let Drupal know that an earlier version of PHP will not work for this module.

On rare occasions, I have heard programmers argue that it is "bad practice" to not support PHP 4, since the Drupal Core supports it. This is not the case. PHP 4 has long been deprecated and unsupported. There is no good reason to write applications for it. By noting in the configuration file that our module requires PHP 5.2, we are abiding by good coding practices.

That is all we need for our `.info` file. At this point, if we were to look in **Administer | Site building | Modules**, we would see our module listed there.

The next thing to do is create `bettereditor.module`. This also, goes in `sites/all/modules/bettereditor/`. As you may recall, this is the file that will store our PHP code.

But before we open that file for editing, we will create two more files. These files aren't required by all modules, but our particular module will need them.

The first is a CSS file, and the second is our JavaScript library. These will be called `bettereditor.css` and `bettereditor.js`, respectively. They will go in the `bettereditor/` directory along with our `.info` and `.module` files.

We now have four files in our module. The simplest one, `bettereditor.info`, is already done. Let's take a quick look at the CSS file.

The CSS file

The `bettereditor.css` file provides a few definitions that will be used to style the editor. To be more precise, it contains four class definitions:

```css
.editor-button {
  border: 1px solid gray;
  padding: 3px;
  text-align: center;
  background-color: #eee;
  float: left;
}
.editor-button:hover {
  background-color: #ccc;
}
.button-bar {
  clear: both;
  height: 2em;
}
.strikethrough {
  text-decoration: line-through;
}
```

The first two define how the buttons on our editor should look. The third class definition defines how our button bar should look. The last one, `.strikethrough`, is intended to be applied to text-containing elements. It will display the text as having a single line through it. We will use this last class to demonstrate an additional feature of our new editor.

That's all there is to our CSS file. Next up, we will turn to the `.module` file.

The bettereditor.module file

Our new `.module` file will implement the same pair of hooks that the previous module used, which are `hook_help()` and `hook_init()`:

```php
<?php
// $Id$
/**
 * A better version of the simple editor.
 * @file
 */
/**
 * Implementation of hook_help().
```

```
 */
function bettereditor_help($path, $args) {
  if($path == 'admin/help#bettereditor') {
    return t('This module provides a JavaScript based text \
      editor.');
  }
}
/**
 * Implementation of hook_init().
 */
function bettereditor_init() {
  $buttons = array();
  $buttons[] = array(
    'name' => 'B',
    'tag' => 'strong',
    'style' => 'font-weight: bold',
  );
  $buttons[] = array(
    'name' => 'I',
    'tag' => 'em',
    'style' => 'font-style: italic',
  );
  $buttons[] = array(
    'name' => 'S',
    'tag' => 'del',
    'cssClass' => 'strikethrough',
    'style' => 'text-decoration: line-through',
  );
  $buttons[] = array(
    'name' => 'ul',
    'tag' => array('ul', 'li'),
  );
  $buttons[] = array(
    'name' => 'ol',
    'tag' => array('ol', 'li'),
  );
  $buttons[] = array(
    'name' => 'li',
    'tag' => 'li',
  );
  $buttons[] = array(
    'name' => 'table',
    'tag' => array('table', 'tbody', 'tr', 'td'),
  );
```

```
$buttonJS = json_encode($buttons);
$script = 'BetterEditor.buttons = ' . $buttonJS;
$path = drupal_get_path('module', 'bettereditor');

drupal_add_css($path . '/bettereditor.css');

drupal_add_js($path . '/bettereditor.js');
drupal_add_js($script, 'inline');
}
```

The help function, `bettereditor_help()`, does the same thing here as it did in the previous project. It provides very basic help that will be shown on the help screen for this module. Again, when building a production-quality module, it is a good idea to write longer, more descriptive help text.

The more important part of our module is the `bettereditor_init()` function. As in `jsloader_init()` in the previous project, this function implements Drupal's `hook_init()` hook. This means it will be called toward the beginning of the page-rendering cycle, right after Drupal has finished its own initialization.

Here, we will insert all of the necessary code to load our JavaScript. In our new editor, this will be a little more complex than our previous example.

We will do two things in this function. First, we will define all of the buttons that our editor should have. We will then add the appropriate JavaScript library (`bettereditor.js`) and export our button properties.

Once Drupal has executed our hook, which is called at the beginning of every page load, it will continue with the rest of the processing and finally deliver the finished HTML document to the user. Our goal in using `hook_init()`, is to make this script available to all pages, since we don't know which pages will have text areas and which won't.

Let's look at the first part of the `bettereditor_init()` function:

```
function bettereditor_init() {
  $buttons = array();
  $buttons[] = array(
    'name' => 'B',
    'tag' => 'strong',
    'style' => 'font-weight: bold',
  );
  $buttons[] = array(
    'name' => 'I',
    'tag' => 'em',
    'style' => 'font-style: italic',
```

```
    );
    $buttons[] = array(
       'name' => 'S',
       'tag' => 'del',
       'cssClass' => 'strikethrough',
       'style' => 'text-decoration: line-through',
    );
    $buttons[] = array(
       'name' => 'ul',
       'tag' => array('ul', 'li'),
    );
    $buttons[] = array(
       'name' => 'ol',
       'tag' => array('ol', 'li'),
    );
    $buttons[] = array(
       'name' => 'li',
       'tag' => 'li',
    );
    $buttons[] = array(
       'name' => 'table',
       'tag' => array('table', 'tbody', 'tr', 'td'),
    );
```

This is a big block of very repetitive code. What's going on here?

We are building a nested series of arrays. The $buttons variable contains an array and each position in that array, contains another array. In other words, this is a two-dimensional array (in fact, it is deeper in some places).

In the previous project, I mentioned that PHP arrays can be either numerically indexed arrays ($array[0], $array[1], $array[2]...) or associative arrays with keys and values ($array['key1'], $array['key2']...). In this example, we have both.

The $buttons array is numerically indexed. Here, we do array assignments like this:

```
    $buttons[] = 'something';
```

This has the practical effect of pushing a new value to the end of the array, similar to the JavaScript practice of appending values like this: myArray.push('new value').

Inside each array item in this array, we build a new associative array. The first entry looks like this:

```
$buttons[] = array(
    'name' => 'B',
    'tag' => 'strong',
    'style' => 'font-weight: bold',
);
```

The `array()` function in PHP works as an array constructor of sorts. It builds a new array.

 Unlike their JavaScript counterparts, PHP arrays are not objects. Arrays are a special type in PHP.

The `array()` function can be initialized with a set of data. Here, we are initializing an associative array with a list of keys and values. The syntax is `'key' => 'value'`, and each pair is separated by a comma.

Associative arrays in PHP can be used for most of the purposes that JavaScript object literals are used. In that respect, you might think of the "first entry" we just saw as a PHP equivalent of a JavaScript structure such as this:

```
var buttons = [
  {
    'name': 'B',
    'tag': 'strong',
    'style': 'font-weight: bold'
  }
]
```

While these two constructs are certainly not identical (JavaScript is much more object-oriented than PHP), the basic analogy certainly works as a heuristic when mentally translating between PHP and JavaScript.

 When defining arrays in PHP, it is OK to leave a trailing comma after the last pair or item. In fact, in Drupal, this is a recommended practice because it reduces errors when new array items are coded in at the end of a list.

In this snippet, we add a new array to the first index of the `$buttons` array. This new associative array contains three elements:

```
'name' => 'B',
'tag' => 'strong',
'style' => 'font-weight: bold',
```

Basically, we have invented a data structure that describes our buttons. The data structure is designed to tell us how the button should look and what tag the button should represent.

So in this case, the `name` shown on the button will be B. The `tag` that will wrap selected text will be `strong`. This will be translated to `<strong></strong>` by our JavaScript. Finally, we might want to style the button a little, so we add the `style` property to make the B on the button show as bold text.

Some of the other elements in this array use different properties:

```
$buttons[] = array(
   'name' => 'S',
   'tag' => 'del',
   'cssClass' => 'strikethrough',
   'style' => 'text-decoration: line-through',
);
```

This button also has a `class` set to `strikethrough`. We're going to use this to add a class, not to the button, but to the `tag` before it is inserted. The above definition should create an **S** button that will, when clicked, insert tags such as this:
`<del. class='strikethrough'></del>`.

In our `bettereditor.css` file, we defined a `.strikethrough` class. This is the item for which that class is used.

We will now add a new feature to our editor. So far, we've created buttons that can insert a single tag. What about cases where we want to add multiple tags with the click of a button?

Let's extend our `tag` attribute, allowing it to have an array of values. Here are a few examples:

```
$buttons[] = array(
   'name' => 'ul',
   'tag' => array('ul', 'li'),
);
$buttons[] = array(
   'name' => 'ol',
   'tag' => array('ol', 'li'),
);
$buttons[] = array(
   'name' => 'li',
   'tag' => 'li',
);
```

```
$buttons[] = array(
  'name' => 'table',
  'tag' => array('table', 'tbody', 'tr', 'td'),
);
```

The highlighted rows show cases where more than one tag is provided. We want our editor to automatically nest the tags, with the left-most tag being the outermost tag. Then, the first unordered list definition should create tags like this:

```
<ul>
  <li></li>
</ul>
```

Likewise, the `tag` for `table` should render like the following. It has `table`, `tbody`, `tr`, and `td`:

```
<table>
  <tbody>
    <tr>
      <td></td>
    </tr>
  </tbody>
</table>
```

This data structure describes how we would like our buttons to look and function. It will be the responsibility of the JavaScript code to take these definitions and interpret them. But before we can turn to the JavaScript, we have a few more items to work on in PHP.

Namely, we need to take the `$buttons` array and translate it into JavaScript. We then need to have that data, and the `bettereditor.js` and `bettereditor.css` files, sent back to the client. Let's take a look at the last part of the `bettereditor_init()` function to see how this is done:

```
$buttonJS = json_encode($buttons);
$script = 'BetterEditor.buttons = ' . $buttonJS;
$path = drupal_get_path('module', 'bettereditor');
drupal_add_css($path . '/bettereditor.css');
//drupal_add_js(array('buttons' => $buttons), 'setting');
drupal_add_js($path . '/bettereditor.js');
drupal_add_js($script, 'inline');
```

At this point, we have two interesting choices to make.

Earlier, I mentioned that there were three ways of calling `drupal_add_js()`. Already, we have seen how it can be called to include an entire script file. It can also be used to inject scripts, either in whole or in part, or to add settings to the `Drupal.settings` object.

Right now, we have the buttons defined in $buttons. Should these be added to the Drupal.settings object or sent as a script fragment? Technically speaking, either one can be done.

Adding things to the Drupal.settings array has the advantage of being easier to code (by a few characters). Modules, such as JavaScript Theming, make liberal use of Drupal.settings. But this is not actually a good idea most of the time.

Earlier in the book, we talked about namespaces. The chief rationale for namespacing applies even here. If we just add our settings to Drupal.settings, we may eventually encounter problems where other JavaScript files which use settings with the same name. This will lead to conflicts as two different libraries will try to store their data in the same place. The Drupal API docs (http://api.drupal.org/api/function/drupal_add_js/6) have this to say on the matter:

> *You might want to wrap your actual configuration settings in another variable to prevent the pollution of the Drupal.settings namespace.*

Is the suggestion that we ought to wrap settings in another variable and then use Drupal.settings (creating something like Drupal.settings.BetterEditor.buttons), or that we should use an altogether different variable?

The first option is not good. Frankly, repartitioning a namespace like this is silly. We've now created another namespace inside of a namespace, and for what purpose?

In addition to this, calling the function is even more difficult. That's because we have to add another layer of testing to our array. Our array would look more like this:

```
$buttons = array(
  'BetterEditor' => array(
    'buttons' => array(
      array(
        'name' => 'B',
        'tag' => 'strong',
        // ...
      ),
      array(
        'name' => 'I',
        // ...
      ),
      // and more buttons....
    ),
);
```

Gaining another layer of complexity on the server isn't the only place. When this is encoded as JavaScript, we now have to reference the settings with unwieldy calls like this:

```
alert(Drupal.settings.BetterEditor.buttons[0].name);
```

This does nothing to improve the readability of the code and, given the additional typing we must do to call the variables, increases the probability of typos.

It doesn't really make sense to add all of this complexity just to work with the `Drupal.settings` object.

Instead, let's look at the third form of `drupal_add_js()`. Let's add a script inline. The idea here is to pass a valid snippet of JavaScript code into `drupal_add_js()`. It takes on the responsibility of wrapping this inside of the `<script></script>` tags, and placing it in the document (after all of the other scripts).

This does put a little more of the scripting burden back on you, the coder. But if used correctly, it has the advantage of reducing code complexity on both the client and server side.

This is the approach taken in our code:

```
$buttonJS = json_encode($buttons);
$script = 'BetterEditor.buttons = ' . $buttonJS;
$path = drupal_get_path('module', 'bettereditor');
drupal_add_css($path . '/bettereditor.css');
drupal_add_js($path . '/bettereditor.js');
drupal_add_js($script, 'inline');
```

Here, we need to accomplish the following:

- Turn our big $buttons array into a valid JavaScript fragment
- Include the CSS and the JavaScript file
- Include our script

The order of these last two is not really important. Drupal will sort things out in a particular order. It will always order things with CSS first, then JavaScript libraries, and then custom scripts.

First, we should ask ourself this question. How do we translate $buttons into JavaScript?

It turns out that we have two options again. First, there is a Drupal built-in function, `drupal_to_js()`, that takes an array and converts it to JavaScript. Second, since we are using PHP 5.2, there is a JSON encoding function, `json_encode()`, which can convert PHP data structures to JSON data.

The JSON notation is identical to the JavaScript literal notation. In other words, `json_encode()` will create valid JavaScript.

How do we choose?

There are three key differences between the two:

1. `drupal_to_js()` is available in all platforms that Drupal 6 supports. `json_encode()` requires PHP 5.

2. `json_encode()` is implemented in C code, which means it is very fast. `drupal_to_js()` is written in PHP and is not terribly efficient.

3. `drupal_to_js()` does an extra encoding routine. It encodes HTML-reserved characters (<. >, and &). `json_encode()` adheres strictly to the standard and does not do this encoding.

 In Drupal 7, `drupal_to_js()` has been re-implemented using `json_encode()`. When Drupal 7 is released, the last point will be the only difference.

Choosing the function depends on your needs. We don't need the extra encoding (that would just make one more decoding run on the client), and the speed improvement is nice to have. So I have chosen to use `json_encode()`. But again, this argument can go either way.

With two lines, we can generate a script suitable for sending to the client:

```
$buttonJS = json_encode($buttons);
$script = 'BetterEditor.buttons = ' . $buttonJS;
```

On the second line, we simply create JavaScript that will assign `BetterEditor.buttons` the value of our JSON-encoded `$buttons` array. The variable `$script` will hold the JavaScript data.

We can now add the CSS and JavaScript in three calls:

```
drupal_add_css($path . '/bettereditor.css');
drupal_add_js($path . '/bettereditor.js');
drupal_add_js($script, 'inline');
```

The `drupal_add_css()` function does the same thing for CSS files, that `drupal_add_js()` does for JavaScript.

The first `drupal_add_js()` call adds the `bettereditor.js` script, which we have not yet created.

The last line adds the `BetterEditor.buttons` data as an inline script. Note that the string `inline`, which is passed in as the second parameter, tells Drupal to include this as an inline script, instead of interpreting `$script` as a file name.

If we were to enable the module (you can do this now) and then load a page, we would see something like this in the source code:

```
<script type="text/javascript">
BetterEditor.buttons = [
  {"name":"B","tag":"strong","style":"font-weight: bold"},
  {"name":"I","tag":"em","style":"font-style: italic"},
  {"name":"S","tag":"del","cssClass":"strikethrough",
     "style":"text-decoration: line-through"},
  {"name":"ul","tag":["ul","li"]},
  {"name":"ol","tag":["ol","li"]},{"name":"li","tag":"li"},
  {"name":"table","tag":["table","tbody","tr","td"]}
]
</script>
```

This array of object literals is the result of running `json_encode()` over the PHP array. When our script loads and is executed, the previous data will all be available to it.

That's all there is to our module file. The last thing to do is work on the `bettereditor.js` script.

The bettereditor.js script

The last file of the project is the `bettereditor.js` script. This file will contain a modified version of the `simpleeditor.js` script we created in Chapter 4. Since we won't go over the repeated pieces, you may find it helpful to skim the relevant section of that chapter again.

The script has undergone a few changes. First, the namespace object is now `BetterEditor` instead of `SimpleEditor`. Second, there are three new theming functions. Third, the internals of a few functions have changed to accommodate the new server-provided `BetterEditor.buttons` data.

Let's start with a quick glance at the code:

```
// $Id$
/**
 * A better version of the simple editor.
 * @file
 */
```

```
var BetterEditor = BetterEditor || {};
BetterEditor.selection = null;

/**
 * Record changes to a select box.
 */
BetterEditor.watchSelection = function () {
  BetterEditor.selection = Drupal.getSelection(this);
  BetterEditor.selection.id = $(this).attr('id');
};

/**
 * Attaches the editor toolbar.
 */
Drupal.behaviors.editor = function () {
  $('textarea:not(.editor-processed)')
    .addClass('editor-processed')
    .mouseup(BetterEditor.watchSelection)
    .keyup(BetterEditor.watchSelection)
    .each(function (item) {
      var txtarea = $(this);
      var txtareaID = txtarea.attr('id');

      var buttons = [];
      for (var i = 0; i < BetterEditor.buttons.length; ++i) {
        button = BetterEditor.buttons[i];
        buttons.push(Drupal.theme('button', button));
      }

      var id = 'buttons-' + txtareaID;
      var bar = $(Drupal.theme('buttonBar', buttons, id));

      $(bar).insertBefore('#' + txtareaID)
        .children('.editor-button')
        .click(function () {
          var txtareaEle = $('#' + txtareaID).get(0);
          var sel = BetterEditor.selection;
          if (sel.id == txtareaID && sel.start != sel.end) {
            var buttonName = $(this).html();
            var targetButton = null;
            for (i = 0; i < BetterEditor.buttons.length; ++i) {
              if (BetterEditor.buttons[i].name == buttonName) {
                targetButton = BetterEditor.buttons[i];
                break;
              }
            }

            if (targetButton) {
```

```
                    txtareaEle.value = BetterEditor.insertTag(
                      sel.start,
                      sel.end,
                      targetButton,
                      txtareaEle.value
                    );
                }
                sel.start = sel.end = -1;
            }
        });
    });
};
/**
 * Insert a tag.
 *
 * @param start
 *   Location to insert start tag.
 * @param end
 *   Location to insert end tag.
 * @param tag
 *   Tag to insert.
 * @param value
 *   String to insert tag into.
 */
BetterEditor.insertTag = function (start, end, tag, value) {
    var front = value.substring(0, start);
    var middle = value.substring(start, end);
    var back = value.substring(end);
    var formatted = Drupal.theme('addTag', tag, middle);
    return front + formatted + back;
};

/**
 * Theme a button bar.
 *
 * @param buttons
 *   Array of buttons that should be added.
 * @param id
 *   ID for the button bar. This is used to distinguish button
 *   bars on screens where there are multiple editors.
 *
 * @return
 *   Themed button bar as a string of HTML.
 */
```

```
Drupal.theme.prototype.buttonBar = function (buttons, id) {
  var buttonBar = $('<div class="button-bar"></div>')
    .attr('id', id);

  jQuery.each(buttons, function (i, item) {
    buttonBar.append(item);
  });

  return buttonBar.parent().html();
};
/**
 * Theme an individual button.
 *
 * @param button
 *   Individual button object.
 *
 * @return
 *   Themed button HTML as a string.
 */
Drupal.theme.prototype.button = function (button) {
  var tag = $('<div class="editor-button"></div>');

  if (button.style) {
    tag.attr('style', button.style);
  }

  return tag.html(button.name).parent().html();
};
/**
 * Theme a tag before inserting it into the text area.
 * This wraps text inside of the appropriate tags. If the
 * button object contains an array of tags, then the tags
 * will be nested, with the text in the innermost tag.
 *
 * @param button
 *   Button object that describes what the button does.
 * @param text
 *   Text that the tag will be wrapped around.
 */
Drupal.theme.prototype.addTag = function (button, text) {
  var tag = null;
  if (button.tag instanceof Array && button.tag.length > 0) {

    var placeholder = $('body')
      .append('<div class='placeholder'></div>')
      .children('.placeholder').hide();
    var current = placeholder; // Copy for working with
```

```
        jQuery.each(button.tag, function (i, data) {
          var newTag = '<' + data + '>\n</' + data + '>\n';
          current.append(newTag);
          if (button.cssClass) {
            current.addClass(button.cssClass);
          }
          current = current.children();
          if (i == button.tag.length -1) {
            current.html(text);
          }
        });
        var html = placeholder.html();
        placeholder.remove();
        return html;
      }
      else {
        tag = $('<' + button.tag + '></' + button.tag + '>');
        if (button.cssClass) {
          tag.addClass(button.cssClass);
        }
        return tag.html(text).parent().html();
      }
    };
```

This is the largest chunk of code we have seen in any single project. Fortunately, much of it is repeated from our earlier project.

Other than the transition from `SimpleEditor` to `BetterEditor`, the first part of the code has not changed. For that reason, we will skip the opening definitions and the `BetterEditor.watchSelection()` function, which simply track what part of the text area is selected.

The editor() behavior

We will begin with the behavior `Drupal.behaviors.editor()`. This function is called when the document is ready, as well as any time a major DOM change results in behaviors being reattached:

```
Drupal.behaviors.editor = function () {
  $('textarea:not(.editor-processed)')
    .addClass('editor-processed')
    .mouseup(BetterEditor.watchSelection)
    .keyup(BetterEditor.watchSelection)
    .each(function (item) {
```

```
        var txtarea = $(this);
        var txtareaID = txtarea.attr('id');

        var buttons = [];
        for (i = 0; i < BetterEditor.buttons.length; ++i) {
          button = BetterEditor.buttons[i];
          buttons.push(Drupal.theme('button', button));
        }

        var id = 'buttons-' + txtareaID;
        var bar = $(Drupal.theme('buttonBar', buttons, id));

        $(bar).insertBefore('#' + txtareaID)
          .children('.editor-button')
          .click(function () {
            var txtareaEle = $('#' + txtareaID).get(0);
            var sel = BetterEditor.selection;
            if(sel.id == txtareaID && sel.start != sel.end) {
              var buttonName = $(this).html();
              var targetButton = null;
              for (i = 0; i < BetterEditor.buttons.length; ++i){
                if (BetterEditor.buttons[i].name == buttonName){
                  targetButton = BetterEditor.buttons[i];
                  break;
                }
              }
              if (targetButton) {
                txtareaEle.value = BetterEditor.insertTag(
                  sel.start,
                  sel.end,
                  targetButton,
                  txtareaEle.value
                );
              }
              sel.start = sel.end = -1;
            }
          });
      });
  };
```

The main jQuery chain has not changed:

```
$('textarea:not(.editor-processed)')
    .addClass('editor-processed')
    .mouseup(BetterEditor.watchSelection)
    .keyup(BetterEditor.watchSelection)
    .each( /* anonymous function here */);
```

This finds all unprocessed text areas and adds a few things. First, it adds the class to indicate that the textarea has been processed. Next, it adds two event handlers. When a mouse button is released, or when a key on the keyboard is released, the `BetterEditor.watchSelection()` function will be executed.

Finally, it uses the `$().each()` function to loop through every textarea and adds the editor.

Let's turn to the function called inside of `$().each()`:

```
function (item) {
  var txtarea = $(this);
  var txtareaID = txtarea.attr('id');

  var buttons = [];
  for (i = 0; i < BetterEditor.buttons.length; ++i) {
    button = BetterEditor.buttons[i];
    buttons.push(Drupal.theme('button', button));
  }

  var id = 'buttons-' + txtareaID;
  var bar = $(Drupal.theme('buttonBar', buttons, id));

  $(bar).insertBefore('#' + txtareaID)
    .children('.editor-button')
    .click(function () {
      var txtareaEle = $('#' + txtareaID).get(0);
      var sel = BetterEditor.selection;
      if(sel.id == txtareaID && sel.start != sel.end) {
        var buttonName = $(this).html();
        var targetButton = null;
        for (i = 0; i < BetterEditor.buttons.length; ++i) {
          if (BetterEditor.buttons[i].name == buttonName) {
            targetButton = BetterEditor.buttons[i];
            break;
          }
        }

        if (targetButton) {
          txtareaEle.value = BetterEditor.insertTag(
            sel.start,
            sel.end,
            targetButton,
            txtareaEle.value
          );
        }
```

```
                sel.start = sel.end = -1;
              }
          });
```

The basic job of this function is to attach the editor to the passed-in textarea. The highlighted sections represent the areas where changes have been made.

The function starts by setting up a few variables with information about the target textarea element. After this is a `for` loop:

```
var buttons = [];
for (i = 0; i < BetterEditor.buttons.length; ++i) {
  button = BetterEditor.buttons[i];
  buttons.push(Drupal.theme('button', button));
}
```

The buttons array, which was declared on the first line, will hold all of the themed buttons. How do we get those? We loop through the values in `BetterEditor.buttons` (this is the array we created on the server) and pass that data into a theming function. Later, we will see how the `Drupal.theme.prototype.button()` function themes buttons.

We now have information about the target text areas and a themed list of buttons. The next step is to turn our buttons into a button bar:

```
var bar = $(Drupal.theme('buttonBar', buttons, id));
```

This uses another new theme, `Drupal.theme.prototype.buttonBar()`. This takes a list of buttons and returns a single chunk of HTML which will function as the button bar.

The next thing to do is insert our new button bar into the document immediately before the textarea. This is also done with a jQuery chain:

```
$(bar).insertBefore('#' + txtareaID)
  .children('.editor-button')
  .click( /* anonymous function here */ );
```

This inserts the new button bar, and then adds a `click` handler to every child of the button bar. What are the children of the button bar? Those are the nodes one-level down (the individual buttons we created before. Therefore, each one of these buttons will be assigned a `click` event handler.

The `click` handler has changed since the `SimpleEditor` version. Let's take a look at this new version:

```
function () {
  var txtareaEle = $('#' + txtareaID).get(0);
```

```
    var sel = BetterEditor.selection;
    if(sel.id == txtareaID && sel.start != sel.end) {
      var buttonName = $(this).html();
      var targetButton = null;
      for (i = 0; i < BetterEditor.buttons.length; ++i) {
        if (BetterEditor.buttons[i].name == buttonName) {
          targetButton = BetterEditor.buttons[i];
          break;
        }
      }

      if (targetButton) {
        txtareaEle.value = BetterEditor.insertTag(
          sel.start,
          sel.end,
          targetButton,
          txtareaEle.value
        );
      }
      sel.start = sel.end = -1;
    }
});
```

The code above has been highlighted even more carefully to show the particular lines that were changed.

This function handles the response to a button click. For example, when a user clicks on, the **B** button, this event handler needs to figure out what button was clicked. Then it takes the appropriate action, which means it finds the selected text and surrounds it with the `<strong></strong>` tags.

The first `if` statement in this function determines whether or not a portion of the document has been selected. As you may recall, our initial design for the editor only wrapped HTML around the existing selected text (it did not insert empty tags).

Once inside of the `if` statement, we need to find out what button was called. To do this, we will match the button's name with the text inside of the button element. Here's why this works.

We know that the bold button will be named B. That is, we know that the text displayed to the user will be **B**. We also know that this value comes directly from the `button` object's `name` property.

So in the click handler function, we can get the HTML value of the button using `$(this).html()`. This gets stored in `buttonName`. We can then loop through all of the buttons in `BetterEditor.buttons` looking for an object with a name equal to the value of `buttonName`. Using our previous example, if a user clicks on a button with the name B, `buttonName` would have the value B. As this code loops through `BetterEditor.buttons`, it will hit the first object:

```
{"name":"B","tag":"strong","style":"font-weight: bold"},
```

It has the name B. So that object will be stored in `targetButton` and the loop will be terminated by the `break` statement. After all, there's no point continuing to loop through the list of buttons if we have already found a match.

Now that we have identified the correct button object, we can find what tag(s) we should use when inserting that button.

The following part of the code simply checks to make sure a button has been found. There is the possibility that something might go wrong and a bogus button may be displayed on the button bar:

```
if (targetButton) {
  txtareaEle.value = BetterEditor.insertTag(
    sel.start,
    sel.end,
    targetButton,
    txtareaEle.value
  );
}
```

If a button object has been found to answer the `click` event, the `BetterEditor.insertTag()` function is executed. In the old version, some HTML formatting was passed in the third argument of the function. Now, the target button object is passed.

Let's turn to that function and see what it does.

The insertTag() function

This function is responsible for finding the correct piece of text and inserting the HTML. It is largely unchanged from the Simple Editor version in Chapter 4. However, we will cover some differences that exist here:

```
BetterEditor.insertTag = function (start, end, tag, value) {
  var front = value.substring(0, start);
  var middle = value.substring(start, end);
  var back = value.substring(end);
  var formatted = Drupal.theme('addTag', tag, middle);
  return front + formatted + back;
};
```

As you may recall, this function proceeds by finding the selected text (captured in the `middle` variable). It then surrounds the selected text with tags, rebuilds the content, and then sends it back to the calling function.

This function has been changed slightly. Instead of building the HTML markup, it passes the button data (stored in the `tag` variable) to a theming function. The theming function, `Drupal.theme.prototype.addTag()`, does the actual formatting and returns a formatted string.

`BetterEditor.insertTag()` simply rebuilds the contents of the textarea and sends the data back to the calling function.

Not much is new in this function. However, the functionality of the `addTag` theme is surprisingly complex. We have three functions left to look at. Let's begin with `Drupal.theme.prototype.addTag()`.

The addTag() theme

The three theming functions, which we are about to look at, are all new in `BetterEditor`. We will begin with the most complex.

`Drupal.theme.prototype.addTag()` is responsible for taking some text and wrapping it in the appropriate HTML. It is passed two arguments. First, the `button` object for the button that was just clicked. This contains the data passed from the server. The second argument is the text that should be surrounded:

```
Drupal.theme.prototype.addTag = function (button, text) {
  var tag = null;
  if (button.tag instanceof Array && button.tag.length > 0) {
    var placeholder = $('body')
      .append('<div class='placeholder'></div>')
      .children('.placeholder').hide();
    var current = placeholder; // Copy for working with
    jQuery.each(button.tag, function (i, data) {
      var newTag = '<' + data + '>\n</' + data + '>\n';
      current.append(newTag);
      if (button.cssClass) {
        current.addClass(button.cssClass);
      }
      current = current.children();
      if (i == button.tag.length -1) {
        current.html(text);
      }
    });
```

```
     var html = placeholder.html();
     placeholder.remove();
     return html;
   }
 else {
   tag = $('<' + button.tag + '></' + button.tag + '>');
   if (button.cssClass) {
     tag.addClass(button.cssClass);
   }
   return tag.html(text).parent().html();
 }
};
```

To get our bearings before we look at this code, let's look back at the `button.tag` property that we defined.

Here's the JSON data for the **B** button:

```
{
  "name":"B",
  "tag":"strong",
  "style":"font-weight: bold"
},
```

Now compare that to our `table` button:

```
{
  "name":"table",
  "tag":[
    "table",
    "tbody",
    "tr",
    "td"
  ]
}
```

The `table` button has an array of tags, while the B button only has a single tag value. So when a user clicks on the B button, the highlighted text will only be surrounded by one pair of tags: `<strong></strong>`.

But if the user were to click on the table button, the text should be nested in the middle of this tag set: `<table><tbody><tr><td> </td></tr></tbody></table>`. The `Drupal.theme.prototype.addTag()` function that we are now examining is responsible for handling these two cases.

The function begins by making a quick choice based on the type of data inside of the button.tag object:

```
if (button.tag instanceof Array && button.tag.length > 0) {
  // Complex case: Nested tags
}
else {
  // Simple case: One tag.
}
```

If the button.tag object is an array, we should assume that we will be working with nested tags. Otherwise, we will assume that there is only one tag.

> If we were building a production quality version of this, we would spend more time evaluating the button.tag object. We might try to streamline the case where the button.tag array has only one item. We might also try to account for cases where no tag data was supplied on the server (an issue that doesn't concern our closed-system example here). But for the sake of brevity, we will cover a simplified case.

Let's quickly dispense with the second case, where button.tag is not an array. In this case, we simply take the value of the tag and create start and end tags out of it. We then wrap that in a jQuery object named tag:

```
if (button.tag instanceof Array && button.tag.length > 0) {
 /* Handle array case */
else {
  tag = $('<' + button.tag + '></' + button.tag + '>');
  if (button.cssClass) {
    tag.addClass(button.cssClass);
  }
  return tag.html(text).parent().html();
}
```

If the button.class object is set (recall that the s button had a class property), we add that too. Finally, wrap the tag around the passed-in text, and return a text representation of the HTML.

Let's now turn back to the more complicated case of nested tags:

```
if (button.tag instanceof Array && button.tag.length > 0) {
  var placeholder = $('body')
    .append('<div class='placeholder'></div>')
    .children('.placeholder').hide();
```

```
        var current = placeholder; // Copy for working with
        jQuery.each(button.tag, function (i, data) {
            var newTag = '<' + data + '>\n</' + data + '>\n';
            current.append(newTag);
            if (button.cssClass) {
                current.addClass(button.cssClass);
            }
            current = current.children();
            if (i == button.tag.length -1) {
                current.html(text);
            }
        });
        var html = placeholder.html();
        placeholder.remove();
        return html;
    }
    else {
        tag = $('<' + button.tag + '></' + button.tag + '>');
        if (button.class) {
            tag.addClass(button.class);
        }
        return tag.html(text).parent().html();
    }
```

There are a couple of ways to do this sort of tag building. I chose a method that made use of jQuery, and that seemed simple to me.

Let's start with the first few lines:

```
var placeholder = $('body')
    .append('<div class='placeholder'></div>')
    .children('.placeholder').hide();
var current = placeholder; // Copy for working with
```

First, we need a root jQuery object to work with. But we don't have any tags to work with at the beginning. So we just create a pair of tags that we don't really need. However, IE requires that these tags be a part of the document. So we append them to the end of the body, and then hide the div so that it won't disrupt the user experience. Once we have the placeholder, the first thing we do is make a copy of it in current. Why is this done? We are going to use current to traverse down the DOM as we create it, but placeholder will always point to the top-level placeholder node.

Next, we will loop through each of the items in `button.tag`, create an element, and then set that as the root element. In essence, we are creating the DOM and descending it as we go.

Here's how that happens. The anonymous function is called once for each tag. It begins by constructing a string representing the new tag:

```
jQuery.each(button.tag, function (i, data) {
  var newTag = '<' + data + '>\n</' + data + '>\n';
      current.append(newTag);
  if (button.class) {
    current.addClass(button.class);
  }
  current = current.children();
  if (i == button.tag.length -1) {
    current.html(text);
  }
});
```

The `newTag` variable holds the new tag data, and `current` points to the current node (starting with the `placeholder` that we created).

 Note that the `newTag` string has `\n` line endings encoded into it. This causes the output to be displayed with line breaks and makes it easier to read in an HTML editing environment like the one we are creating.

The `newTag` is appended to as the last child of `current`.

Next, if there is a `class` property on this button, we add the class to the current element.

 According to this setup, the same class is added to all of the tags in `button.tag`. In practice, that is not usually desirable. Alternatives to this may be to ignore the `button.class` properties for nested tags, or to simply add the class only to the first tag in a nested series.

After this, we reset `current` to `current.children()`:

```
current = current.children();
```

Here, we are changing the jQuery object to point at the new element that we just created. For example, let's take the case of an unordered list. We will begin with a DOM representable like this:

```
<div class='placeholder'></div>
```

The `current` variable points to this element. The first time through the `jQuery.each()` iterator, the DOM is changed to this:

```
<div class='placeholder'>
  <ul></ul>
</div>
```

First the tag is added. Next, when `current = current.children()` is executed, the current node is moved from `<div></div>` down to the child element `<ul></ul>`.

The next time through the loop, the new tag `<li></li>` will be added. It is appended to the end of `current`, and `current` points to the `<ul></ul>` element. The result is a DOM fragment looking like this:

```
<div class='placeholder'>
  <ul>
    <li></li>
  </ul>
</div>
```

All we need to do now is add the text. This is easy because we know from the outset how deep the DOM fragment will be, based on the number of things in the `button.tag` array:

```
if (i == button.tag.length -1) {
  current.html(text);
}
```

Once our counter (maintained by `jQuery.each()`) is only one less than the length of the array, we know we are in the innermost tag and can add the text here. This results in a DOM fragment looking something like this:

```
<div class='placeholder'>
  <ul>
    <li>Text Here!</li>
  </ul>
</div>
```

We are done creating the DOM fragment. Since we still have our placeholder variable pointing to the main `div`, we can get our newly marked up text with a call to `placeholder.html()`. Remember, since `$().html()` returns only the children of the present node, the current node is not returned. In other words, given the HTML we have in the previous DOM fragment, the following will be returned by `placeholder.html()`:

```
<ul>
  <li>Text Here!</li>
</ul>
```

The placeholder is not present in the results as only the children of the placeholder were returned. Once we are done with our special-purpose placeholder, we remove it from the DOM using `placeholder.remove()`.

At the end of the `Drupal.theme.prototype.addTag()` function, a string containing the HTML markup is returned. As this gets passed back to the `BetterEditor.insertTag()` function, the contents for the textarea are recreated. The new text is returned back to the click event handler, which inserts the text into the textarea. And, voila! The user sees the new HTML wrapped around the selected text as seen here:

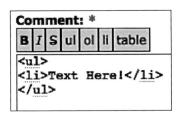

We have made it through the most complicated parts. Just two theme functions are left.

The button() theme function

While looking at `Drupal.behaviors.editor()`, we saw the `Drupal.theme.prototype.button()` theme get called. That theme is responsible for taking a button object and turning it into an HTML button. In Simple Editor, this was handled by some very generic string concatenation and a little bit of jQuery. We haven't gained much sophistication in moving to themes. The code is simple:

```
Drupal.theme.prototype.button = function (button) {
  var tag = $('<div class="editor-button"></div>');

  if (button.style) {
    tag.attr('style', button.style);
  }

  return tag.html(button.name).parent().html();
}
```

The button object is passed in. We create a jQuery object with the base `<div></div>` tag. If the `button` object has a `style` property, we add a `style` attribute to the `div` tag. For example, with the **B** button, we add `style='text-weight: bold'` to the `div` tag.

Finally, we run one last jQuery chain, adding the button name as the text content of the `div` tag. We then returning the whole thing as a string containing HTML.

Every button is passed through this theme function. Together, all of the buttons are handed over to the `Drupal.theme.prototype.buttonBar()` function for additional theming.

The buttonBar() theme function

The `Drupal.theme.prototype.buttonBar()` theme is also very straightforward. It's job is to take an array of buttons and combine them into a single button bar. Since more than one button bar may exist on a page, each button bar needs to have its own ID.

Here's the theme:

```
Drupal.theme.prototype.buttonBar = function (buttons, id) {
  var buttonBar = $('<div class="button-bar"></div>')
    .attr('id', id);
    jQuery.each(buttons, function (i, item) {
    buttonBar.append(item);
  });
    return  buttonBar.parent().html();
}
```

First, the new button bar jQuery object is created and the ID is appended.

Next, we loop through each of the items in the `buttons` array and append each one to the button bar.

Finally, the button bar is converted to an HTML string and returned. It is then inserted by our main behavior, `Drupal.behaviors.editor()`, into the appropriate place in the DOM.

We have made it through our largest project. Although we began with an existing project, there has been a substantial amount of information to cover. However, we have created a second module. A module tied closely to server-generated content.

A last question

There is a question that might arise in regard to this last project. Why involve the server in the process the way that we did? Why not simply create the buttons in JavaScript to begin with?

The point of this project was to exhibit how data could be passed from the server. However, if we wanted to delve into a little more PHP, we could derive even more from server integration. We could, for example, use the Forms API (FAPI) to create an administration form, which would allow system administrators to select the buttons that should appear on a form, or even define their own buttons.

We could also use the input filter logic (which determines what tags are allowed in a given input box) to determine which buttons are displayed to the user.

In short, there are many directions we could go with our server-side development. But we have hit the boundaries defined for this book. Delving into serious PHP programming is beyond our scope. Of course, if you are interested in Drupal 6 PHP development, you might like my book *Learning Drupal 6 Module Development*, Packt Publishing, *978-1847194442*.

Summary

The focus of this chapter was on module development. We set out to use Drupal modules as a way to encapsulate JavaScript functionality. We did this in a way that would be portable across themes and even across Drupal installations. During this chapter, we created two projects. The first was a script autoloader that provided module-side .info file processing for scripts. This essentially replicated the behavior of themes and their .info files.

Our second project was more ambitious. Starting with the code from the Simple Editor that we created in Chapter 4, we created a Better Editor. This editor obtained configuration information from the server, allowing the JavaScript editor to be customized from PHP.

In the next and final chapter, we will focus again on Drupal JavaScript libraries and add-ons. Now that we know how to create modules, we have a more robust toolset for future projects.

Integrating and Extending 9

In this final chapter, we will look at a few advanced topics. We will look at integrating existing Drupal JavaScript tools with our own site design, and then we will see how to extend the JavaScript libraries with the jQuery UI library. Finally, we will take one more step and extend jQuery's library with our own functions, building a jQuery plug-in in the process.

We will cover the following:

- Using the `autocomplete.js` Drupal library
- Installing and using the jQuery UI library
- Building a custom jQuery plug-in
- Using a custom jQuery plug-in both inside and outside of Drupal

As with the previous chapter, the focus of this chapter will be on completing projects.

Project: autocompletion and search

One of the more successful Web 2.0 uses of JavaScript has been autocompletion. Start typing a search term in a text entry field and the browser displays a list of suggested terms. Type a few more characters and the list changes as you type, refining and narrowing the terms that might be completions of what you are typing. This is known as **autocompletion**.

How does autocompletion work? Here's what happens behind the scenes. As you type text into the field, a piece of JavaScript is monitoring the field, sending AJAX requests to the server to tell it what text you have entered so far. The server then does some preliminary searching or matching routine and returns data to the JavaScript. The script then displays the choices that match. Usually, the script displays the options in a way that makes them look like part of a combo box (a text entry field with a selectable list).

There are a lot of nuances to autocompletion scripts. How often should the script perform its AJAX query? If queries happen too often, autocompletion becomes a performance burden. If they happen too rarely, the autocomplete functionality will be useless. Should the script send short strings (such as 'is') to the server? How many results should it show? These and other such questions make implementing autocompletion a sizable task.

The Drupal Core makes use of autocompletion in several places. For that reason, Drupal developers created a special-purpose JavaScript library that provides the client-side facilities. This library can then be used to add autocompletion to other text fields on your site.

One area where autocomplete is not enabled in Drupal is on the search pages. As always, there are a variety of reasons for this, the most important being performance. Having lots of autocompletion scripts, on various clients, all running numerous searches would significantly increase the load on the search engine.

In our first project, we are going to devise a simple autocompletion tool for searches.

The theory

At one time I was on a team charged with analyzing a large-scale search implementation for a web site that handled hundreds of thousands of hits a day. Sifting through the search data, we were surprised to find that while there were many thousands of unique searches; most of the searches were for one of the eighty different search strings. We could reduce the load on our server by almost 75 percent simply by caching the results for those eighty search strings.

We can extrapolate from this example. Perhaps autocompletion would be useful if the server only returned a subset of all of the possible search terms. That subset would have to reflect the popular information on the site in order to be useful. Implementing things this way could cost less performance-wise, while still being useful to the user.

Our plan

For our implementation, we will add autocompletion to the search field in the search module's block. But rather than running a search for each autocompletion request, we will build a scaled-down list of terms that we will define. Only that list of terms will be used for autocompletion.

If this were a book on PHP development, I would suggest writing some server-side code to collect and analyze search engine data, and then use that information to pre-populate an autocompletion field. But we can't readily get that information. So we will try another approach.We will use a Drupal taxonomy as the source for our suggestions.

Taking this approach, we will allow content creators to add keywords to articles. Those keywords will then be used for autocompletion.

First step: creating the taxonomy

We are going to use a taxonomy to seed our search terms. Drupal taxonomies are collections of terms that are sometimes structured (such as a hierarchy of categories) and sometimes unstructured (such as user-entered tags). Using taxonomies you can add keywords, categories, and tags to the content on your site. But there are many other uses for taxonomies. Ours will be used for providing our search autocompletion with a list of suggestions.

 On occasion, Drupal uses the term **vocabulary** instead of taxonomy. Sometimes, a tenuous distinction is made (a taxonomy is made up of vocabularies, which are in turn made up of terms). Practically speaking, the term 'vocabulary' is a synonym for taxonomy.

The taxonomy will be created through Drupal's administrative interface. Our new taxonomy will be called **Tags**. Here is the relevant portion of the taxonomy creation page:

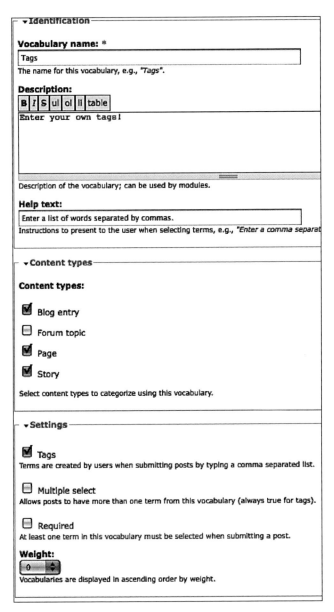

The taxonomy defined in the screenshot will be applied to all of our content types and will use a tagging structure. When a user creates new content, she or he can add tags, which in turn will be used by our autocompletion tool.

Since it has been applied to all content types, any time we go to the **Create content** page and create a new node, we should have the option of tagging that content. Here's a new piece of content:

Title: *
> Story with lots of tags

Tags:
> access, alabama, alba, albacore, albania, albatross, alexander, alexy, algeria, allowed, almost, altimeter, anaximander

Enter a list of words separated by commas.

-- ▸ **Menu settings**

[Split summary at cursor]

Body:
B *I* S ul oi li table

> Albatross and Albacore traveled from Albania to Alabama, and then went on to algeria. There, they almost allowed Alexander, called Alexy, and his brother Anaximander access to an altimeter.

Here we added just over a dozen tags to the story. When we finish with this project, those tags should be displayed as autocompletion recommendations when a user types the appropriate text into a search box.

Next, we need to go into **Administer | Site building | Modules** and turn on the **Search** module (if it's not already on). Once you have enabled that, you should also go to the **Administer | Site building | Blocks** page and put the **Search** block into one of the regions. Our script will turn that **Search** block's text field into an autocompletion field.

We are now finished with our preparations. We can move on to the code.

> It is wise to manually run Cron before continuing. The new content we just created will not be available to your search engine until the re-indexing operation has been run. Cron will run that operation.

The new module

We are going to implement our new package as a module. Creating JavaScript-centered modules was covered in the previous chapter. Nothing new will be introduced here.

To begin with, we will create our new module in the appropriate directory. Under the Drupal root, we create the directory `sites/all/modules/search_autocomplete/`. In that directory, we will create the `.info`, `.module`, and `.js` files.

Here are the contents of `search_autocomplete.info`:

```
; $Id$
name = Search Autocomplete
description = Provide autocompletion for search fields
dependencies[] = search
core = 6.x
```

We only need the bare minimum for our module. We added one new directive `dependencies[]`, which indicates that this module depends upon another module. In this case, it is the `search` module that comes with Drupal.

> The square brackets (`[]`) at the end of the dependencies directive indicate that the directive can have multiple lines. If we need to declare another dependency, we should do so by adding another line like this: `dependency[] = another_module`.

Next, we need some boilerplate PHP code to add the appropriate JavaScript files and set a few variables that will be sent to the JavaScript. This code is similar to the modules we created in the previous chapter. Here is the `search_autocomplete.module` file in its entirety:

```php
<?php

/**
 * Provide autocomplete functionality to Drupal search.
 * @file
 */

/**
 * Implementation of hook_help().
 */
function search_autocomplete_help($path) {
  if ($path == 'admin/help#search_autocomplete') {
    return t('Provide autocompletion to Drupal search.');
  }
}

/**
 * Implementation of hook_init().
 */
function search_autocomplete_init() {
  $path = drupal_get_path('module', 'search_autocomplete');
```

```
    // The Taxonomy ID.
    $tid = 2;

    $autocomplete_uri = url('taxonomy/autocomplete/' . $tid);
    $inline = 'SearchAutocomplete.url = "' .
      $autocomplete_uri . '";';

    drupal_add_js($inline, 'inline');
    drupal_add_js('misc/autocomplete.js');
    drupal_add_js($path . '/search_autocomplete.js');
}
```

The `search_autocomplete_init()` function is very important. It implements the Drupal `hook_init()` hook, which means this function will be run when Drupal initializes on each request.

For our module, the duty of this function is to send the correct JavaScript to the client.

The first line simply gets the URL path to the current module. `$path` can then be used to construct URLs.

Next, we do a little bit of hard coding. We set `$tid` (the Drupal shorthand term for **Taxonomy ID**) to 2. This is the TID of the taxonomy we just created.

Finding the ID of a taxonomy

One easy way of finding an ID for your taxonomy is to go to **Administer | Content management | Taxonomy** and then click **list terms** for your taxonomy. Your browser will display a URL like this: `http://example.com/admin/content/taxonomy/2`. The number at the end (**2**) is your TID.

For the sake of simplicity, this has been hard coded. If we were to spend some more time coding with PHP, we might create an administrative interface for choosing the taxonomy we want to use. We could then augment the previous function , to retrieve the appropriate taxonomy ID from the database. But since our focus is on JavaScript, and not PHP, we will forgo the better solution in favor of the most expedient.

Our AJAX form, when we create it, will need to callback to the server. The server will need to provide the correct taxonomy terms to the client. How are we going to get that list?

Fortunately, Drupal again has a tool that we can use. There is a built-in taxonomy autocompletion script that comes standard with the taxonomy module. We can reuse that feature. All we need to do is pass the correct URL down to the client-side JavaScript, which we will do in three simple steps:

```
$autocomplete_uri = url('taxonomy/autocomplete/' . $tid);
$inline = 'SearchAutocomplete.url = "' .
  $autocomplete_uri . '";';

drupal_add_js($inline, 'inline');
```

First, we use the `url()` function, a Drupal built-in, to create a URL pointing to the relative path `taxonomy/autocomplete/2`. (2 is the ID of our taxonomy and is stored in `$tid`.)

Next, we build that into a JavaScript fragment, which will look something like this:

```
SearchAutocomplete.url =
  'http://example.com/taxonomy/autocomplete/2';
```

That data is stored in `$inline`.

On the third line, we send the previous code to the client in the form of an inline script. This is similar to the way we passed settings to the Better Editor in the previous chapter.

We have now finished the brunt of the configuration for our autocompletion script. The last thing to do is make sure that our two necessary JavaScript libraries are loaded by the client. That is done with the following two lines:

```
drupal_add_js('misc/autocomplete.js');
drupal_add_js($path . '/search_autocomplete.js');
```

The first script added is the Drupal `autocomplete.js` library, which is stored in the `misc/` directory.

The second script added is our `search_autocomplete.js`—a file that we will look at next.

That is all that there is to our server-side component.

The search autocomplete JavaScript

The last thing we need to do is create a JavaScript tool that will turn our plain old search box into an autocomplete-capable search box.

We will put this code in `search_autocomplete.js`, the last JavaScript file that we added in our `hook_init()` implementation.

The main task of this code will be to modify the search block in order to turn it into an autocomplete function, and then let the Drupal autocomplete behavior do the requisite processing on that field.

Here is the code in its entirety:

```
// $Id$

/**
 * Turn the search block into an autocomplete form.
 * @file
 */

var SearchAutocomplete = SearchAutocomplete || {};

$(document).ready(function () {
  $('input[name="search_block_form"]:not(.form-autocomplete)')
    .each(function () {
    var newId = $(this).attr('id') + '-autocomplete';
    var newElement = $('<input type="hidden"/>')
      .addClass('autocomplete')
      .attr('id', newId).attr('disabled','disabled')
      .attr('value', SearchAutocomplete.url);

    $(this).after(newElement);

  }).addClass('form-autocomplete');

  Drupal.attachBehaviors();
});
```

The first thing done here is to create an empty `SearchAutocomplete` object. This will be our namespace. In our PHP code, we added an inline script that adds the `SearchAutocomplete.url` object, so we need to make sure that that namespace exists here in order for that script to successfully run.

Next, we handle the remainder of our code using the jQuery `ready` event.

But wait! Why aren't we doing this in a behavior? After all, this is the situation that behaviors are good for, right?

Here is the reason for our choice: We need to make sure the behaviors are run again after we finish processing. But if we put code to run `Drupal.attachBehaviors()` inside of a behavior, we then have to write some extra code to prevent infinite recursion. In our case, the simplest solution to this problem is to run our code in the `ready` event handler instead of trying to write a recursion detection device.

Let's take a look at the beginning of this function:

```
$('input[name="search_block_form"]:not(.form-autocomplete)')
  .each(function () {
    // More code here...
  }).addClass('form-autocomplete');
```

This first jQuery object grabs elements that match the query `input[name="search_block_form"]:not(.form-autocomplete)`. This is a little longer than our usual query, but it is not difficult to understand.

The query is composed of three parts: an element query (`input`), an attribute query (`[name="search_block_form"]`), and a negation pseudo-class (`:not(.form-autocomplete)`). In short, the query looks for all `<input/>` elements with an attribute `name` that has the value `search_block_form`. But due to the negation pseudo-class, only elements that don't have the class `form-autocomplete` match.

> The `search_block_form` name is used by the search module when it creates a block containing a search text field. This part of the script could be extended to find other text fields and turn them into autocompletion fields. For example, to enable autocompletion in your theme's search box, you would use the name `search_theme_form`.

In short, it matches all search text boxes that don't already have an autocomplete feature. This query should match any Drupal search block, which typically looks something like this:

```
<input type="text" maxlength="128" name="search_block_form"
  id="edit-search-block-form-1" size="15" value=""
  title="Enter the terms you wish to search for."
  class="form-text" />
```

As we can see from the previous code, it iterates through each of the matching elements. In a moment, we will look at what happens to each element as it is iterated over. Then, once that is done, the class `form-autocomplete` is added to each of the matching elements.

Adding this class serves two purposes. First, it makes sure that the same code cannot be run on it again (not a likely event, given that we run the code in the `ready` handler). Second, it identifies that element as an autocomplete form. The Drupal CSS then styles the element accordingly, adding the standard autocomplete throbber inside the text box:

Note the grey circle near the end of the search box. That is the location of the throbber icon. When the autocompletion AJAX script is running, the throbber icon will be displayed as a spinning circle.

Let's now turn to the anonymous function that is run inside the `each()` function:

```
$('input[name="search_block_form"]:not(.form-autocomplete)')
    .each(function () {
      var newId = $(this).attr('id') + '-autocomplete';
      var newElement = $('<input type="hidden"/>')
        .addClass('autocomplete')
        .attr('id', newId).attr('disabled','disabled')
        .attr('value', SearchAutocomplete.url);

      $(this).after(newElement);

    }).addClass('form-autocomplete');
```

In a nutshell, the highlighted code creates a new hidden element that contains instructions for the autocomplete handler. This hidden element is then added after the search box input element.

The anonymous function called by `each` does the following. First, it creates a new ID based on the `id` attribute of the current `input` element. This ID will be assigned to the new hidden element. The `autocomplete.js` library will use the ID to correlate the new hidden element with the field that it describes. So the naming convention used (original ID plus `-autocomplete`) is important.

Next, the script creates the new element:

```
var newElement = $('<input type="hidden"/>')
  .addClass('autocomplete')
  .attr('id', newId).attr('disabled','disabled')
  .attr('value', SearchAutocomplete.url);
```

Once created, the new hidden element is assigned a new class (`autocomplete`), an ID, and a value.

The `class` is used by Drupal's autocomplete behaviors to identify autocompletion fields. The `value` attribute is expected to contain a URL that will be used for AJAX operations.

In the last line of our anonymous function, the new element is added after the search box input element:

```
$(this).after(newElement);
```

Once the main jQuery is done, only one thing remains in the function:

```
$(document).ready(function () {
  $('input[name="search_block_form"]:not(.form-autocomplete)')
    .each(function () {
    var newId = $(this).attr('id') + '-autocomplete';
    var newElement = $('<input type="hidden"/>')
      .addClass('autocomplete')
      .attr('id', newId).attr('disabled','disabled')
      .attr('value', SearchAutocomplete.url);

    $(this).after(newElement);

  }).addClass('form-autocomplete');

  Drupal.attachBehaviors();
});
```

Lastly, `Drupal.attachBehaviors()` is run. This will load and run all of the behaviors.

This line raises an interesting point. We know that all behaviors are run during the jQuery `ready` event. This function is also run during the jQuery `ready` event. But it is run after Drupal's behaviors and modifies the DOM. We need to give the behaviors another chance to process the new material we just added. So we have to run `Drupal.attachBehaviors()` again to be sure that the autocomplete behavior correctly attaches.

This shouldn't cause any problems. After all, behaviors are intended to be run multiple times.

That's all there is to our autocomplete module. To enable this module, simply go to the administration menu **Administer | Site building | Modules**, and enable **Search Autocomplete**.

Once the module is enabled, search dialogs should respond automatically. Here's a screenshot showing the autocompletion in action:

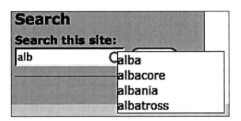

Typing in the first three letters, we get a list of four matching words from our tag list.

Now we are done with our first project. In the next one, we will use the jQuery UI plug-in to add richer user interface elements to our site.

Project: jQuery UI

Although we are going to write a small amount of code in this project, we are going to get some big results with it. We will focus on integrating the jQuery UI with Drupal. We already have a sufficient background to make this task a breeze.

What is jQuery UI?

The jQuery library has received considerable attention in this book, and deservedly so. After all, not only does jQuery come packaged with Drupal, but much of Drupal's own JavaScript code uses jQuery.

The small jQuery library doesn't provide widgets or other components popular in JavaScript libraries. Instead, it is focuses on providing a rich toolset for working with the DOM, CSS, events, and AJAX.

Interested in calendar widgets, or tabs, or sliders, or drag-and-drop support? You won't find any of those in jQuery. But you will find them in an official jQuery add-on package called the **jQuery UI**. The jQuery UI library provides a huge repository of tools for building rich user interfaces. It builds on the solid foundation of jQuery, but it adds much more.

The official jQuery UI web site is co-located with the jQuery home page. Visit `http://ui.jquery.com` to learn more about the project and to view some of the demos.

Here's a partial list of the things you will find in jQuery UI:

- Drag-and-drop support: Declare elements as draggable or configure them as dropable containers.

- Over a dozen additional effects (in addition to `slide` and `fade`): Some, like explode, are tantalizingly elaborate.

- Make elements or containers resizable: you can even add drag bars to images, allowing your users to click and drag on an image border to make the image larger.

- Sortable lists: Turn a list or group of items into a sortable list with drag-and-drop support.

There are even more features, but these should whet your appetite In this project, we will use the accordion tool to turn our menus into an elaborate expanding and collapsing accordion widget.

But the best part about this library is that, like jQuery, the tools are compact. Much can be done with only a few lines of code.

Getting jQuery UI

The jQuery UI library does not come standard with Drupal nor is it to be included in the near future. So to use it with Drupal, you will need to download the library from `http://ui.jquery.com`.

 There is a jQuery UI Drupal module which adds some convenience functions for PHP developers working with jQuery UI. While we won't use it here (our PHP code isn't complex enough), it is a good option for PHP module developers looking to integrate with jQuery UI. For more information, see `http://drupal.org/project/jquery_ui`.

There are several ways of getting jQuery UI, including building a custom package. (See `http://ui.jquery.com/download` for all of the options.)When learning jQuery UI, the best bet is the **Development bundle** distribution. This includes the entire library along with examples and unit tests.

The library is constructed in a modular fashion. Individual features are stored in separate files. For the most part, it is easy to pick and choose which elements you want to install on your server.

When you are ready, download a version of the jQuery UI. We will be using the `ui.core.js` and `ui.accordion.js` files, so make sure you at least have these two. If you get the Development bundle, you will have everything. Later on, we will copy the necessary files into our module.

The next step in our project will be to create a new module.

The accordion module

We are going to write a small module, using the jQuery accordion library, to turn our left-side navigation blocks into an accordion widget. This will keep our site navigation compact and easy to use.

 Earlier in the book, we added a Drupal behavior to our blocks to make them collapsible. Before proceeding, that behavior should be turned off because it will conflict with our accordion widget. To do this, comment out `scripts[] = behaviors.js` in the `frobnitz.info` file, or simply switch to another theme.

As usual, the first thing we need to do is create a new module directory in the appropriate location under the Drupal root directory. Our module will be named `accordion`, so we will be creating `sites/all/modules/accordion`.

Inside of that folder, we will be creating four files:

1. `accordion.info`.
2. `accordion.module`.
3. `accordion.css`.
4. `accordion.js`.

These four files should all be familiar by now. The `.info` file will describe the module. The `.module` file will hold some spartan PHP code. The `.js` file will hold our JavaScript, and the `.css` file will hold our CSS.

Along with these four files, we will create a directory named `ui/`. This is where our jQuery UI files will go. How you downloaded jQuery UI will determine how you need to copy the appropriate files:

- If you downloaded the Development bundle, you can simply copy the bundle's `ui/` folder into `sites/all/modules/accordion/`

- If you built a custom package, copy `ui.core.js` and `ui.accordion.js` into `sites/all/modules/accordion/ui/`

Next, we will create the `accordion.info` and `accordion.module` files.

The .info and .module files

The `accordion.info` file will follow the same structure as our previous `.info` files:

```
; $Id$
name = Accordion
description = Display the left-hand blocks as an accordion.
core = 6.x
php = 5.2
```

There should be nothing surprising here.

Next, we will create a very simple module file. The PHP code for our module will simply add the requisite JavaScript libraries. Like our previous module, it will implement only the `hook_help()` and `hook_init()` hooks:

```php
<?php
// $Id$

/**
 * Attach an accordion effect to menus.
 * @file
 */

/**
 * Implementation of hook_help().
 */
function accordion_help($path, $args) {
  if ($path == 'admin/help#accordion') {
    return t('This module adds accordion effects to menus.');
  }
}

/**
 * Implementation of hook_init().
 */
```

```
function accordion_init() {
  $path = drupal_get_path('module', 'accordion');
  drupal_add_css($path . '/accordion.css');
  drupal_add_js($path . '/accordion.js');
  drupal_add_js($path . '/ui/ui.core.js');
  drupal_add_js($path . '/ui/ui.accordion.js');
}
```

The `accordion_init()` function adds four files.

First, the `accordion.css` file (which we will create in a moment) contains styling information. It is a CSS file, not a JavaScript file. Therefore, we add it with the `drupal_add_css()` function.

Next, we have three JavaScript files that need to be added:

1. `accordion.js`: This holds our custom JavaScript code. We will take a close look at the contents of this file shortly.

2. `ui/ui.core.js`: This is the base library for jQuery UI. It contains functions used by the rest of the jQuery UI components. Any time you use jQuery UI you will need to include this library.

3. `ui/ui.accordion.js`: This contains the jQuery UI accordion widget code.

That is all there is to our module. Next, we will look at the JavaScript.

The accordion JavaScript

Our module code was short, but our JavaScript code is going to be even shorter. In `accordion.js`, we need to write the necessary *glue code* to find the right part of our document and turn it into an accordion. With jQuery at our disposal, and jQuery UI tightly integrated, this process is as easy as writing a simple jQuery chain.

To make things even simpler, we will wrap this in a Drupal behavior and allow Drupal to control the initialization of our widget:

```
// $Id$

/**
 * JavaScript for initializing and adding accordion effect.
 * @file
 */
Drupal.behaviors.accordion = function () {
  $('#sidebar-left:not(.ui-accordion)').accordion({
    header: 'h2'
  });
};
```

The body of our newly defined behavior has a single jQuery chain that consists of two parts. First, the jQuery call executes this query:

```
#sidebar-left:not(.ui-accordion)
```

This will look for an element with the ID `sidebar-left` that does not have the class `ui-accordion`.

The `sidebar-left` ID is a standard ID for Drupal. It identifies the lefthand region where blocks are typically located. Here's what my `sidebar-left` column looks like before running the previous code:

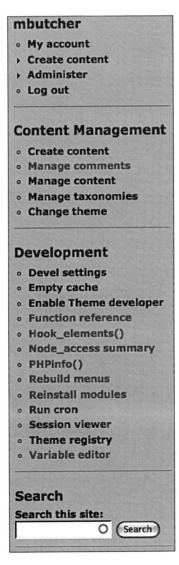

This is the area that the ID identifies. But there is the additional `:not(.ui-accordion)`. The `ui-accordion` class is added by an accordion widget. As with other behaviors, we add this extra check to ensure if the behavior is run multiple times, we won't try to repeatedly turn the left column into an accordion widget.

Let's now take a look at the second part of the query:

```
$('#sidebar-left:not(.ui-accordion)').accordion({
  header: 'h2'
});
```

The jQuery UI functions are added onto the main jQuery object (we will see how to do this in our final project). So adding the accordion is as simple as calling the `accordion()` method.

That method takes an object literal containing settings. There are over half a dozen possible settings for the accordion, all documented at `http://docs.jquery.com/UI/Accordion/accordion#options`, but we will only use one.

We need to tell the accordion effect what element to use as header information. To explain this, let's take a quick look at the structure of the HTML in the left sidebar:

```
<td id="sidebar-left">
  <div class="block block-user" id="block-user-1">
    <h2 class="title">
      mbutcher
    </h2>
    <div class="content">
      <!-- Menu content -->
    </div>
  </div>
  <div class="block block-menu" id="block-menu-menu-custom-content-
management">
    <h2 class="title">
      Content Management
    </h2>
    <div class="content">
      <!-- Menu content -->
    </div>
  </div>
  <div class="block block-menu" id="block-menu-devel">
    <h2 class="title">
      Development
    </h2>
    <div class="content">
```

```
        <!-- Menu content -->
      </div>
    </div>
    <div class="block block-search" id="block-search-0">
      <h2 class="title">
        Search
      </h2>
      <div class="content">
        <!-- Search form -->
      </div>
    </div>
  </td>
```

In the previous code, I have removed the content of every block to simplify the HTML. It's the general structure that we are interested in.

First, the `<td></td>` element has the ID `sidebar-left`. That is going to be the main container for our new accordion widget.

The blocks are inside of the `<td></td>` element. The blocks have the following structure:

```
<div class="block other-class" id="block-ID">
  <h2 class="title">
    <!-- TITLE -->
  </h2>
  <div class="content">
    <!-- CONTENT -->
  </div>
</div>
```

Each of these blocks will be a collapsible region in our accordion. A collapsible region looks like this:

Looks familiar? This is a block. The title of the block becomes the header of the collapsible region, and the block's content becomes the body of the collapsible region.

The jQuery UI accordion widget assumes that all direct children of the container element (the `<td></td>`, in our case) are collapsible regions. However, it needs information about what element holds the title of the collapsible region. So when we call `$().accordion()`, we pass it the needed information:

```
$('#sidebar-left:not(.ui-accordion)').accordion({
  header: 'h2'
});
```

We tell it that the header of the region should be composed from the `<h2></h2>` elements inside of each block.

 This will not work well for blocks that do not have headers. Regions in an accordion are expanded by clicking on the header. If no header exists, there is no way to expand the region. On possible remedy would be to use jQuery to dynamically add titles to all blocks before adding an accordion. Of course, the more pragmatic solution is to avoid using blocks with no titles in an accordion.

That is all there is to our code. The accordion widget is added to the `<td></td>` element with the ID `sidebar-left`, and we get something that looks like this (or will look like this once we add a little CSS):

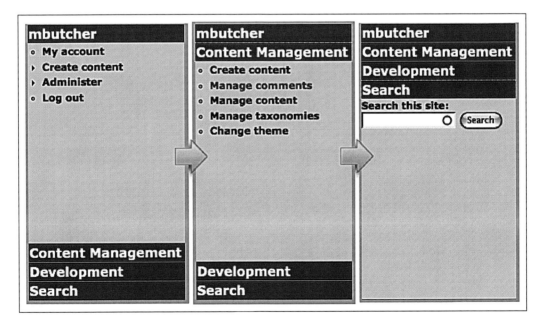

The previous screenshots capture the accordion in three different states.

The leftmost screenshot shows the accordion as it looks when it initially loads. The main Drupal menu block is expanded and the remaining blocks are collapsed.

If we click on the title of the second block, **Content Management**, the second block slides upward and hides the first. The middle screenshot shows the block in this state.

Now if we click on the last item in the accordion — **Search** — it too slides up, pushing the **Development** section upwards. The rightmost screenshot shows the end result. The **Search** block is displayed in its entirety, and the other blocks are collapsed above it.

If we click on **Content Management** again, it would expand downward until its contents are displayed. At that point, it would again look like the screenshot in the middle.

By using the jQuery UI library, we added this sophisticated component in just five lines of JavaScript. However, to get it to look as it does in these screenshots, a little CSS is needed. We won't go through the styles in detail, but in the interest of completeness, here is the `accordion.css`:

```
/*
 * Accordion module CSS.
 */

.ui-accordion div.block {
  background-color: #efefef;
  margin-bottom: 0px;
  padding-bottom: 0px;
}

h2.ui-accordion-header {
  border: 1px solid black;
  background-color: #6699CC;
  color: white;
  margin-bottom: 0px !IMPORTANT;
}
```

There are two selectors in this code. The first selects all of the blocks in the UI accordion and sets the background color to light-grey. It also fixes the bottom padding and margin to prevent gaps between titles in our accordion.

The second item styles the accordion header. It makes it look more like a clickable area by surrounding it with a black border, setting the background color to blue, and setting the text color to white. Here too, we need to adjust the bottom margin. This adjustment is marked as `!IMPORTANT` to prevent the default style sheet from overriding it.

That wraps up our accordion widget project. Even though this has been an easygoing project, I hope it has done three things. First, I hope it has illustrated the ease with which jQuery UI effects and widgets can be integrated into Drupal. Second, I hope it inspires further experimentation with the library. Other widgets, such as tabs, spinners, dialogs, grids, and so on, are just as easy to work with. These widgets can really make a site stand out.

My third objective was a little more subtle. By looking at $().accordion(), we have seen how a jQuery extension can integrate cleanly with jQuery. For our final project, we will go back to the main jQuery library and write a simple plug-in.

Project: writing a jQuery plug-in

Earlier in the book, we talked about jQuery plug-ins. Plug-ins are to jQuery what modules are to Drupal—a tool for extending functionality. In this project, we will write a small jQuery plug-in.

Throughout the book, we have looked at numerous ways to work with JavaScript in a Drupal site. We are going to look at one final way. A jQuery plug-in extends the capabilities of jQuery. This is not a Drupal-specific feature, but a feature of the jQuery library.

Why would we learn this technique if we can already write JavaScript in a Drupal site?

There are a few reasons for this:

- With close integration into jQuery, we can build compact code using jQuery's fluent interface pattern.
- When it comes to manipulating DOM and CSS, managing events, or working with effects, you can often make the coding task easier by writing it as a jQuery plug-in.
- A plug-in is more portable than a Drupal module and you can use it in non-Drupal (or even non-PHP) web applications. Thus, reusability is good.
- The jQuery architecture makes plug-in writing easier, simpler in some respects than adding a Drupal behavior.

Our example here will be very basic. Robust and complex jQuery plug-ins can certainly be written (many such plug-ins are available for download at `http://jquery.com`). Our project should give you the tools needed to write more complex plug-ins.

The plug-in code

The basic principle of writing a jQuery plug-in is very simple: You write a function and attach that function to the jQuery object. We are going to add a new method to the jQuery object.

The most basic pattern for writing such a plug-in is similar to this:

```
jQuery.fn.myNewPlugin = function () {
  // Do something.
}
```

The new plug-in could then be called like this:

```
$('p').myNewPlugin();
```

What are we doing here? The `jQuery.fn` object is where jQuery functions are attached to the jQuery prototype object. In other words, all of the functions that are attached to `jQuery.fn` will be available to jQuery objects, and can be called (as in the previous example) by `$().someFunction()`.

 As a de facto rule, a plug-in should use only one namespace inside of the `jQuery.fn` namespace. When adding multiple functions to jQuery, these functions should be grouped into another namespace. Instead of `jQuery.fn.myPluginFirst()` and `jQuery.fn.myPluginSecond()`, it should be `jQuery.fn.myPlugin.first()` and `jQuery.fn.myPlugin.second()`.

We now have a basic idea about how to write a plug-in. Following this prescribed pattern for plug-in development, we are going to create our own simple plug-in.

Plug-ins for jQuery should be stored in files named `jquery.<plug-in>.js`, where `<plug-in>` is replaced with the name of the plug-in (all in lowercase). Our plug-in is going to wrap matched elements in a `<div></div>` tag. For example, we might create a jQuery object that finds all anchors:

```
$('a');
```

Our little tool could then be applied in order to enclose each of those anchor elements inside of a div:

```
$('a').divWrap();
```

This would transform something like `<a href="http://example.com">` into `<div><a href="http://example.com"></div>`. Though our plug-in may never win any awards for innovativeness, it is a good starting point for investigating jQuery plug-ins.

We are going to call this plug-in `divWrap`, so it should be stored in a file called `jquery.divwrap.js`.

 This library will work just like any JavaScript library in Drupal. You can add it to a theme using the theme's `.info` file, or you can include it in a module with the `drupal_add_js()` function. While developing, you might find it handy to simply start with a static HTML file and include only jQuery and your plug-in.

Here's the code that we will put in `jquery.divwrap.js`:

```
(function ($) {

  /**
   * Wrap the selected element or elements in <div></div>
   * tags.
   *
   * @param attributes
   *   An object containing name/value pairs for attributes.
   */
  jQuery.fn.divWrap = function () {
    var attrs = (arguments.length > 0) ? arguments[0] : {};

    this.each(function (index, item) {
      var div = $(item).wrap('<div></div>').parent();

      if (attrs) {
        div.attr(attrs);
      }
    });
    return this;
  };
}) (jQuery);
```

The first thing to note about this plug-in is the outermost wrapper, which looks like this:

```
(function ($) {
  // Code here
}) (jQuery);
```

What is this? In JavaScript, you can both define and call a function in one step, and this is how it is done. The previous code performs a task similar to what this code does:

```
myFunc = function ($) {
  // Code here
}
myFunc(jQuery);
```

There are two important reasons why we begin a jQuery plug-in with code such as this:

1. We can conveniently work with jQuery using the `$()` function alias.
2. We also create a closure that protects our plug-in's context.

Neither of these may be obvious, so let me explain.

Although we have used the `$()` function many times in this book. However, the name `$` is sometimes overridden, or turned off, by other JavaScript libraries. In short, there is no guarantee that `$` refers to jQuery. The convention that we saw overcomes this uncertainty by wrapping the entire plug-in in a function that takes an argument named `$`. The function is then called with the globally scoped `jQuery` object. In effect, it re-maps `$` to `jQuery` so that we can confidently use the `$()` function in our code.

Second, this convention creates a closure around our plug-in. Closures are often treated as an advanced aspect of JavaScript development. In fact, they are used frequently in a variety of contexts. (We have used them a few times already, but without the fancy name and in a subtler fashion.) We will take a brief look at this topic, and you will find that they are not as mysterious as they may seem at first.

A brief introduction to closures

A **closure** provides a convenient way of providing a context in which we can store local variables and functions that we don't want other outside scripts to have access to. A closure basically seals-off a context for us.

Inside of a closure, we can create variables and functions that would not be accessible to the outside world. However, code inside the closure can access these functions and variables. With a closure, we can hide data from outsiders, while making it available to the code inside.

 If you have done object-oriented programming in Java, PHP, or other languages, you can compare the closure method of protecting access to the `private` keyword used in class variable declarations. While they are technically quite different, they are functionally similar.

All of this may sound abstract, and perhaps even a little lofty and impractical. However, a quick look at some simple code should make things clear.

Let's start with a simple test:

```
var text = 'This is a test';
console.log(text);
```

If we were to run this in Firefox with Firebug turned on, we would see the contents of the `text` variable printed to the Firebug console.

But what if we wrapped the `text` variable inside of a closure as shown:

```
(function () {
  var text = 'This is a test';
})();


console.log(text);
```

In this case, Firebug would show an error saying something like **ReferenceError: text is not defined**.

This happens because `text` in the previous code is scoped only to the anonymous function. In other words, the `text` variable is not available outside that anonymous function.

This comes in handy when we want to have private variables or functions (variables or functions that are available only inside of our plug-in and not to code outside). To see how this works, let's make a few additions to the previous code:

```
var MyObject = {};
(function () {
  var text = 'This is a test';
  MyObject.getText = function () {
    return text;
  };
})();
console.log(MyObject.getText());
console.log(text);
```

The highlighted lines were added.

The first `console.log()` call will print **This is a test** to the console. However, the second one will give the same **ReferenceError** that we saw earlier. Let's see why.

In this new addition, we have done the following:

- At the top, we create an object, `MyObject`, which is globally scoped (since it is outside of the function).
- Inside of the closure we add a new function, `MyObject.getText()`, that returned the value of the private `text` variable. Note that this new function is attached to the globally scoped `MyObject` object.
- Outside of the closure, we run `MyObject.getText()` and print the returned value to the console.

In our simpler example, we saw that `console.log(text)` fails. What will happen when `console.log(MyObject.getText())` is run? It will print **This is a test** to the console.

The reason why this happens is simple: When we create `MyObject.getText()`, we create it in a context that has access to the `text` variable. We might say that `MyObject.getText()` can *see* `text`. Also, it can see `text` because `text` is in its context. Both are inside of the closure.

Even when we call the `MyObject.getText()` method outside of the closure, as we do in the `console.log()` call, that function can still see the `text` variable, and so it can return it. Since `text` is available only to code inside of the closure, we can say that `text` is a private variable.

The `getText()` function is attached to `MyObject`, which makes it available in any context where `MyObject` is available. Since `MyObject` is a globally scoped object, `MyObject.getText()` is available just about anywhere.

 Should we need, we could also create functions inside of the closure. By not attaching them to an object outside of the closure, we can create private functions.

Returning to our closure, the `(function ($) {}) (jQuery)` construct is not fundamentally different from the code we just wrote. The `jQuery` object is globally scoped, and anything we explicitly add to `jQuery.fn` will be available outside of our closure. However, anything else we define in our closure will be accessible only to other code in the same scope.

That's the general strategy we are using with our plug-in. We define the entire plug-in inside of a closure so that we can carefully control access to the code we write.

Glancing back at the code, you may notice that we don't really make use of this feature. There are no private variables or functions. But writing it this way will make it easier to extend later, if we so choose, and conforms to suggested practices for jQuery plug-in development. And we are still getting the benefit of the aliasing of `$` to `jQuery`.

Now that we understand the basics of closures, let's get back to our plug-in.

The divWrap() function

Inside of our closure we define one new function:

```
jQuery.fn.divWrap = function () {
  var attrs = (arguments.length > 0) ? arguments[0] : {};

  this.each(function (index, item) {
    var div = $(item).wrap('<div></div>').parent();

    if (attrs) {
      div.attr(attrs);
    }
  });
  return this;
};
```

This function takes all of the items wrapped in the current jQuery object and wraps each in `<div></div>` tags. It takes an optional parameter—an object. The attributes of that object will be used as attributes for the new `div` element.

The first thing our `divWrap` function does is check to see if any arguments were passed in. Recall that JavaScript's built-in `arguments` variable is an array-like object that lists all of the parameters passed into the function.

The first line checks to see if `arguments.length` is greater than `0`. If it is, then the `attrs` variable will be assigned the first argument. Otherwise, `attrs` will be assigned an empty object (`{}`).

Next, we use `this.each()` to loop through all of the objects currently wrapped by jQuery. This works because a plug-in added to `jQuery.fn` is part of jQuery. It's `this` variable—a variable automatically created by JavaScript—that points to the object of which this function is a part. So in this case, it points to a `jQuery` object.

To understand this, let's look at how we would call our new plug-in:

```
$('a').divWrap();
```

In this line of code, we use `$()` to search for all `<a></a>` elements. So when `divWrap()` is called, the jQuery object should contain a list of all `<a></a>` elements. When `divWrap()` is executed, `this` will point to the current `jQuery` object—the very object that contains the list of `<a></a>` elements.

Now returning to our code, we want to loop through each element in the current jQuery object and wrap it in a `div` tag. We do that with the anonymous function inside of `this.each()`:

```
function (index, item) {
  var div = $(item).wrap('<div></div>').parent();

  if (attrs) {
    div.attr(attrs);
  }
}
```

Recall that the `$().each()` function receives two arguments: `index`, which is the numeric index of the current object within jQuery's list of objects, and `item`, which is the current object.

> This anonymous function acts as a closure. Inside of the context of the `$().each()` method, this anonymous function has access to the `attrs` variable. But for the rest of jQuery that variable is out of scope. We've been creating closures all along!

The first thing we do in this function is run a jQuery chain to wrap the current item inside of a `<div></div>` tags. At the end of this chain, we call `parent()`, which will select the `div` element we just wrapped with. This is done for the sake of the second step.

In the `divWrap()` function, we assigned `attrs` the value of `arguments[0]` or `{}`. Here, we add the contents of `attrs` as attributes to the `div`. A quick look at an example will clarify this.

We could call our plug-in like this:

```
attrs = { style: 'background-color: #F0F' };
$('a').divWrap(attrs);
```

In this case, the `attrs` object would be used to add attributes to the `div` that wraps any found `<a></a>` elements. The result of this would look something like this:

```
<div style='background-color: #F0F'>
  <a href='http://example.com'>Some link</a>
</div>
```

Notice how `attrs` was turned into attributes for the `<div></div>` tag.

That's all there is to this anonymous function executed by the `$().each()` function. There's only one more thing our plug-in function does:

```
(function ($) {
  jQuery.fn.divWrap = function () {
    var atLrs = (arguments.length > 0) ? arguments[0] : {};

    this.each(function (index, item) {
      var div = $(item).wrap('<div></div>').parent();

      if (attrs) {
        div.attr(attrs);
      }
    });
    return this;
  }
}) (jQuery);
```

Notice the highlighted line in the code? Why do we `return this`? We are returning the jQuery object so that other functions can be chained off to this one. We could, for example, do something like this:

```
$('a').divWrap().text();
```

This would return the text of each `<a></a>` element after wrapping all of the `<a></a>` elements inside of the `div` tags.

So that's the basic method for creating a jQuery plug-in. How do you make use of this tool inside of Drupal? This is done the same way you would use any JavaScript library. In a theme, you might add it to the `.info` file using a `scripts[]` directive. Or in PHP (such as a module), you can add it with the `drupal_add_js()` function.

Other references for writing jQuery plug-ins

There are two very helpful jQuery basic plug-in writing tutorials that may be helpful. The official plug-in writing guide is at `http://docs.jquery.com/Plug-ins/Authoring`. The standard plug-in writing pattern is explained here: `http://www.learningjquery.com/2007/10/a-plug-in-development-pattern`.

When should you write a jQuery plug-in instead of JavaScript in Drupal? To a large extent, the answer will depend on your own needs. However, here are some guidelines:

- If you might need to use the code outside of Drupal, a plug-in is easier to port. In fact, you may want to release a generic plug-in to the jQuery community at `http://jquery.com`.

- If your code would work well as part of a jQuery chain, you might consider adding it as a jQuery plug-in, even if it does depend on Drupal.

- If you find a jQuery plug-in that already does much of what you want, you might consider writing another plug-in that extends the base jQuery plug-in. Even in this case, it is easier to work from within jQuery than from Drupal's JavaScript library.

As we have seen throughout this book, the JavaScript integration in Drupal is very robust. Whether it's a jQuery plug-in or a Drupal-centered library, or even an unrelated JavaScript library, Drupal makes it easy to integrate.

Summary

In this chapter we covered three projects. In the first project, we saw how we could integrate another existing Drupal JavaScript library—`autocomplete.js`—into our site. We used a taxonomy to add suggestions to our search box.

After that, we integrated one of the jQuery UI tools—the accordion widget—into our site. Using this tool, we turned our lefthand navigation into a compact, but elegant accordion menu.

Finally, we learned how to extend jQuery by writing a jQuery plug-in. In a couple dozen lines of code, we wrote a complete plug-in that takes advantage of jQuery's DOM tools and looping structures. During this section, we talked about closures and discovered that we'd been writing them all along.

This is the final chapter of the book. In our earlier chapters, we started out with some fairly clumsy JavaScript, just barely integrated into a Drupal theme. Now, seven chapters later, we know how to write Drupal-centred JavaScript with the use of jQuery, Drupal's own JavaScript libraries, and even external libraries such as jQuery UI. We've worked with both themes and modules. We've even written a little bit of PHP code.

The purpose of this book has been to give you access to the JavaScript tools which are often used for Drupal development, and to show you how to use them in this context. We have only scratched the surface of what can be done with these tools. This book, if I have been successful, gives you a foundation. From here, you can begin building the next generation of JavaScript-enabled Drupal web applications.

Index

T

template system 184
TextMate 24
theme
  about 43
  Bluemarine theme 44
  Chameleon theme 44
  creating 45
  CSS file 52
  full theme, creating 44
  Garland theme 44
  JavaScript, adding 52
  requisites 43
  subtheme 44
theme, creating
  fields, required 47
  files, adding to theme 48
  frobnitz.info file, creating 47
  Frobnitz theme, creating 48
  .info file, creating 47
Theme Engine 18
theming project
  about 161
  block, adding with menu 162, 164
  block, theming 164
  block, theming in JavaScript 166, 167
  block, theming in PHP 164
  menu, theming 168-173
translation functions
  about 128, 129
  advantages 133
  Drupal.formatPlural() function 136
  Drupal.t() function 134
  uses 133
translation system
  english language, default 129
  language, installing 129
  languages 128

U

user module
  about 19
  anonymous user 19
  authenticated user 19

roles 19
special user 19
utilities
  about 107
  Drupal.checkPlain() function 108
  Drupal.encodeURIComponent() function 112
  Drupal.getSelection() function 113
  Drupal.jsEnabled 107
  Drupal.parseJson() function 111

V

views 220
Views Datasource 220

W

Web 2.0
  about 198
  AJAX's role 199
web clips tool, AJAX project
  creating 207
  WebClips behavior 209-216
  WebClips.showItem() function 217, 218
weekend countdown project
  about 139
  array of weekdays, creating 141
  Day.banner() function 141
  dayFields object 143
  day.js 140
  day namespace object, creating 140
WSDL 198

X

XHR
  about 200, 201
  data transfer 202
XML 13
XMLHttpRequest 200
XML-RPC 198

Y

YUI 60

Thank you for buying
Drupal 6 JavaScript and jQuery

Packt Open Source Project Royalties

When we sell a book written on an Open Source project, we pay a royalty directly to that project. Therefore by purchasing Drupal 6 JavaScript and jQuery, Packt will have given some of the money received to the Drupal project.

In the long term, we see ourselves and you—customers and readers of our books—as part of the Open Source ecosystem, providing sustainable revenue for the projects we publish on. Our aim at Packt is to establish publishing royalties as an essential part of the service and support a business model that sustains Open Source.

If you're working with an Open Source project that you would like us to publish on, and subsequently pay royalties to, please get in touch with us.

Writing for Packt

We welcome all inquiries from people who are interested in authoring. Book proposals should be sent to author@packtpub.com. If your book idea is still at an early stage and you would like to discuss it first before writing a formal book proposal, contact us; one of our commissioning editors will get in touch with you.

We're not just looking for published authors; if you have strong technical skills but no writing experience, our experienced editors can help you develop a writing career, or simply get some additional reward for your expertise.

About Packt Publishing

Packt, pronounced 'packed', published its first book "Mastering phpMyAdmin for Effective MySQL Management" in April 2004 and subsequently continued to specialize in publishing highly focused books on specific technologies and solutions.

Our books and publications share the experiences of your fellow IT professionals in adapting and customizing today's systems, applications, and frameworks. Our solution-based books give you the knowledge and power to customize the software and technologies you're using to get the job done. Packt books are more specific and less general than the IT books you have seen in the past. Our unique business model allows us to bring you more focused information, giving you more of what you need to know, and less of what you don't.

Packt is a modern, yet unique publishing company, which focuses on producing quality, cutting-edge books for communities of developers, administrators, and newbies alike. For more information, please visit our website: www.PacktPub.com.

Learning Drupal 6 Module Development

ISBN: 978-1-847194-44-2   Paperback: 310 pages

A practical tutorial for creating your first Drupal 6 modules with PHP

1. Specifically written for Drupal 6 development

2. Program your own Drupal modules

3. No experience of Drupal development required

4. Know Drupal 5? Learn what's new in Drupal 6

5. Integrate AJAX functionality with the jQuery library

Building Powerful and Robust Websites with Drupal 6

ISBN: 978-1-847192-97-4   Paperback: 362 pages

Build your own professional blog, forum, portal or community website with Drupal 6

1. Set up, configure, and deploy Drupal 6

2. Harness Drupal's world-class Content Management System

3. Design and implement your website's look and feel

Please check **www.PacktPub.com** for information on our titles

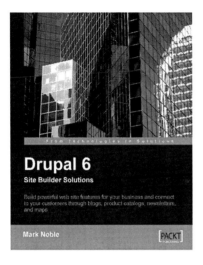

Drupal 6 Site Builder Solutions

ISBN: 978-1-847196-40-8   Paperback: 333 pages

Build powerful website features for your business and connect to your customers through blogs, product catalogs, newsletters, and maps

1. Implement the essential features of a business or non-profit website using Drupal

2. Integrate with other "web 2.0" sites such as Google Maps, Digg, Flickr, and YouTube to drive traffic, build a community, and increase your website's effectiveness

3. No website development knowledge required

4. Complete example of a real world site with clear explanation

Drupal 6 Themes

ISBN: 978-1-847195-66-1   Paperback: 291 pages

Create new themes for your Drupal 6 site with clean layout and powerful CSS styling

1. Learn to create new Drupal 6 themes

2. No experience of Drupal theming required

3. Techniques and tools for creating and modifying themess

4. A complete guide to the system's themable elements

Please check **www.PacktPub.com** for information on our titles

3772692

Made in the USA
Lexington, KY
21 November 2009